HERITAGE NOW

Irish Literature in the English Language

ANTHONY CRONIN

St. Martin's Press New York

For information write:
St. Martin's Press, Inc., 175 Fifth Avenue, New York, NY 10010

First published in the United States of America in 1983

ISBN 0-312-36993-X

Library of Congress Cataloguing in Publication Data

Cronin, Anthony.
Heritage now.

1. English literature—Irish authors—History and criticism. I. Title.
PR8711.C66 1983 820′.9′9415 82-42719
ISBN 0-312-36993-X

Jacket design: Robert Ballagh
Author photograph: *Sunday Tribune*
Printed and bound in Great Britain by
Biddles Ltd, Guildford and King's Lynn

CONTENTS

FOREWORD 5

INTRODUCTION 7

MARIA EDGEWORTH:
The Unlikely Precursor 17

THOMAS MOORE:
The Necessary National Bard 31

WILLIAM CARLETON:
Idyll and Bloodshed 37

JAMES CLARENCE MANGAN:
The Necessary *Maudit* 47

CHARLES LEVER:
Enter the Stage Anglo-Irishman 51

WILLIAM ALLINGHAM:
The Lure of London 61

GEORGE MOORE:
The Self-Made Modern 69

EDITH SOMERVILLE AND MARTIN ROSS:
Women Fighting Back 75

WILLIAM BUTLER YEATS:
Containing Contradictions 87

JOHN MILLINGTON SYNGE:
Apart from Anthropology 95

JAMES JOYCE:
The Advent of Bloom 105

JAMES JOYCE:
Footnote for a Poet 143

JAMES STEPHENS:
The Gift of the Gab 147

THOMAS MacGREEVY:
Modernism not Triumphant 155

FRANCIS STUART:
Religion Without Revelation 161

SAMUEL BECKETT:
Murphy Becomes Unnamable 169

PATRICK KAVANAGH:
Alive and Well in Dublin 185

LOUIS MacNEICE:
London and Lost Irishness 197

FLANN O'BRIEN:
The Flawed Achievement 203

BIBLIOGRAPHICAL NOTE 215

FOREWORD

Though some of the chapters in this book had their genesis in previously published essays, book reviews, radio talks and prefaces, scarcely anything stands as it originally stood and much has been altered almost out of recognition by revision, combination, addition and deletion. The fact that pieces have been combined and synthesised as well as extensively added to and re-written makes the task of individual acknowledgement difficult; but anyway my thanks are due to the BBC, *Hibernia*, *The Irish Times*, RTE, *The Sunday Press* and *The Times Literary Supplement*, both for providing me with the original impulse and with permission to reprint. 'The Advent of Bloom' appeared more or less as it now is in *A Question of Modernity*, published by Secker and Warburg (London, 1966).

Anthony Cronin,
Dublin, April 1982.

INTRODUCTION

> Anglo-Irish literature, though far less characteristic of the nation than that produced in the Irish language includes much that is of lasting worth. Ireland has produced in Dean Swift perhaps the greatest satirist in the English language; in Edmund Burke probably the greatest writer in politics; in William Carleton, a novelist of the first rank; in Oliver Goldsmith a poet of rare merit. Henry Grattan was one of the most eloquent orators of his time – the golden age of oratory in the English language. Theobald Wolfe Tone has left us one of the most delightful autobiographies in literature. Several recent, or still living, Irish novelists and poets have produced work which is likely to stand the test of time.

The words are Eamon de Valera's. The date of their enunciation was the 6th February 1933. The occasion was the opening of the Athlone broadcasting station. And however surprising it may seem that Mr. de Valera should have expressed such sentiments at all, among the things to be noted is the general weakness of the claim.

And it is not that the then hale and lusty President of the Executive Council was playing it down. The probability is the contrary one; he was pitching it as high as he could, probably with the unease that all stern critics feel when they are laying it on a bit. (He was, by all accounts, a sparse reader and infrequent encomiast.) But his faith in what he called Anglo-Irish literature was not strong. And neither possibly, in spite of all the guides and summaries, the digressions on the national character and references to the wit of such as Congreve and Goldsmith, Sheridan and Bernard Shaw, was anybody else's.

One reason was, of course, that the thing had fuzzy edges. Not only were you faced with problems like that of Sterne, who happened to be born in Ireland as the Duke of Wellington's proverbial horse might have been born in a stable; or that of Congreve, whose formative years were spent in Kilkenny and Trinity College, but who was otherwise no more Irish than Queen Anne herself; but you also had the rather more various and complicated difficulties posed by some of those that Mr. de Valera mentioned – Swift, Burke and Goldsmith.

And it was not merely a matter of pedigree or up-bringing. All but the most obdurate of Gaelic racialists – and they had, after all, really no more right to a say in the matter than anybody else – would have to admit the Irishness of Goldsmith as the son of his father; while all but the most insensitive to the display of national characteristics would recognise the sometimes heartbreakingly Irish modes of his behaviour.

But the many *belles lettres*istic or guidebook attempts to place the never failing brook, the busy mill, the decent church that topped the neighbouring hill in the neighbourhood of Lissoy and to make 'The Deserted Village' a specifically Irish poem could not disguise the fact that outside the pot-boiling histories of England and the *Life of Thomas Parnell* there are only two actual discursions about Ireland in his works. As subject matter, whether in its corporeal or incorporeal aspects, Ireland might as well have disappeared off the map as far as Goldsmith was concerned after he left the place, never to return, at the age of twenty-two. His career thereafter was that of the London literary gent who was jack of all literary trades: reviewer, translator, compiler, editor, essayist, novelist, playwright, historian, poet and populariser of the scientific and philosophical knowledge of his day.

But it was not, as so many other successful careers have been since, that of a purveyor of Irish colour, Irish frustration, Irish violence, Irish pastoral or anything else. He never expressed an Irish (or any) point of view about current affairs or his country's plight. He wrote no *Drapier's Letters*, no *John Bull's Other Island*. He never mentioned Ireland in his well documented conversations with his London literary friends. His ambition was to take rank as the typical English man of letters of his time, an up-to-date critic of thought and manners who was *au courant* with English and Continental life, thought and literary fashion. His expressed values and standards of conduct were those of the emergent English bourgeoisie of the late eighteenth century: nor was Goethe so far wrong when, seeking to express the admiration he felt for *The Vicar of Wakefield*, he said that its author "can thankfully acknowledge that he is an Englishman and reckon highly the advantages which his country and his nation afforded him", for *The Vicar of Wakefield* contains all the English vices – whimsicality, sentimentality, plain hypocrisy and the confusion of mere respectability with some sort of morality.

And if Goldsmith, so patently and even pointlessly Irish in aspects of his personal conduct, so over-ridingly Irish perhaps in his great allegorical poem, posed problems of this sort for the compilers of histories of Anglo-Irish literature, so, in one way or another, did almost everybody else they chose to boast of; and this gave much of what was written on the subject an air of mere assertion and enthusiasm; coloured, as in the case of Mr. de Valera, by a recognisable unease.

So, for the most part they fell back, as he did, on the "Ireland has produced" line of argument. No matter that Burke was more concerned with the fortunes of his own Whig faction than he was with those of Grattan's Parliament; or that he was more cut up about the iniquities of Warren Hastings and the wrongs done to the French royal family than he was about the desperate plight of the Irish peasantry. Ireland had "produced" him. The bit about Marie Antoinette and the swords leaping from their scabbards could go in *The Cabinet of Irish Literature* alongside Grattan and Philpot Curran; or a piece from *The Sublime and Beautiful* could be put beside Bishop Berkeley on *Human Knowledge*.

For the fact is that most critics used the term Anglo-Irish as critics will, because it got them off the hook: it obscured divisions rather than enhanced them. For the purpose of these critics, anybody born in Ireland of whatever stock, and whether or not he had shaken the bog mire off his shoes at an early age, or ever referred to the Irish and their ridiculous manners, customs or problems thereafter, was an Anglo-Irish author.

Thus, faced with the task of compiling an anthology for a London publisher, you could happily stick in Thomas Parnell as well as George Darley. Landed with the job of finding something to say from an Irish angle about George Bernard Shaw, you could discuss the tradition to which, according to you, he really belonged, beginning with Congreve and going on to Sheridan and Wilde. For there were those still alive when the Athlone radio station was being opened to the strains of Tom Moore's 'Let Erin Remember' played by the Number One Army Band who posed problems for Mr. de Valera or anybody else who cared to discuss the matter analogous to those posed by Burke and Goldsmith.

Bernard Shaw's mother had not betaken herself to London until he was well into his twenties. His miscellaneous writings on Ireland when finally collected and edited in 1961 by David

H. Greene and Dan H. Laurence would fill a decent sized volume. He had turned his attention to his native land for one brilliant moment in a play that for some extraordinary reason is never reprinted and seldom produced. He himself never tired of adverting to the Irish nature of his gift and the Jaeger tweeds that he went about in could be taken for the uniform of an Irish man of letters. But in the totality of his literary output Ireland was no more than a wry note in the margin; and he had said more than once that the full development of his talents had required that he should flee forever from the place and its problems.

It was true also, of course, that in 1933 the Irish Literary Revival, the Celtic Renaissance or whatever one chooses to call it was a well established literary landmark. From an early age Yeats had established himself as an Irish writer, even perhaps an "Oirish" one, in both English and Irish eyes, by making Irish saga and legend, peasant lore and faery lore, his subjects – or one of his subjects, for within the space of a poem, a line, or, as Joyce was to demonstrate, a word, there is room for several "subjects" to co-exist. He had influenced a whole generation (many of them the sort of minor writers who can only deal with one subject at a time) to do likewise. And to balance Oscar Wilde, who had adopted the Goldsmith attitude and eschewed all mention of the place, there was George Moore, who had turned his redoubtable talents loose on it and produced masterpieces in the process.

It was true also that in 1933 or thereabouts there was an alleged new school of Irish writing, sometimes referred to as poetic realists, who represented the nascent state proudly both in the lists of English and American publishers and in the growing schedule of books which had attracted the attention of the censorship of publications board. Liam O'Flaherty's *The Informer*, which won a well-known literary prize, had come out in 1926; Frank O'Connor's *The Saint and Mary Kate* in 1932; while Sean O'Faolain's *A Nest of Simple Folk* appeared in the very year that Mr. de Valera came to the microphone and proclaimed that we now had a broadcasting station as well as all the other appurtenances of statehood.

But two impressions nevertheless remained and they are both contained in what Mr. de Valera said. One was that Irish literature in English was hard to de-limit and define, so hard that its very existence, or its existence as other than a branch of English literature, was a matter for special pleading and involved a sort of patriotic act of faith, a feeling admitted to in the very use of the term "Anglo-Irish". The other impression was equally widespread; and it is given succinct enough expression in the words that Mr. de Valera actually used. Anglo-Irish literature, in so far as it was a literature and belonged to, or was produced by Ireland, was "far less characteristic of the nation than that produced in the Irish language".

Of course, speaking in 1933, less than a full year after the Eucharistic Congress, and on a state occasion at that, there was much that Mr. de Valera could not mention except in a very peculiar fit, or through the medium of such a sentence as the one about Irish poets and novelists producing work likely to stand the test of time. There was, for example, *Ulysses*, which had been in the world for upwards of a decade; had incurred the wrath of legal authorities in both Britain and America; and was a distant and not too savoury rumour in Ireland.

But if the picture had changed since the publication of *Ulysses*, it has changed even more radically since. To put it briefly, confronted with the phenomenon of *Ulysses*, with the poems of Yeats's full maturity, with Kavanagh's poems or *Finnegans Wake* or *At Swim-Two-Birds* or *Black List, Section H* or the Beckett trilogy, there is not much point in talking about Anglo-Irish literature. Whatever else these works are, they are not Anglo-anything, unless, that is, the work of Whitman or Hart Crane or Melville or Dos Passos or Scott Fitzgerald is Anglo-something. And the truth is that Ireland now has quite a considerable literature of its own in the English language to which the term Anglo-Irish, though still used in universities, is entirely inapplicable.

And, leaving literature aside for a moment, it may as well be said that whoever invented the term in the first place did no service at all to his countrymen, whoever they were. In so far as notions about ethnology play a part in politics – and they do, alas, play a large part – it has done its share of damage in the political sphere also. In literature the amount of confusion, if not damage, it has caused may be assessed by harking back to the work of two influential users in the era immediately prior to Mr. de Valera's speech. Daniel Corkery and Thomas MacDonagh were nationalists: indeed MacDonagh, Pearse's "helper and friend" who was, according to the Yeats poem, "coming into his force" and"might have won fame in the end/So daring and sweet his thought/So delicate his nature seemed" proved his nationalist convictions by dying before an English firing squad in 1916.

As employed by Corkery, a critic of very real influence in the decade or so before Mr. de Valera came to the microphone, it was a term of opprobrium. Whatever his ethnological origin, an Anglo-Irish writer was one divorced from that Gaelic and

Catholic tradition which was the mainstream of "Irishness". He might belong to the ascendancy class. He might even be, in origin and upbringing, "one of our own", a noble peasant who had sold his birthright for a cheque from Scribners. But if he did not reflect the experience of the "people", he was not Irish, but Anglo-Irish.

Strangely enough, though, MacDonagh, whose "nationalist" credentials were entirely above reproach, used the term in an entirely different and much less pejorative sense. He believed, and was certainly one of the first to say outright in so many words, that Ireland was witnessing the birth of a specifically Irish literature in the English language, a literature which "could come only when English had become the language of the Irish people, mainly of Gaelic stock; and when the literature was from, by, of, to and for the Irish people".

He based his claim for a separate identity first on the assertion "that the ways of life and the ways of thought of the Irish people – the manners, customs, traditions and outlook, religious, social, moral – have important differences from the ways of life and thought which have found expression in other English literature" – and secondly on the fact that "the English language in Ireland has an identity of its own, and the rhythm of Irish speech a distinct character". And for this nascent literature, which was to him Irish of the Irish, and in no sense a product of an ascendancy or an alien culture, he adopted as a mere matter of description and not in any pejorative sense the term "Anglo-Irish".

But although MacDonagh seems now more attractive, both as a thinker and a person, than the overtly racialist Corkery, there were still dire confusions inherent in what he was saying. If an Irish writer, or an Irish critic was to worry about these things, he would have to worry himself about matters which were taken for granted everywhere else. Whatever about "from" or "by", were the works of Beckett, for example, not to mind those of Joyce, really "to" and "for" the Irish people? Except in so far as they were "to" and "for" everybody? And come to that, were they?

Of course, worrying about matters which are taken for granted everywhere else is an endemic Irish occupation; and by applying a well-known psychological law we may conclude that if the Irish continue to do it, they in some sense enjoy it. Still, it is certainly no part of the present writer's purpose to indulge himself in this particular national pastime, however diverting he might find it. As far as literature is concerned most of the unnecessary worries are created by the use of the term Anglo-Irish to describe a now quite voluminous literature in the

English language of which the only definition that might be hazarded is that unlike much of the work of Goldsmith, say, or, to come down a bit, Robert Lynd or Conan Doyle, it was not written as a contribution to English literature, or any compartment or sub-section thereof.

This most certainly does not mean that it is always by any means Irish with malice aforethought. In fact the principal self-imposed obstacle to the production of work of genuine merit in Irish literature has been the concentration on certain kinds of alleged Irishness as subject matter. By a sad paradox the claim made for these subjects, at least implicitly, has often been that they belonged to the timeless or Irish-Irish aspects of the Irish experience, a claim which foreign critics have usually been too ready to endorse, Ireland being in their eyes preferably a never-never land rather than a real place. The prose writers have had more commercial inducement than the poets for their indulgence in the tawdry picturesque and the phoney primitive, but the poets with their fairground characters, travelling people, thimble-riggers and trick o' the loop men have not been guiltless either. Nor have what Beckett called, almost half a century ago, "the antiquarians, delivering with the altitudinous complacency of the Victorian Gael the Ossianic goods" yet, alas, vanished from the same scene. "Thus", he said, and the words are about as true today as when he wrote them "contemporary Irish poets may be divided into antiquarians and others, the former in the majority . . . This position, needless to say, is not confined to Ireland or anywhere else. The issue between the conventional and the actual never lapses, not even when the conventional and the actual are most congruent. But it is especially acute in Ireland, thanks to the technique of our leading twilighters". Of course, poets being poets the metrical and prosodic devices employed had also to come into a claim to be more Irish than the other man. It is not so long since Austin Clarke was elevated by Irish criticism over Kavanagh on the grounds of his use of assonance, which was supposed to be a specifically Irish mode, a use he was said to have learned from a certain Jeremiah Joseph Callanan. It linked him, it was said, up with the Gaelic and made him an unmistakeably Irish poet, whereas others were . . ? Roibeard O'Farachain even wrote a book which suggested that assonance was the way in which we could all strengthen our Irishness and was, therefore, the way forward. Ah well.

The present writer does, as it happens, believe that it is important for Irish people anyway to recognise the "Irishness" of their literature. The reflection any country or people obtains from its literature is at least as important a means of strengthening and exploring identity as is anything else. The possession of a literature is as important as is the possession of a language. Again, the establishment of an independent literature is at least as important as the establishment of an independent state; and it could be argued that in many matters the authors have so far shown more signs of independence than the state has.

There is in every country, and in all human affairs, a balance of forces, a balance in which a literature, being itself both reflection and reality, subject and predicate, actor and spectator plays a curious part. The principal characteristics of the best of our literature in English have been its daring, its humour, its humanity, its true internationalism, its willingness to face ultimates and to go to extremes. Those who reflect on the balance of forces in Ireland while leaving it out of account, are doing the wrong sums.

It has not, however, been by any means my primary purpose in the majority of these essays to isolate or analyse the "Irishness" of the authors involved. Only a very narrow-minded critic would be primarily concerned to do that. Nevertheless in some cases, most notably that of Maria Edgeworth's solitary masterpiece, I have dwelt at some length on the specifically Irish characteristics which I believe it shares with the work of some of her notable successors: the devouring interest in speech as a mode and monologue as a form, the stancelessness, the disdain for plot. I have done this in the belief that by doing so one illuminates, to some extent, both her work and theirs. Irishness may not be the most important thing, but there is no use saying that it is not of any importance, that it does not help to understanding or provide its own illumination. And, to an extent, I have used Maria to get some aspects of Irishness out of the way. Likewise, in the case of one or two minor figures, like Thomas Moore or Lever, or more major ones such as Carleton, Louis MacNeice or Flann O'Brien, I have adverted to the totality of their relationship with Ireland in the belief that it was a factor in their achievement or lack of it. But there are equally those, of whom Synge, and to a degree, Kavanagh, may stand as examples, where the Irishness or otherwise has been a source of confusion to criticism and where I have believed it important to put it in its place.

In conclusion I ought perhaps to say, though, that it has not been my aim, as it was of Austin Clarke's admirers, to encourage others to become more Irish, in technique, vision or otherwise. From now on, I rather imagine, Irishness will take care of itself. I do believe that at this point we need some sort of summing up. I think it is important to see where we stand: whether some modes come, for whatever reasons, more naturally to us than others; who among our predecessors faced the same or analogous problems; whom we might recognise as *confrères*. And I agree with Octavio Paz when he says: "We know . . . that criticism cannot, by itself, produce good literature. That is not its mission. On the other hand we know that it alone can create that space – physical, intellectual, moral – in which a literature can evolve."

MARIA EDGEWORTH:
The Unlikely Precursor

If Irish literature in English begins anywhere, it begins with Maria Edgeworth's *Castle Rackrent*; and the key dates in Maria's life as far as the composition of the novel is concerned have a melancholy aptness. Born in England, she had been given a brief, tantalising glimpse of Ireland as a child of six; and then whisked back to become, at the age of eight, a boarder at Mrs. Lataffier's academy for the daughters of gentlefolk at Derby; and – at thirteen – a pupil at Mrs. Davis's seminary in Upper Wimpole Street. When she was fifteen her admired father had decided to settle in the land which his ancestors had called home for upwards of two hundred years; and the family had come back to Edgeworthstown, to an inclement Irish summer when snow fell in June and was cupped for a while in the roses. But the year was 1782; and in April Henry Grattan, still pale and weak from a recent illness, had told the House of Commons in College Green: "Having given a Parliament to the people, the Volunteers will, I doubt not, leave the people to Parliament, and thus close specifically and majestically a great work . . . . Ireland is now a Nation."

Since *Castle Rackrent* has twice in recent years been described by eminent critics as a "regional novel", it is as well to emphasise straightaway that Maria belived in that nationhood: believed in it in 1782; and believed in it seventeen years or so later when she wrote her little masterpiece; for the title page of that work echoes something of the pride with which the claim to nationhood had been made and, up to then, sustained:

CASTLE RACKRENT
AN
HIBERNIAN TALE
Taken From Facts,
And From
The Manners of the Irish Squires,
Before The Year 1782

The phrase, "An Hibernian Tale" may, it is true, give us a little pause. It is hard to savour now because the word Hibernian went from bad to worse; or perhaps from good to worse; and so probably did the word tale, at least in association with Hibernian. She is addressing an English audience, if only by virtue of the fact that her book was first published in London (it was published in Dublin in the same year). But if it is difficult for us now to recapture the exact nuance of what she meant by describing her short novel on its title page as "An Hibernian Tale", it is even more difficult for us to hear again the faint but unmistakeable note of sennet and triumph contained in the phrase, "before 1782".

For, if not after Parnell, then certainly after Arthur Griffith, Ireland began to scorn the nationhood presided over by the Protestant assemblage in College Green. In doing this, it would doubt the evidence of its own senses, for everywhere in Ireland the remains of the extraordinary upsurge of energy and confidence which Grattan's Parliament inspired are visible: in the Georgian streets and squares of the capital; in the great buildings of its centre; in the canals enclosing them and stretching Westward as engineering miracles across the bogs; in many of the big houses with their attendant demesnes; in the great mills and still-standing granaries of the South-East. It was a time of almost unexampled and unbelievable prosperity, affecting many more sections of the population than those at the very top. Tradesmen, artisans and day-labourers benefited in their thousands; and if it did not all begin like a clockwork mechanism released by the Declaration of 1782, the commercial independence gradually extended and finally secured by the Irish Parliament was at the root of it. Even the poorest in their wretched cabins on the worst-managed estates could sniff something, however distant, of the air of prosperity; and around Edgeworthstown, in spite of the snow on the roses, it was a balmy and health-giving breeze.

For Richard Lovell Edgeworth threw himself immediately into the management and improvement of his estate with the energy and optimism which often amused or dismayed the more languid among his contemporaries. He built good slated stone houses. He sacked bailiffs and dispossessed middlemen. He reclaimed bog and mountainside. He chose tenants for their willingness to work and share in the general scheme of improvement rather than for their initial ability – or fancied ability – to pay. He even built a little railway to carry limestone from one place and marl from another. The husband of four wives and father of many children in amorous fact, he was paternalist landlordism personified; though as a saving grace he had serious doubts about the quality of the governing classes in general. The upper and middle classes in Ireland, he said, were poor stuff; the peasants, for all their ignorance, superstition and cruelty had great qualities. Government could bring out the best in them and make Ireland a great country. And at the centre of all this whirl of optimism and activity was his eldest daughter, for it was no part of Richard Lovell Edgeworth's philosophy to exclude women from the government of anything. "Not only his wife but his children knew all his affairs", Maria was to remember. "Whatever business he had to do was done in the midst of the family, usually in the common sitting-room, so that we were intimately acquainted not only with the general principles of conduct, but with the most minute details of their everyday application. I further enjoyed some peculiar advantages; he wished to give me habits of business and allowed me during many years to assist him in copying his letters of business and receiving his rents."

1782, the year of the return to Edgeworthstown, was a memorable year in Maria's life. But more than that, it was a memorable year in the history of her country. In adding the phrase "Before the Year 1782" to her title page, she was hoping to make one thing about her novel abundantly clear. She was writing about "the bad old days".

But she was also, as a matter of probable if not absolutely established fact, writing in 1798: the year of the French landing, the Wexford rebellion and the first serious mootings of a Union with England. Her book was published in 1800 and by that time the failure of nerve and the inner corruption of the aristocracy of which her father had such a low opinion were apparent to all. She was constrained to add two notes; one by way of preface, the other in the form of an afterword. The prefatory reference to the Union is the more ambiguous of the two:

> The Editor hopes his readers will observe, that these are "tales of other times"; that the manners depicted in the following pages are not those of the present age: the race of the Rackrents has long since been extinct in Ireland, and the drunken Sir Patrick, the litigious Sir Murtagh, the fighting Sir Kit, and the slovenly Sir Condy, are characters which could no more be met with at present in Ireland, than Squire Western or Parson Trulliber in England. There is a time when individuals can bear to be rallied for their past follies and absurdities, after they have acquired new habits and a new consciousness. Nations as well as in-

> dividuals gradually lose attachment to their identity, and the present generation is amused rather than offended by the ridicule that is thrown upon their ancestors.
>
> Probably we shall soon have it in our power, in a hundred instances, to verify the truth of these observations.
>
> When Ireland loses her identity by an union with Great Britain, she will look back with a smile of good-humoured complacency on the Sir Kits and Sir Condys of her former existence.

If this is doubtful, the afterword is bleak:

> It is a problem of difficult solution to determine, whether an Union will hasten or retard the amelioration of this country. The few gentlemen of education who now reside in this country will resort to England: they are few, but they are in nothing inferior to the men of the same rank in Great Britain. The best thing that can happen will be the introduction of British manufacturers in their places.

She was clear-headed enough to see the decline of Irish industry and the abandonment of a wretched country by a wretched aristocracy. She was short-sighted enough to believe that the Union would work; and that the collapse of the "Protestant nation" would be the end of the Irish nation. But perhaps the main thing to note is her conviction that there was, or had been, a separate identity; and if she is Protestant and aristocratic enough to confuse that identity with the character of her own class, she believes that the exploration of it is proper employment for a writer.

In this she is at one with most of her successors, even the less nationally-minded, such as Joyce with his "uncreated conscience", or Kavanagh with the specifically Irish types of his satires. The exploration of the Irish identity is at least a subtheme with most of them, its glorification a major theme with Yeats. Often it gets in the way of criticism, as with J.M. Synge, so that their real theme is obscured. Often it gets in their own way, conflicting with the claims of an art which, they feel, should be more clearly universal, or achieve universality by some other route. Frequently, in the case of lesser writers, it is the exploitation rather than the exploration of identity which provides what can only be called a stock-in-trade. The differences (usually from the English character or identity) are what are important: the mode is, however "realist" it may claim to be, the picturesque, with all that the word implies in the way of charm, oddity, weakness.

In Maria's case the exploration, in *Castle Rackrent* anyway, superseded the claims of the sort of educative guidance and provision of moral examples which she believed to be the main business of an author. The strange thing in her case, though, is not that it merely superseded these or anything else, but that it seems to have brought something along with it as a sort of bonus, or revealed something in her the presence of which could scarcely have been suspected, even by the most enthusiastic among her friends and well-wishers. For all the things that might have been said about or wished upon Byron's "nice little, unassuming 'Jeanie Deans-looking body' . . . . if not handsome certainly not ill-looking", about whom "one would never have guessed that she could write her name", though her father "talked, not, as if he could write nothing else, but as if nothing else was worth writing", the last the most effervescent admirer would have claimed for her was that she was an artist of the greatest subtlety.

She is said to have believed that Macbeth's speech "To-morrow and to-morrow and to-morrow . . ." was a warning on the evils of procrastination. Her only book before *Castle Rackrent* was *The Parent's Assistant*, written to exemplify the principles contained in her father's treatise, *Practical Education*. She was all her life under the influence of that worthy, inventive, energetic, supremely high-minded man – Byron's "supreme bore" – and his corrective hand lies heavy on all her other work. She followed *Castle Rackrent* with *Early Lessons and Moral Tales*. The eighteenth-century illusion that all could be improved – that all *would* be improved – by dint of example and precept, precept and example, an illusion soon to vanish and give way to Dickens' rather more plausible (and for artists marginally more fitting) belief that you could haunt, or terrify or move people into bringing change about has dated her almost beyond redemption. Most of her other work is, whatever thesis writers or variously commissioned literary gents may say, ruined in varying degree and extent by pedagogic and moral purpose. Only *Castle Rackrent* escapes into the realm of non-assertion. It is as delicate, as deliberate and as duplicious as is Henry James.

Now to attribute all this to the fact that in *Castle Rackrent* she was exploring aspects of what she saw as the Irish identity – more especially the quarrelsome, intemperate and extravagant aspects of that identity – may be to oversimplify. But the fact remains that here, and only here, the preacher in Maria, to whom the mere writer, let alone the great artist latent in her was too often made subservient, is kept firmly in its place. Here are none of the sermons, the digressions, the warnings to young ladies, the reproofs to society in general, which mar her other work. Creative excitement, that least definable but most recognisable of any writer's possible qualities, possesses her from the beginning. Though what she has to tell about varies from the merely melancholy to the grotesque to the tragic; though incompetence, waste, callousness and lost possibilities are her themes, the miracle of an art which is its own annealment is accomplished on every page. Something within this material is giving its manipulator something akin to joy. The wonder with which we may be sure the fifteen-year-old had opened her eyes to Ireland's contradictions and her ears to its speech is not lost in the woman of thirty-three. Indeed it is the discovery of a technique which will allow her to use that speech, with its evasions and ambiguities bewilderingly intertwined with stabs of perception and ruthless honesty, which, more than any other single factor, makes her first and freshest book her greatest.

The story is told – it would probably be more accurate to say that the events are chronicled – by an old family retainer, Thady Quirk. By the standards of an improving eighteenth-century landlord, or a progressive eighteenth-century reformer of any description, he is an obtuse old idiot. In his eyes, no Rackrent, however proud, spendthrift, callous or downright cruel (and most of them are these things in good measure) can do any wrong. His virtue is loyalty: to the head of the house, the chief, if you like of the clan. In the century and upwards that had elapsed since the not quite complete dispossession of the native Irish aristocracy, the Cromwellian and Williamite intruders had come to see themselves as, more or less, the inheritors of ancient Irish ways and customs. Maria's successors, Charles Lever and Lady Morgan, nearly always conferred a Gaelic lineage on their aristocratic principal figures; but this was post-Walter Scott; and, for an author with an eye on the public, a way of cashing in on the romanticism about the clan system that prevailed after *Waverly* and *Rob Roy*. That Maria was aware of the difference that existed in the two, admittedly contiguous and somewhat intertwined aristocracies, the one barely surviving amid the other, is proved by the attitude of his fellow-landowners to the eccentric Count O'Halloran, with his Continental title, his gold-laced coat and his Irish wolfhounds in *The Absentee*. She must also have been aware that the commonly advanced claim to Gaelic lineage was in part an alibi: a way of saying "I can't help it" about your faults of character; and in part snobbism: an admission that the old barbarians were in truth more aristocratic in lineage than their dispossessors. It was also a simple matter of fact that there had been a good deal of inter-marriage; and a rather more complicated matter of fact, related to the conditions and psychology of subservience, that there had been a transference of the old sort of loyalty to the new sort of chieftain, at least by poets, house servants and the like. Maria anticipates Scott and anticipates much in popular romanticism by giving the Rackrents a Gaelic lineage and their servant an essentially Gaelic loyalty. Their real name is O'Shaughlin, changed for inheritance purposes. His attitude is that of a retainer rather than a servant. Thus she solves an early problem of moral stance. The Rackrents have a sort of entitlement to be going downhill, not up. Thady Quirk's loyalty is not servility: it has something of the nobility of Yeats's "My fathers served their fathers before Christ was crucified" in it. We are on somewhat appealing romantic ground to begin with; and she has also performed for herself a distancing trick. If Thady has a totally different way of seeing things from that of his creator, it is one which we can not only understand but with which we are subtly compelled to sympathise. It is a romantic sympathy, not yet exhausted, the appeal of which is proved by the fact that it was soon to sweep Europe. In using Thady to recruit it for the unfeeling Rackrents, Maria is playing a double game.

Of course, this sort of ambiguity was not new. The obtuse narrator – obtuse by the standards of the author's intelligence and moral values – was already a type in eighteenth-century literature. Defoe's woman criminals, Moll Flanders and Roxana, see the world with different eyes from those with which their creator might have been presumed to regard it; and in allowing these inveterate liars, self-deceivers and tricksters to present themselves, Defoe builds up sympathy by presenting also their defenceless situation in a cruel, predatory and exclusivist male world.

What was new was Thady's perfectly modulated, colloquial manner: his loose but pellucid syntax with its sustained natural flow, ideally fitted not only to narration but to a rich and complex mixture of self-deception, self-revelation and devastating realism. And this was not only new, but was to prove Irish. Maria is truly delighted and absorbed by the flow of natural speech, as no major English novelist has been at such length, brief as it is, even yet; as no major American novelist was to be until Mark Twain; and she has given us a central character's thought-process and speech process combined in a way that had to wait until *Ulysses* for its culmination.

The speech-process is integral to the ambiguity. We think in syntax of some sort. We deceive ourselves in syntax of some sort. We justify and asssert ourselves in syntax of some sort. We judge and condemn in syntax of some sort. In the matter of Sir Kit's brutal treatment of his Jewish wife, of which the breakfast sausages are a part, Thady is seen at his best:

> Her honey-moon, at least her Irish honey-moon, was scarcely well over, when his honour said one morning to me – "Thady, buy me a pig!" – and then the sausages were ordered, and here was the first open breaking out of my lady's troubles – my lady came down herself into the kitchen to speak to the cook about the sausages, and desired never to see them more at her table. – Now my master had ordered them, and my lady knew that – the cook took my lady's part because she never came down into the kitchen, and was young and innocent in house-keeping, which raised her pity; besides, said she, at her own table, surely, my lady should order and disorder what she pleases – but the cook soon changed her note, for my master made it a principle to have the sausages, and swore at her for a Jew herself, till he drove her fairly out of the kitchen – then for fear of her place, and because he threatened that my lady should give her no discharge without the sausages, she gave up, and from that day forward always sausages or bacon or pig-meat, in some shape or other, went up to table; upon which my lady shut herself up in her own room, and my master said she might stay there, with an oath; and to make sure of her, he turned the key in the door, and kept it ever after in his pocket – We none of us ever saw or heard her speak for seven years after that – he carried her dinner himself – then his honour had a great deal of company to dine with him, and balls in the house, and was as gay and gallant, and as much himself as before he was married – and at dinner he always drank my lady Rackrent's good health, and so did the company, and he sent out always a servant, with his compliments to my lady Rackrent, and the company was drinking her ladyship's health, and begged to know if there was anything at table he might send her; and the man came back, after the sham errand, with my lady Rackrent's compliments, and she was very much obliged to Sir Kit – she did not wish for any thing, but drank the company's health. – The country, to be sure, talked and wondered at my lady's being shut up, but nobody chose to interfere or ask any impertinent questions, for they knew my master was a man very apt to give a short answer himself, and likely to call a man out for

> it afterwards – he was a famous shot – had killed his man before he came of age, and nobody scare dare look at him whilst at Bath . . . .

In this astonishingly punctuated passage, the real emotion, the pity aroused by the friendless young woman's situation is barely allowed through and one shudders to think what Maria in her preacher-moralist role would have made of it. As it is, there are the sly insights about the cook's happiness in having a housewife she can cheat, the degree of her pity and affection being measured by her swift turnabout. Above all, there is the fact that, at the end, Sir Kit's credentials as a gentleman have been emphasised rather than diminished. It could not have been managed in other than the vivid, colloquial mode in which it is, in which the interest of the situation is shared with the interest of the thought-process and the speech-pattern, and it was not to be managed again until *The Master of Ballantrae*, in which the narrator's syntax is, to a degree, archaic and unStevensonian, but neither so colloquial nor so capable of ambiguity as this.

And so Maria stands at the beginning of that devouring interest in speech, which was to run right through to the twentieth century. Beckett's four or five major prose works have in common with Maria's solitary masterpiece the fact that they are speech-novels, monologues. So, in effect, has *Ulysses*, even if the monologues are interior ones. Less obviously, they all share an interest in syntactical lapses, bathos, irony and a curious sort of ironic eloquence, common to Thady, Leopold Bloom and Malone, but difficult to match elsewhere in the world's literature: and if Flann O'Brien never employed a colloquial narrator to produce these effects, he would be nowhere without the intrusion of the colloquial into the formal, the bathetic into the eloquent, the ironic under-cut as well as the ironic enrichment that nearly all his dramatis personae employ. One does not suggest, of course, that Maria's influence was so great as to confer on Irish prose literature in English that pervasive talking quality which was to have such magnificent results. It was simply that confronted with an artistic necessity she found a natural mode. The appalling Rackrents could not have been presented directly, least of all by an insensate educator and moralist like herself. If they were to be the subject of a work of art, the presentation had to be suitably oblique. That the mode she found was not only a natural but a national one is proved by its continuance. And it could also be said that she provides the first example of the curious stancelessness of the Irish novel at its best. Since the Rackrents are indefensible morally, since Thady can neither explain nor justify but only present and praise them, we are free from the omniscient narrator, with his clearly defined moral certitudes, who was to weigh down Dickens, Thackeray and so many others, spoiling even, to an extent, the novels of D.H. Lawrence. When Thady speaks we are almost, already, in the territory of *Ulysses*. She was, of course, a Protestant. But she lived in a Catholic country where habits of evasion and mendacity had, within five generations, overtaken the straight-backed puritan soldiery of Oliver Cromwell. It was a long way still to Flann O'Brien's "Conclusion of the book, ultimate: Evil is even, truth is an odd number and death is a full stop". Because of Maria's all too well-developed and well-known moral attitudes; because her work is embellished with artistically unfitting footnotes and afterwords, we are aware of her; we know what she feels herself. Indeed on occasion, in the text itself even, Thady falters a bit and she sometimes shows through, but all the same, the suspension of judgment, moral and philosophical, perhaps the product of a reaction from dogma and religious certitude, and the equivocal, enigmatic and even oracular qualities of many of her successors are, in retrospect at least, and however peculiarly, present in Thady's way of telling his story.

And another dominant feature of the Irish novel which she foreshadowed was to be its absence of plot. It may be that certain great Irish writers have been simply incapable of constructing an ordinary machinery of dramatic causation. It may be that some of them, like Joyce, were uninterested in doing so. The line is hard to draw because novelists, like everybody else, turn their failings and weaknesses to advantage. In a later chapter of this book I shall suggest that *The Real Charlotte* is the only major work of prose fiction by an Irish writer which follows the pattern of implanted and pre-arranged dramatic causation which we call plot. The native genius is for the discursive, the anecdotal, the pseudo-historical, in other words chronicle; or else for construction of quite a different and often more complex kind than mere plot constructions. In her own later work Maria Edgeworth was to show herself quite capable of rather wearisome plot devices – the prolonging of Lord Colambre's misunderstandings about Miss Nugent in *The Absentee* for example. But *Castle Rackrent* is a chronicle novel. It, or rather Thady, simply unfolds. He throws away, incidentally, about a hundred possible plot situations while he does so: indeed for a dreadful moment towards the end when it seems as if Sir Condy might, after all, marry Judy McQuirk and somehow procure himself a happy ending, we begin to fear that the author was about to develop one. But happily, she doesn't. Life, she seems to say, is not like that. There is a beginning: Sir Patrick, Sir Kit, Sir Condy come into their inheritance. There is a life-path: in Sir Patrick's case of drunkenness, with the house over-flowing with fellow debauchees and even the chicken-house fitted up for the accommodation of intoxicated guests; in Sir Murtagh's case of all-consuming litigation; in Sir Kit's of gambling and quarrelling, marriage and philandering; in Sir Condy's of elation and despair as funds are raised and squandered. There are even choices of a sort, as when Sir Condy flips the coin to decide between Judy and Miss Isabella. There is an end: often, considering the characters involved, one of a curious pathos and tattered grandeur. But there are no carefully devised causative mechanisms, no concealed circumstances with a trumpery of possibility and coincidence leading to sudden *bouleversements* and revelations. Maria is a superb story-teller, in *Castle Rackrent* at least: but she does not keep us in suspense; and in this she anticipates, strange though it may seem, both Joyce and Beckett.

She lived to be eighty-two, a life of apparent composure, of more than average fulfilment and, certainly, of fame. She wrote several more novels of which *The Absentee, Ormond, Patronage* and *Ennui* are the most praised. Yet she never repeated the oracle; and there is no use saying she did, though people will say it, for there is a little Maria Edgeworth industry; and of the making of books and articles there is no end. *Castle Rackrent* is the reason why we are interested in Maria; and if it were not for *Castle Rackrent* she would be very nearly forgotten: certainly if it were not for this one little book we would say that she was a worthy, likeable, extremely intelligent person who turned to fiction as a means of doing good; displayed observation, intelligence and even flashes of artistry in the writing of it; but was, in the end, no artist .

But whether or not for the reason that when she wrote it her interest in and excitement about her native land was at its keenest; or whether, even, the brutish but curiously stylish Rackrents released something in her deepest sexual nature which a stick like Lord Colambre could not, *Castle Rackrent* is a great work of art. In nothing is this shown more clearly than in our simultaneous knowledge of the Rackrents' worthlessness and their pathos: indeed, in the case of Sir Condy, squandering the golden guineas even on his deathbed, and dying with a terrible aloneness, she rises above pathos into tragedy:

> The fever came and went, and came and went, and lasted five days, and the sixth he was sensible for a few minutes,

> and said to me, knowing me very well – "I'm in burning pain all within side of me, Thady," – I could not speak, but my shister asked him, would he have this thing or t'other to do him good? – "No, (says he) nothing will do me good no more" – and he gave a terrible screech with the torture he was in – then again a minute's ease – "brought to this by drink (says he) – where are all the friends? – where's Judy? – Gone, hey? – Aye, Sir Condy has been a fool all his days" – said he, and there was the last word he spoke, and died. He had but a very poor funeral, after all.

Where are all the friends? It was a question any of them might have asked, including the grasping, litigious Sir Murtagh. The Rackrents may be extreme in their behaviour, but they are in no real sense "Irish eccentrics"; and in death, if not in life, with wives, mistresses, boon companions, fled or gloating in their downfall, their aloneness gives them a share in the human condition which they perhaps do not deserve. Amidst noise and riot and even gaiety, they are truly as alone as Crusoe. They put their faith in marriages of convenience, in boon companions, in political associates; and they have neither intimates, nor, in any true sense, and within any true definition of feudalism, dependants. The land passes into the hands of avaricious middlemen, the wives greet their deaths as an escape from bondage; the boon companions have already deserted them. And Sir Condy dies with his lips framing a terrible question.

Maria went on to write of worthier people; to intelligent discussions of the state of Ireland after the Union in *The Absentee*, from which Ruskin said there was more to be learned about Irish problems than from a thousand blue books; to the creation of some real Irish eccentricity in *Ormond*. But as P.H. Newby shrewdly points out:

> Quite apart from the natural tendency of didactic fiction to deal in types and humours, there was, tucked away at the back of her mind, a deference to the audience for which she was writing, the aristocracy and landed gentry of England . . . . Even so, her readers would probably have accepted much more of the joyous extravagance of the original material than she allowed herself to use. The reception given to *Castle Rackrent* should have shown her that.

After 1817, though she was to live for thirty odd years, and to spend her strength and money on the relief of her tenants during the Famine, she deserted Ireland altogether as a subject. But she had already thrown away the speech weapon, amounting, as her footnotes and glossary suggest she believed, almost to a foreign language to her English readers, which had stood her in such splendid stead. For as long as she wrote about it Ireland brought out the best in her; but reading even *The Absentee* and *Ormond*, which have something of the excitement Ireland always gave her, the reader must agree with Mme. de Staël that, "*Vraiment, Miss Edgeworth est digne de l'enthusiasme mais elle se perd dans votre triste utilité*". Thady had provided her not only with what the years to come were to prove was a characteristically Irish verbal mode, but, because he was a mask, with a mode of perception as well. She wrote some good passages afterwards and created, in Grace Nugent and Dora O'Shane, women characters who had something of the cool attractiveness that she herself may have possessed. But the ambiguities of *Castle Rackrent* she never found again.

THOMAS MOORE:
The Necessary National Bard

At a breakfast party in the house of the poet M.P., Richard Monckton Milnes, Walter Savage Landor, one of the least compromising and most acute critics the English language has known, told Thomas Moore, "I think you have written a greater number of beautiful poems than anyone that ever existed". It is a judgment that might have been echoed by an astonishing number of Moore's contemporaries, but by no-one at all since. Moore's reputation began to sink from the shining height of that estimate during his own long lifetime; and if it has not sunk so low as that of some other admired poets of his day – Anna Letitia Barbauld, Joanna Baillie, Samuel Rogers, William Bowles – criticism has not much to say about him that is not, in one way or another, dismissive. In spite of Auden's affectionate advocacy, to English criticism he is a very minor lyricist who may just be allowed his place in the anthologies. To Irish criticism – which, apart from anything else, dates everything from what is called the Irish Literary Revival – Thomas Moore is a bit of an embarrassment. No-one denies that he occupies an important place in the history of Irish writing in English, or in the relationship of that writing to the rest of the writing in the English language, but the uncertainty about the nature of the place is only equalled by a distaste for the remembrance that he was once our "national bard", or, as the subtitle of Terence de Vere White's recent book has it, "The Irish Poet".

Indeed the sagging of Moore's reputation was probably hastened by the fact that as his merely literary or critical reputation began to sink, his place in the popular pantheon remained for a long time secure. Naturally, this did not please criticism and speeded up the process of decline. The popular notion of a "national bard", deriving from Walter Scott, the romantic movement and the rise of European nationalism, did not, as the critics knew, fit the facts of Moore's particular case. For all that one of his finest poems, the one beginning

Dear harp of my country, in darkness I found thee
The cold chain of silence had hung o'er thee long
When proudly my own island harp I unbound thee
And gave all thy chords to light, freedom and song

gratefully acknowledged that his country had a literary tradition far prouder, grander and more ancient than others acknowledged it to be, it staked at the same time his claim to be the "national poet" in the specific sense in which every then emergent country had one; and it was decided as the years passed that the claim did not stand up. For one thing, we came to have, even before the "Literary Revival" and even in English, better poets who were also better patriots. Moore's longer poems were said to be unreadable. His satires were in fact unread. The sentiments of the *Irish Melodies* were declared to be "trite"; the language "hackneyed"; and when, in order to inflate the early nineteenth century pages of the sort of anthology of Irish verse which English publishers were forever commissioning and Irish poetasters compiling, a clutch of them were included, it was all too sadly obvious that the words did not "stand up" on the printed page.

The truth is, though, that while Moore was not the poet his contemporaries thought him to be, he was not as bad or as boring a poet as it became fashionable to assume. *Lalla Rookh* is by no means unreadable; and while Moore did a great deal of research into Eastern material while putting off the writing of it, he had the sense in the end to give his imagination fairly free rein. The result is an "Eastern tale" not untypical of the passing century, the eighteenth, to which he and Byron still owed a sort of allegiance. It may be remarked, however, as evidence of Moore's "foreignness" to England, that the blend of erotic fantasy modified and coloured by the sentimentalities of the boudoir – which sentimentalities were, in the case of Moore, "a lady's man", never far away – was commoner elsewhere than in England. If the poem is not, in the end, highly interesting, that is because Moore's imagination was neither interesting nor intense; and though the thought is bound to occur to an Irish reader that it may have been a pity to put the amount of imagination that he did put into a tale of the orient when the occidental island from which he had come offered subjects enough, the author neither could nor would have treated his native land in the same way. "Mr. Moore, I have not read your Larry O'Rourke. I don't like Irish stories," said Lady Holland; but while Ireland may perhaps regret such diversions of effort on the part of its writers we may console ourselves with the reflection that if he had chosen a Hibernian subject sentimentality would have been uppermost. Doubtless Ireland could have provided almost everything that is in *Lalla Rookh*, including even the touch of necrophilia, but it is doubtful if Moore would have dwelt on such ingredients in Ireland's case. He made the enormous continent of Asia into a sort of Wardour Street Mahommedan's paradise; and he, above all men, would not have done anything even so interesting as that with the "emerald gem of the Western world".

Of late there has been an attempt to rescue the satires at the expense of his other achievements, an attempt which, as de Vere White remarks, could only end in the extinction of his reputation, for if the satires are better as any sort of poetry than the *Melodies*, then the *Melodies*, as poetry, must be very poor indeed. Great satire can universalise anything and doubtless a great satirist would have found in Whig and Tory politics and in the doings and misdoings of the Prince Regent matter enough for bitter reflection on the foibles of mankind, but whatever is the trick of universalisation, Moore missed it. Perhaps because he was so anxious to prove himself an insider he missed the combination of treating the subject as important and seeing it *sub specie aeternitatis* at the same time. To Moore it really is important: he comes hotfoot with the news and gossip from St. James's; and the result is breathlessness and boredom.

And so, finally, we come back to the *Melodies*, into which Moore poured his soul, such as it was; but that they also no longer command even the popular affection which once was theirs is evidenced by the fact that his recent bi-centenary (he was born at Number 12 Aungier Street, Dublin, on the 28th May 1779) passed almost un-noticed in his "own loved island of sorrows".

A hundred years before the celebrations of his centenary were loud, tearful, melodious and convivial; and the era of Tom Moore the national bard did not finally vanish until much later than that. At least until the mid-nineteen-thirties, nearly every household in Ireland that had a book at all had a copy of *Moore's Irish Melodies*, sometimes a very ornate copy, embossed with harps and shamrocks and embellished with engravings of rather long-jawed maidens seated on rocks near round towers, with a wolfhound at foot and a harp improbably balanced on the muddy ground. Every household that boasted a piano had a copy with music, the thin words elongating and ingratiating themselves among the crotchets and quavers. Almost everybody knew a dozen or so of the songs by heart; and on every occasion and in every place where Irish people foregathered the familiar pieces were sung with genuine feeling.

It was of course the era of the drawing-room (or more likely, parlour) song. Moore was the beneficiary of people's willingness to do it themselves when it came to entertainment. But there was more to the place he held in what the toastmasters of 1879 doubtless called "the hearts of his countrymen" than that; and the principal reason was that when he died in 1852, mentally helpless, having sunk under the weight of his *History of Ireland* and the loss of many children, his death coincided with an extraordinary era of cultural and emotional deprivation for the Irish people. There was the seemingly total failure of the repeal movement and the eclipse of the burgeoning national consciousness represented by Young Ireland. There was the apparently final decline of the Irish language and all, including the literature, that went with it. Neither the new shopkeeping middle class nor those beneath them in the Irish scheme of things, least of all, of course, the emigrants pouring ashore in the English-speaking lands beyond the seas, had even a national imagery, let alone a national literature, to sustain them. And for half a century or more the vacuum was only to be filled, in so far as it was filled at all, and improbable as it may seem now, by the songs and poems to music, the harps, the round towers, the swords and the sunbeams of Tom Moore.

It was, of course, his second lease of life, for, as has been said, the reputation of the poet who had been the equal and accounted the friend of Byron, who had secured an advance of three thousand pounds for *Lalla Rookh* and received such astonishing praise from Landor, was gone almost before the man was in his grave. Still, it was not the author of *The Odes of Anacreon, The Twopenny Post Bag* or a rather indecent Eastern epic that the Irish clung to. It was the arranger and provider of words for certain traditional airs, the restorer (and admittedly perhaps despoiler) of the musical fabric which was our heritage, the lyricist of easy sentiment, the celebrant of past glories, above all perhaps the celebrant of futile but heroic sacrifice, the celebrant of defeat.

Nor, of course, must we forget the sheer merit of the songs as songs; indeed it is precisely their merit and their memorability which has made it impossible and unfair to judge the *Irish Melodies* as poetry: impossible for the Irish people who can never divorce the words from the music; and unfair for anybody else, including those critics not familiar with the airs, for it is the first and most peculiar requirement of great song that the words should be subservient to the music and just that much weaker than it to ensure that they will never attract too much attention to themselves.

Three things, in fact, are necessary for good lyric writing (or perhaps one should say for good lyric writing on a secondary level, for there is a small body of supreme song which disobeys these rules and triumphs nonetheless). First, the words must be, to some extent, deficient in very striking or very difficult imagery; second, the imagery they do contain must be general rather than particular; and third, to make a very rough distinction, the thought must be subservient to the emotion. Moore's "gems", "rosebuds", "lips" and "flowers", not to mention his "harps" and "chains" fitted the first and second specifications perfectly. Thought bothered him rather less even than it bothers most second-rate poets – certainly less than it bothered the Restoration lyricists with whom his contemporaries liked to compare him. And, over all, he sought for and obtained effects as a song-writer which are not conveyed by the words on the printed page – even though some of his technical devices, such as the use of syllabics, show a high degree of originality and are now fashionable again.

Because the air is always dominant, therefore, the *Melodies* are not great poetry, though it is extraordinary nonetheless how often Moore achieves a great line, almost Elizabethan in its intensity and magic or fundamental appeal:

> I'll not leave thee, thou lone one
> To pine on the stem;
> Since the lovely are sleeping
> Go, sleep thou with them.

But Coleridge, in a beautiful image not unrelated to Moore's own, went to the heart of the matter when he spoke of "the music, like the honeysuckle round the stem, twining round the meaning, and at last over-topping it".

Yet great though the merits of Moore's songs, judged, as they should be, "merely" or purely as songs, are, their merits do not account for the place that up to a short while ago he held in the consciousness of the Irish people, or for the role that the *Melodies* played in the history of the Irish imagination, providing images round which a sense of nationhood could focus, providing, almost of themselves, the curious illusion of a golden age before the intrusion of the rude stranger, acting as a balm for injured national pride, and, above all, for a sense of national betrayal and defeat.

That was a historical accident; and between Moore as the supreme representative of the Irish soul, such as it was throughout the greater part of the nineteenth century, and ourselves, there come, one is very glad to say, a number of crucial and important things: the birth of an Irish historiography and an adult sense of Irish history (dating from James Connolly); the revival, or partial revival of the Irish language and a knowledge of its literature; the revival of Irish traditional music, the creation of a vibrant and original literature in the English language which can boast with certainty of more interesting and more relevant poets; and of course a successful or partially successful assertion of political identity which renders the sweet, sweet songs of perpetual betrayal and defeat, of the minstrel always fallen and the harp strings always rent assunder, no longer so sweet-seeming as they were.

The Irish no longer need Tom Moore in the way they needed him when he was, very nearly, their all in all. But in saying that we should have the grace to remember what he meant when he was, single-handed, repository, re-vivifier and reviver; when to the facile sadness and sense of loss of the minor romantics he brought, as a darker colouration, the greater and somewhat more serious sense of loss of an entire people.

WILLIAM CARLETON:
Idyll and Bloodshed

William Carleton is one of the great oddities of European literature, a writer with no ancestor and no successor. The life he depicted had never been written of before and in the nature of things could never be written of again; for, though much in his work is still instantly recognisable, he stands just before the point of historical change: before the Great Famine, the final decline of the Gaelic language and the last pathetic remnants of Gaelic culture, the eventual cracking of the systems of property ownership which had, as it were, roofed over the secret, half-Gaelic, world of the people, with their lately proscribed religion, their all but proscribed schools and their almost unknown language. For the people Carleton wrote of had, up to then, been almost totally sealed off from change. Even to the most intelligent members of the Protestant landlord class, the Catholic peasantry were a matter of indifference or a mystery. Their vices were well enough known: their drunkenness, their occasional ferocity and, perhaps still more disgusting, fecundity; but their secret mores, the corrupted but organic loyalties that sustained them were not, nor were the grotesque caricatures of ancient and higher ways which still lived on among them recognised for what they were, but were regarded simply as further proofs of barbarism. The drunken rakes among the squireens and smaller landlords must have known them well enough, but they were scarcely literate. And though Sir Condy Rackrent in Miss Edgeworth's best book was fostered in a cabin and drank his eggshell of whiskey from the saddle at many a cabin door, through her eyes we glimpse the aboriginal Irish only as family retainers, helpless victims or objects of philanthropy.

When Lord Colambre, in her novel *The Absentee*, returns to his heritage and his native land he drives in his carriage through just such a village as Carleton imagines a stranger riding through at the beginning of *The Hedge School*, past the miserable, mud-walled cabins with the smoke pouring through the door or through a hole in the roof, the green puddles and the dunghills, the almost naked children; but in Carleton we enter the cabins and the school itself, an astonishing manifestation of a civilisation degraded and cut off from organic development – we enter in fact the dark world of which Carleton is the solitary voice. There are things in that world which are mediaeval and earlier, for what are the disputations and the challenges by which one hedge-schoolmaster drove out another but a comic, grotesque and degraded caricature of the great contests that enlivened the universities of the Middle Ages? And there are things which go back further, to early Christian Celtic Ireland, and perhaps even beyond that again to the lake dwellings of La Tène.

An alien, largely absentee landlord system, foreign in language, religion and fundamental outlook, regarded the so-called peasantry as at best but people to be remodelled on the lines demanded by the progressive liberalism of the eighteenth century, or a sub-structure on which the classical edifice of Georgian Dublin might be reared, at worst but a source of money to be squandered in the familiar ascendancy fashion. But the accident of the system's imposition had secured that vestigial remnants of the most ancient things should live on in semi-secrecy among the people. Nobody knew them so well as Carleton, for though there is a certain amount of Irish reality in Lever, his knowledge of them is confined to their serio-comic relationship with their masters; and though Griffin and the brothers Banim belonged to the older race and its religion, they belonged also to the small-town shopkeeper classes rather than to the country people, nor are they even remotely in Carleton's class as writers.

In fact Carleton is not only the first great prose-writer to emerge from the ruins of a culture as old as history, but at his best a great writer by any standards, much of that best being contained in the volumes that go to make up the series *Traits and Stories of the Irish Peasantry*. Mere chance made him a writer at all; chance also played a major part in deciding what form his writing should take; and, one could add, has played the oddest tricks since then with his reputation, his startling emergences and disappearances. He was born in the last decade of the eighteenth century, to a father who was famous in his parish as a story-teller and a mother locally celebrated for her singing. The Irish were among the poorest and most thwarted peoples in Europe, but they retained a comic and incredible love for education, or rather for learning, most of it useless. Carleton obtained some of his under the drunken pedant who was the model for Matt Kavanagh in *The Hedge School*; but since it fortunately entered his father's head to make a priest of him he was also sent to a somewhat superior academy which concentrated on the Latin necessary for the achievement of this ambition; and at sixteen or so he was reading the classics fluently and for pleasure and was adept in three languages, Irish, Latin and English. In the matter of his education, as in so much else, he comes out of the Middle Ages.

The priesthood was practically the only method of advancement to comparative power and affluence – even if only among their own – open to the ambitious, and Carleton probably subscribed to the notion with all the enthusiasm of Denis O'Shaughnessy. It bore in the end, as we know, strange fruit, but at least the young priestling was, in spite of the poverty of his family and apart from his classical studies, allowed to spend his entire youth and young manhood in complete idleness. Whatever perils he had to survive on the road to fulfilment of his genius, he never had to escape either from the spade or from the family responsibilities which a more ordinary upbringing might have brought him. Naturally gregarious and, in spite of his pseudo-clerical garb, a noted athlete and dancer, he besported himself wherever the country people congregated. However seriously he took his ostensible vocation, it seems as if he was already preparing himself unconsciously and in idleness for his real one: the vast, sprawling picture of peasant life in all its aspects that his best work constitutes. Also he joined the Ribbonmen, one of those oathbound secret societies which struck back in blind ferocity at landlords, agents and Protestants, and frequently vented their ire in comparative safety on their more peaceable co-religionists. From them he learned something about violence, and he perhaps learned also something about Irish history which is not clear to the liberal and the enlightened yet.

The death of his father and a quick decline from little to less for his family left Carleton's vocation for the priesthood rather in the air. He set off for Munster as a wandering scholar, but quickly returned; the farm was given up, only one cow and that year's crop of oats being salvaged, and he had to impose himself as a budding priest on relatives who, though aware, he testily remarked years later, that he read the classics six hours a day, were sooner or later bound to suggest that he do something more immediately useful. For better or worse he read also *Gil Blas* and under its influence he threw himself on the mercy of the world, becoming a vagrant and, with intervals of hedge-schoolmastering and tutoring, sometimes little better than a beggar; until, towards the end of 1818, chance brought him to Dublin, where a few years later chance made him a writer.

In Dublin he alternated between the starkest poverty and more minor employment as schoolmaster and tutor, becoming eventually acquainted with an enthusiastic anti-Roman who edited a proselytising journal and commissioned Carleton to undertake a series of sketches illustrating the superstitions and tyrannies of Catholicism among the peasantry.

In this devious way, at last, Carleton arrived at himself; for the suggested propagandist tracts turned almost immediately into a detailed, intimate and utterly faithful re-creation of the world he had left. What he re-created when he got into his stride was nothing less than the life of a whole people. It is a strange one, in its grotesqueness, its often savage humour, its perennial violence and its not infrequent horror. Human life was little thought of, though the human emotions of passion, anger, revenge and loyalty were certainly esteemed. Murder, whether in jest or earnest, was frequent, and the gibbets were often seen by the roadside, as Carleton saw them, coming through Louth in that hot summer of 1818, when nobody would eat the fruit because of the flies that clustered on the bodies that hung like tar-sacks at every cross-roads, with "long ropes of slime shining in the light".

But though there is a dark side to Carleton, a part of him that seems to have been both drawn to and repulsed by the perennial murderous ferocity of the human heart, beyond and perhaps above this is a delight in the re-creation of a world which to him, after all, was really the ordinary one. For Carleton is above all, I think, a great comic artist. The grandiose pretensions of Denis O'Shaughnessy; the complicated finesse displayed by all parties in their dealings about the horse; the discomfiture of the Cambridge gentleman by the two scurrilous schoolmasters; the subtle references to the non-existent bed during the match-making in *Phelim O'Toole*; these are the comic touches of a master. And his comic gift was matched, as such gifts usually are, by an ear for dialogue which, to mix the metaphor, never puts a foot wrong. Rarely, except perhaps by Somerville and Ross and by Joyce himself, has the fecund eloquence of the Irish been captued so faithfully. And since he was re-creating out of his memories with such an oblivious faith in their value there is the constant glow of living detail: the small child who is so enraptured by the priest's boots that she forgets to baste the goose, the cow that would move out of the way of its own accord when somebody entered the door behind it. And of course there is the wonderful depth and extent of the picture itself: the pilgrimage with its mixture of prayer and bloodshed, the menace that hangs over the town as the parties separate before the fight, the crowd racing for the bottle at the wedding, the women joining in the battle of the factions.

* * *

I had written thus far in 1961 or thereabouts when the late Patrick Kavanagh objected that there was too much "historicity", as he called it in what I showed him. Carleteon's strength, he said, was not in the changing but in the unchanging. The world he described was one that he, Kavanagh, recognised from his own early experience – not at all dissimilar in terms of immediate parentage, social class and particular geographical location, for Kavanagh's father too had been a man of lore and story, a small farmer with a cobbler's traditional sophistication; and both he and Carleton had been born in what are now the border counties. I was just beginning, he said, to get on the right track; but I should cut out "the historical stuff" that came earlier.

Of course, Kavanagh had not read Carleton's novels; and neither, even yet, has anybody else read them except Thomas Flanagan, Benedict Kiely and a few students and academics who are bent on making something out of him and doing something for themselves at the same time. *Fardouragha The Miser* was re-published in 1974 by the then fairly novel photolithographic process, but such re-publication is merely a matter of re-stocking libraries and is no indication of readership. Though de Valera described Carleton as "a novelist of the first rank" in the passage I have quoted in the Introduction, it is charitable to the former President's reputation as a critic to assume that he had never even seen or handled a novel; while the possibility that he had actually read one is remote, for the novels are not, on the whole, very readable; and in truth the form was an alien one to Carleton, the mode of whose imagination was in general either intimate and profound, or melodramatic and ridiculous. He could not construct or re-arrange; he could only tell stories, which is a different thing. His genius was the native one, nurtured in near-anarchy, or at least in classless, largely propertyless, sloth and cheer, happiness and despair. Besides, his formal, introductory, explanatory and descriptive prose is sometimes clumsy and abstract to a greater degree even than we expect from many nineteenth-century writers, while the words he gives his better-born characters to speak at moments of high emotion are altogether pompous and unreal. Neither of these things is too surprising, since Carleton wrote nothing at all until he was thirty-four and met no high-born characters until after that age; but so atrocious is his prose and his educated dialogue on occasion, that we are forced to remember that not only was the formal English of the Queen's subjects alien to him, but the English language itself was very nearly so: he came from a bilingual household in which Gaelic had been the normal language a generation back.

His novels are theses, about the problems of the day. Like other Irish writers he is intent on explaining the problems to some putative, well-intentioned, educated reader on whose eventual degree of understanding the whole future of the country may depend. It was the spirit in which Maria Edgeworth wrote: uselessly, as it turned out. But if Maria in all but one book is totally and obliviously committed to a certain sort of liberal enlightenment, there is a further dimension to Carleton, perhaps two further dimensions, intimately related to each other. It is not that he is not in earnest about his liberal solutions to what he conceived as the principal socio-economic problems of the day. Although Carleton in large part published in Ireland – a fact often overlooked – as in Maria's case we get the feeling that the reader he has in mind is mis-instructed or misinformed about certain matters which are vital to Ireland's happiness. This reader seems as likely to be a member of the Dublin, Protestant, commercial or professional classes as English; and the matters in queston have mostly to do with the involutions of the Irish system of land tenure: *Valentine M'Clutchy* is about absenteeism, a theme which obsessed the writers throughout the century. Sometimes the urgency to explain is rendered the more desperate by a feeling on Carleton's part that national calamity will follow if certain things are not understood as he understands them; and it is a melancholy reflection on our history that so many of his colleagues have, over and over, been possessed of his feeling. For the most part Carleton's attempts to explain are honourable and unmuddled. He sees more than one point of view, and though this may have been a result of the peculiar "shoneen and proselytiser" position he occupied, it is an advantage to him as social thinker; indeed for someone we pigeon-hole as a primitive Carleton shows a surprisingly clear-headed grasp of economics and other matters.

And even in the novels there are many times when his imagination suddenly comes into its own and we realise that we are again in the presence of a master. The recurrent image of the dark clouds in the sky reflecting the unceasing funerals on earth in *The Black Prophet*, a novel of famine, is no melodramatic device; and the bands of murderous men blundering silently across the dark fields at the end of *Fardouragha The*

Miser are not there merely to bring the novel to a worked up end.

In fact Carleton has a sense of evil which goes beyond melodrama. He has a sense of the frightfulness of certain historical forces – for him, as for Joyce, perhaps, history is a nightmare from which one must struggle to awake – which gives him more urgency than the ordinary reasonable man and he has an, at times, almost unbearable sense of calamity; indeed it is not too much to say that the spectre of the Great Famine of 1847 hangs over even the happiest and most poignant of his pages. In writing of his own youth, Carleton seems to know that he is writing of something which is lost in a double sense; and indeed when the time came, when the cholera sheds were put up by the roadside and the potato-stalks withered in the polluted rain, Carleteon had only to go back to the famines of 1817 and 1822, to remember the horribly silent crowds besieging the grain wagons and the spectres with their mouths stained with nettles, to find the material for description; but even in the interval the memories to which he returned again and again, faithful, as Thomas Flanagan says, to them as to nothing else, were the more vivid and the more actual in his mind because the signs were already plain to him that the whole country was sliding towards a newer and greater calamity than any that had previously been conceived of.

His position, naturally enough, forced him into the role of pundit, preacher and authority. When Captain Moonlight burned and killed with more than his usual ferocity, Carleton was ready enough to purvey his knowledge and his nostrums. He was the educated native who is summoned to Government House for the purpose. When another Paddy Devaun committed another blind atrocity, well-meaning people of all descriptions looked to Carleton, who understood Paddy Devaun as perhaps nobody in his time except Daniel O'Connell himself understood him, for guidance and a moral story.

But if such "natives" often have their tongues in their cheeks, artists are supposed to bear fuller witness. We can exculpate Carleton of the charge that he held back on his feeling of impending economic and social calamity. If we are to judge him by the tests of "reasonableness" and "rightness" about the economics of government, then we must say that he emerges with credit, even to his detriment as an artist. While between the artist's Arcadian note, particularly in the stories, and the informed witness's knowledge of doom there is no conflict whatever.

And yet we get the feeling that he is holding something back. In all his politics and no-politics there is a feeling that he knows something fundamental both about human nature and about the Irish situation which his well-meaning, middle-class readers do not know, and which he sometimes swerves away from, hypocritically moralises about, or turns into a joke, but which he can finally not deny.

It is common for artists to be attracted towards states of mind and feeling of which they would as citizens disapprove; and there can be little doubt in the mind of the honest reader that Carleton was drawn to violence. Some dark streak still exists in the make-up of this reasonable and unmuddled man which he detests but which he can never destroy. It is no doubt part of his background, even part of his upbringing. Horror had stalked the fields of Arcadia in Carleton's youth; and whatever other psychological predispositions or even malformations there had been in him, the burgeoning artist had no doubt been drawn to the flames of 'Wildgoose Lodge' as to an image full of power.

But even beyond this there is something which this former Ribbonman knows; which he is concealing from his liberal readers; something which perhaps explains the shifts of allegiance, the apparent betrayals and disloyalties which made him so disliked in the fiercely partisan Ireland of his day. One can sense it in the cold terror of 'Wildgoose Lodge', the appalling violence of 'The Party Fight', the fearful scene at the Whiteboy meeting in *Fardouragha The Miser*. It is that, for anything his liberal readership can wish for or reform, violence remains endemic in the Irish situation. They could have averted famine. They could – and did eventually – rationalise and humanise the landlord system. But short of a fundamental restoration of grievance which would affect more than landlords and a fundamental abdication of power by people much less well-meaning than Carleton's liberal, Protestant, Dublin audience, violence would still stalk the fields. Carleton knew this, but he did not tell them so.

* * *

Patrick Kavanagh was brought up in Monaghan in the years which saw both a revolution and a civil war, but which were yet among the most peaceful in Ireland's agrarian history. He was a firm believer, like Thomas Hardy, in the things which go on "though dynasties pass"; and, rather illogically for one who was an incisive political satirist, or at least an incisive satirist of a society which had in his own lifetime been brought directly into being by politics, he poured scorn on the idea that public events, movements and calamities could be material for art.

That material, he said, (though, if the satires are art, a large part of his own work does not bear him out) was the humble, the simple and the eternal.

He disliked the first part of this chapter because it seemed to mix the anthropological-historical with other things; and attributed some of Carleton's importance to it, whereas for him what mattered in Carleton were the intimacies with his own world. He was in part right. Although much more of Carleton's world than he was prepared to concede had vanished, much more than I in my ignorance was prepared to admit had remained, though it has vanished now and no mistake. Where we both erred, in emphasis anyway, however, was in making – in so far as we did make – Carleton's importance depend either on what remained or on what had vanished.

He would have disliked the second part even more because it deals with a side of Carleton's work which disdains his own aesthetic and in which Carleton was, anyway, often an artistic failure. In so far as he might have alleged that Carleton's economics were an ephemerality which did not fuse with the other passions necessary to creation and were therefore a bore, he might have been right. But the same can hardly be said of other things, such as the fascination with vengeance and violence in 'Wildgoose Lodge'. These have not so far been proved an ephemerality, as we know all too well. That they did fuse with his other themes and pre-occupations, even his comic sense, and had, over all, an enriching effect is something that as social beings we may not like, but it is a fact nonetheless and one that is of importance to criticism too.

JAMES CLARENCE MANGAN:
The Necessary *Maudit*

Some twenty years or so after James Clarence Mangan's death, the young Arthur Rimbaud, who, of course, had never heard of him, invented the notion of the poet as *maudit*, "accursed". Suffering was an essential part of his role, and it was actually necessary for the poet to become deliberately *"le grand malade, le grand criminal, le grand maudit."* Part of the concept, subsequently developed by Verlaine, and adopted, consciously or otherwise, by many poets, (the otherwise often leading to strange results) was that of the poet as scapegoat, who, by sin and circumstance, getting himself into trouble and generally bashed around, atoned in some way for the sins and hypocrisies of society. By society was meant, of course, bourgeois society; there being by now, in effect, no other; and it was felt by both parties to the contract to be deeply in need of such an animal as a scapegoat. One says both parties for bourgeois society, or that part of it which knew anything about poets, gleefully, if also somewhat inchoately, adopted the idea; and gladly helped the poets to suffer and atone.

Thus, every country has its sacrificial poets. France, where the idea originated, and the self-consciousness of both poets and bourgeoisie was acute, has Baudelaire, Verlaine, and Rimbaud himself. America got off to a good start with Edgar Allen Poe and kept it up with Hart Crane and others. If the major English poets of the nineteenth century were far too disposed towards comfort to accept the role of scapegoat, in the 'nineties a whole generation, including Ernest Dowson, Lionel Johnson and Oscar Wilde cheerfully rushed in to supply a long-felt want. (Yeats's references to Dowson and Johnson suggest some guilt on his part about holding back.) The public rejoicings on both sides of the Atlantic which greeted the final self-destruction of even such a poet as Dylan Thomas demonstrated the strength of the feeling of need. Aspects of Dylan's own psychology amply confirmed that he wanted the role.

And Ireland? Well, Ireland has James Clarence Mangan; and though the poet himself frequently waved aside the proferred purple, Patrick Kavanagh. The late Brendan Behan somewhat incongruously tried to get in on this act too. The role is not in fact a dishonourable one, and the idea has much to commend it. It was invented by a considerable fellow and poets understand it. Of course, suffering is not enough. As has often been made clear, anybody who has money enough to go out and collect a hangover or contrive to get himself muddled up sexually, can do the suffering. A degree of genius or near genius is, alas for some, also desirable. But there is indeed a sort of necessity in the thing; and as far as the poets are concerned it is, whatever their declared beliefs, a religious necessity. Society's motives are probably religious too, if somewhat perverted. The critic, biographer, friend, judge, executioner, patron, whore and perjurer all have a part to play in what is essentially a religious ritual.

But a modern religious ritual, played out when others are no longer believed in; and when what are felt somewhere deep down to be the false gods of materialism and progress are being worshipped. And of course the whole idea of the poet as *maudit* has to be a specifically modern one also because it is related to the poet's loss in post-aristocratic, commercial society of what he feels to be his true, but may in fact only be his old, role. It is in part a protest against the post-aristocratic age which makes no provision for poets. Anyway, to make the claim for James Clarence Mangan that he partially at least knew what it was all about, is to suggest that he was a modern poet.

He has, of course, been ill served by the anthologists, all of them content to take in each other's washing. The representation of Mangan in Irish anthologies would seem extraordinarily repetitive, except that everything in Irish anthologies seems so. 'My Dark Rosaleen', whatever else one thinks of it, is not a modern poem: that is to say it does not relate to any experience realised by anybody walking the streets today. A product of two romanticisms, the literary one and the nationalist one, it is a fair old performance of a kind, but anybody who thinks of Ireland as a maiden, "a saint of saints", making "sweet and sad complaints", whose "holy delicate white hands" will "girdle him with steel" wants to have the general mechanism of his sensibility examined.

Nor is Mangan well served by his prolixity and general indeterminacy of purpose and style. Yeats pointed out that the establishment of a style, even though it might vary at periods of the poet's life, was half the battle. He also remarked rather sadly on the fact that it is possible to bring to birth in verse only a very small amount of one's personality. Mangan seems most of the time to be making little attempt to bring the whole man in. Part of the trouble here is that he was in fact early in the game with a specifically modern notion: that of operating behind masks and personae. All those fake or partial translations, the pretence that poems were from the Ottoman, the Turkish, the Persian, the Arabic, the German, the Irish even (of which he knew very little) may be seen as a rudimentary attempt to use the mask in what is really quite a modern way: the way it is used in 'Homage to Sextus Propertius', etcetera.

At least once he used it superbly. 'Twenty Golden Years Ago', attributed to the non-existent Selber, in other words the self, is an astonishingly modern poem and it establishes Mangan at once as a contemporary whose pain and remorse we can understand. The circumstances are not his but they are real.

> Wifeless, friendless, flagonless, alone,
> Not quite bookless, though, unless I choose,
> Left with naught to do except to groan,
> Not a soul to woo except the Muse –
> O! This is hard for me to bear,
> Me who whilom lived so much *en haut*,
> Me who broke all hearts like chinawear
> Twenty golden years ago.

The imagery is urban; there are no stock properties; no grots, vales or bowers, and nothing, from the coffee in the cup onwards, is too mundane to be unworthy of inclusion. The tone is kept low deliberately; the self-mockery is unindulgent and bitterly ironic, in fact we might almost be in the country of Laforgue, Corbière, and the Eliot of 'Prufrock'; there is no romantic agony, but there is a real agony all the same; and it jumps out of the pages that surround it in poor Mangan's works.

He wrote really a great many more good poems than the anthologists seem to be aware of, but only once did he equal this. 'The Nameless One' seems to me to be the only occasion on which he drops the masks entirely, including the romantic masks, Byronic and otherwise, that the poor fellow, in his general weakness of poetic will, perhaps did not know he was adopting. It might be thought to begin badly with the rhetorical apostrophe to the song to "roll forth . . . . Like a rushing river," etcetera, but the rhythm, even if it is only a slight variation on stock rhythm, is altogether Mangan's own.

Tell how this Nameless, condemned for years long
 To herd with demons from hell beneath,
Saw things which made him, with groans and tears, long
 For even death.

Here is the personal rhythm that is the sure mark of the genuine article. The tone is rhetorical, but it is extraordinary how mundane circumstances prevail at the same time. He admits to the drink, "gulf and grave of Maginn and Burns"; he tells us his age and condition, "old and hoary at thirty-nine"; and he tells us what his life is like: "want and sickness and houseless nights". There is nothing rarer in poetry than a successful cry from the whole encircumstanced heart. This is one.

These two poems seem to me to be not only the first two modern poems written in Ireland in the English language, but among the first in that language anywhere. For once Mangan gets his real agony on paper and it is a modern agony. It is extraordinary that they should have been written in the eighteen-forties. Between the drink and the opium and a hideous romantic love of despair, poor Mangan brought a lot on himself, and he rarely succeeded in bringing that self to poetic birth. The suffering in 'The Nameless One' has a terrible intensity. He was, if the concept has any validity in it, *maudit* all right.

CHARLES LEVER:
Enter the Stage Anglo-Irishman

To drink a toast,
A proctor boast,
Or bailiff as the case is;
To kiss your wife,
Or take your life
At ten or fifteen paces;
To keep game cocks, to hunt the fox,
To drink in punch the Solway,
With debts galore, but fun far more;
Oh, that's "the man for Galway".

The lines, about a Galway landlord and Member of Parliament, Giles Eyre, come from one of Charles Lever's few successful forays into verse; and they make one thing about him immediately plain. He was not the inventor nor the celebrator of the "stage Irishman". That dubious distinction belongs to his contemporary Samuel Lover, who collaborated with Dickens and wrote *Handy Andy*, a book which Patrick Kavanagh professed to find amusing.

Lever was the inventor, laureate and celebrator of an almost equally durable breed, "the stage Anglo-Irishman", whose pedigree carries on through the lesser work of Somerville and Ross into the "hard-drinking country gentlemen" of Yeats's rather rambunctious and sometimes less than honest last poems.

In fact when the Irish people, or, to avoid begging questions, the lower orders of the population of the island, appear in Lever they represent, as often as not, a vein of realism. His ear for the speech of those lower orders is coolly accurate; his respect for their general shrewdness not inconsiderable. Because Lever wrote, and for a long time wrote successfully, for a foreign – that is, a British – audience, his stock-in-trade was, like that of many later Irish writers, the picturesque, the outlandish and the comic. Ireland was, to him as to them, an island of "quare goings on" and laughable surprises; but although Mickey Free following after the heels of the horses provides some of them, the majority are provided by the members of Lever's own class and their hangers-on. They are in fact the Rackrents, their boon companions and their political associates broadened and, in terms of literary technique, coarsened for comic purposes; but dealt with, as perhaps everything that is seen as comic must be dealt with, generously and affectionately, so that there are really two modes of distortion, the comic and the affectionate. And when, in the later books, a genuine disgust and cruelty of portraiture becomes apparent, it is reserved for the lawyers and the middlemen who are seen to have dragged that class down.

The hall-mark of the Rackrents' world was the make-shift: the broken-down sidecar used as a gate, the pillow case that replaces the glass in the upper windows; and the element of the make-shift was strong both in Lever's life and in his literary technique. He seems to have become everything he did become by a sort of accident. He became a doctor (of sorts), a magazine editor (of sorts), and a novelist (again only of sorts) because there was nothing better to hand to become; and he wound up as a consular official in an obscure Continental seaport, the appointment having been made in very haphazard fashion by an unthinking aristocratic patron. Although he hated the place, it was there that he died.

Since his death his reputation has declined further than that of any comparable Victorian figure; but that too is partly an accident. Lever writes of a world whose cruelties and shortcomings have become all too apparent to later generations; and when we expect him to be apologetic he is, on the contrary, full of zest and glee. It comes as something of a surprise to find that he was born in Dublin as late as 1806; and that he is writing, for much of the time, about a world that had vanished before he was even born. The Peninsular War, which preoccupies him so much, was over before he was in his teens. What he knew about it he had heard from hearsay and anecdote and the same largely applies to the Ireland of all except a few later books. It is a ramshackle, corrupt, jovial Ireland; and Maria's distinction between the "bad old" pre-1782 days and the more purposeful, idealistic and forward-looking Ireland of the brief twenty years of partial independence is never emphasised. For Lever "the bad old days" are continued up to 1800 and for a while beyond; but they are in fact "the good old days": the duelling, drunken gamblers, always in money straits but always with a dodge or two up their sleeves are to him admirable figures; the roistering land they inhabit is, on the whole, a happy one. It has a capital city. It has figures of note as well as grotesques and eccentrics. Even in those books which are set, or partly set, after the passage of the Act of Union the memory of College Green is strong and three things about Lever are plain. He is not a realist; he is an artist in nostalgia. He is a perfect example of a writer whose class orientation is so complete as to colour his vision of nearly everything. (The Rooneys in *Jack Hinton* are, consciously, caricature *parvenus*; but in delineating them Lever is unconsciously caricaturing the aristocratic view: Mrs Rooney has the "coarse expression which high living and a voluptuous life is sure to impress upon those not born to be great".) And he is, in his own aristocratic, ascendancy way, a patriot.

One says his class orientation rather than his class loyalty, for he was middle-class himself. Born the son of an architect, he went to Trinity and took a B.A. in 1827. Then, in a rather desultory fashion he embarked on the pursuit of a medical qualification, voyaging to Canada and the United States as an unqualified assistant on an emigrant vessel, on which he dispensed simple medicines and doubtless simple treatment in return for board and passage; attending lectures at Göttingen, where he seems principally to have absorbed some of the more convivial habits of German student life, studying at Stevens's Hospital and the Medico-Chirurgical School in Dublin, by whose doubtless not too astringent standards he was found wanting; finally acquiring the degree of Bachelor of Medicine from Trinity in 1831.

One of his biographers remarks on the "chaotic conditions of medical studies at the time, without any state regulation or interference" and adds that "he was more remarkable for his social qualities than for his devotion to medicine, which would seem at no time to have been congenial to him and in which he certainly won no great professional distinction." Another says of Lever's appointment to dispensary practice under the Board of Health at Kilkee, county Clare, and Portstewart, county Antrim, "the cholera was then in the land and the Board was probably not very particular."

Whether or no, he needed, for he was all his life a gambler, more money than medicine could give him, and in 1837 he began to utilise that talent for anecdote, for the telling of very "Oirish" stories, which was probably the gift he possessed most genuinely, and which was both the making and, in a sense, the ruination of him as a novelist.

He began, in short, to publish *Harry Lorrequer* in the *Dublin University Magazine*. It consists almost entirely of rambling, inconsequentially jointed stories of the kind that were bandied about in the bar library (Lever might have made a better lawyer than doctor); in Trinity common rooms; in garrison towns (he might have made a better soldier than either); in big houses and country inns. Much of it is horse-play at its most unbearable. It was a rip-roaring success; it confirmed Lever's image in the public eye; and it may well be his worst novel.

Yet even here we must not underestimate him. There are fascinating glimpses of Irish lifc during the eighteen hundred and teens. The parish priest of Kilrush, for example, to which assemblage of mud huts and its benighted inn Harry is exiled by his superior officer for his sins, breakfasts from a snow-white cloth on newly-taken trout and buttered toast, has all the metropolitan morning papers airing upon the hearth, offers his guest a choice of tea or coffee and adds: "There's the rum if you like your coffee *chassé*."

Lever followed *Harry Lorrequer* with a multitude of novels all in the same vein: *Charles O'Malley, Jack Hinto* and *Tom Burke of "Ours."* etc. The public, for a while, could not have enough, Lever needed the money. The scene usually alternates between the Ireland of the first years of the century and the Spain of the Peninsular War which was largely fought by Irish regiments or regiments officered by the type of reckless, misfortunate, game-for-anything type of young Irish subaltern that Lever made his hero.

Charles O'Malley is probably the best of these. Some of the opening scenes: the hunt, the country-house dinner, the duel, the election, the review of the Phoenix Park are superbly energetic and often truly funny. But once again we are stuck in the past, in the era before the Act of Union, "the most brilliant period of my country's history" as the dedication calls it. "The rain was dashing in torrents against the window-panes, and the wind sweeping in fitful gusts along the dreary and deserted streets, as a party of three persons sat over their wine, in that stately old pile which once formed the resort of the Irish Members, in College Green, Dublin, and went by the name of Daly's Club House" it begins; though we are soon off to the wars, lightheartedly marching to the treble of the fifes on the breeze, drinking, dicing, looting and philandering as befits our station; and if the reader can forget about the grimmer realities beyond Lever's ken or caring he can follow our hero's adventures at Fuentes D'Onoro, Almeida and the Azava happily enough. Of course our author never was a soldier. The Peninsula with its dark-eyed beauties and its opportunities for glory had been a distant place of rumoured adventure in his boyhood. Yet in certain ways nobody has ever written better, even if we say "superficially" or "heartlessly" about military life or the exigencies of campaign psychology: and right enough he did claim to have had adventures on the warring frontiers of the new world, including a spell among the Indians.

Soon after *Charles O'Malley* Lever made a characteristically haphazard attempt to edit the magazine whose fortunes he had made. Then, in debt as usual, he departed for the Continent, and most of the rest of his life was peregrination.

Not so oddly perhaps, divorced from Ireland he began to treat it more seriously; and he certainly made efforts to become a novelist rather than a grand outpourer of stored anecdote. In *The Knight of Gwynne*, published in 1847, almost half a century after the event, he is still brooding over the Act of Union; but there is a difference in his attitude now: in spite of the light-hearted tone which he attempts to maintain he sees it very plainly as a calamity and one for which he must seriously find a reason. The extraordinary thing to our eyes, though, must be the fact that in "black 'forty-seven", with the people dying in their hundreds of thousands from the famine of which most contemporaries saw the Union as the cause, it is not the people who matter to Lever, but his own class, its dishonour and its loss. The opposing title page of the original edition (by the great Phiz) shows Ireland as a maiden balancing a harp upon a mound of earth. She is trampling underfoot a scroll called "Agitation" and behind her is a city which is doubtless meant to be Dublin, but has more of a look of London about it. The river of this great port is full of shipping, so it is evidently prosperous; and indeed the surround tells us that someplace or other is GREAT in the development of her resources; GLORIOUS in the happiness of her people; FREE from poverty, misery and anarchy.

Given the year that was in it, it was all a little unfortunate; and indeed the illustrator and the publishers (Chapman and Hall) of this "Tale of the Time of the Union" had somewhat simplified Lever's final admission and hope, which went:

> Of the period which we have endeavoured to picture some meagre resemblance, unhappily, the few traces remaining are those most to be deplored. The Poverty, the Misery, and the Anarchy survive; the Genial Hospitality, the warm attachment to Country; the cordial generosity of Irish feeling, have sadly declined. Let us hope that from the depth of our present sufferings better days are about to dawn, and a period approaching when Ireland shall be "Great" in the happiness of her people, "Glorious" in the development of her in-

> exhaustible resources, and "Free" by that best of freedom, free from the trammels of an unmeaning party warfare, which has ever subjected the welfare of the country to the miserable intrigues of a few adventurers.

Even this, however, comes as a bit of a surprise in view of the fact that the happiness, and, even more so, the wishes of the people seem to have been the least of Lever's concerns throughout. There is a Dublin slum scene which makes us regret that his interests were so much narrower than Dickens's until it becomes apparent that his sympathies are so narrow that he could never have written about the Dublin poor with any worthwhile degree of creative enthusiasm: like all apologists for aristocracy he prefers the rural variety and understands it better. The "mob" makes a brief appearance in support of one of the gentlemen who will not vote for the Union and is treated by him with the contempt it deserves:

> The crowd which, growing as it went, followed him from place to place throughout the city, would break forth at intervals into some spontaneous shout of admiration, and a cheer for Bagenal Daly, commanded by some deep throat, would be answered by a deafening roar of voices. Then would Daly turn and, as the moving mass fell back, scowl upon their unwashed faces with such a look of scorn, that even they half felt the insult.

Taunted by a supporter of the government with the possession of such unwashed friends, Daly answers, "Aye and by my soul, for the turning of a straw, I'd make them your enemies"; but suppresses the impulse almost immediately:

> For a second or two Daly's face brightened, and his eyes sparkled with the fire of enterprise, and he gazed on the countless mass with a look of indecision, but suddenly folding his arms, he dropped his head and muttered, "No, no, it wouldn't do, robbery and pillage would be the whole of it," and without raising his eyes again, walked slowly homewards.

The scene makes us realise how deep the memory of Emmet's insurrection and the "mob" unleashed for a moment must have gone. Even more so it is borne in on us that Lever regards the argument about the Union and the fate of Ireland as a quarrel between gentlemen; indeed the whole burden of the story is whether or not the government can manouevre the Knight of

Gwynne into a position which makes it impossible for him, for honour's sake, to abstain or vote against the measure. And while the Knight agonises about his honour, Lever agonises over the question of how the class he loved had been brought to yield up its country so easily:

> Each day revealed some desertion from the popular party of men who, up to that moment, had rejected all the seductions of the Crown, country gentlemen, hitherto supposed inaccessible to all the temptations of bribery, were found suddenly addressing speculative letters to their constituencies wherein they ingeniously discussed all the contingencies of a measure they had once opposed without qualification. Noblemen of high rank and fortune were seen to pay long visits at the Castle, and by a strange fatality were found to have modified their opinions exactly at the period selected by the Crown to bestow on them designations of honour or situations of trust and dignity. Lawyers in high practice at the bar, men esteemed by their profession, and held in honour by the public, were seen to abandon their position of proud independence, and accept government appointments, in many cases inferior both in profit and rank to what they had surrendered.
>
> There seemed a kind of panic abroad. Men feared to walk without the protective mantle of the Crown being extended over them; the barriers of shame were broken down by the extent to which corruption had spread.

The "proud independence" of the lawyers is a particularly strange notion, but except for its historical interest, the whole thing would scarcely be worth the attention of a modern reader were it not for one brilliant and malign portrait, done with a subtlety and care which is surprising in the hitherto nearly always unsubtle and slapdash Lever. Con Heffernan is a politician without office or the desire for office, the sort of parasite on power that exists in all societies. As his name implies, he is probably of lowly enough origin; nobody seems to know. He is, "in secret, far from esteeming the high and entitled associates with whom his daily life brought him in contact" but yet "no man ever went through a longer or more searching trial unscathed, nor could an expression be quoted, or an act mentioned, in which he derogated, even for a moment from the habits of 'his order' ". In other words, Heffernan too obeys the code of honour and therefore reveals a doubt somewhere in Lever of its sufficiency. His role, in the politics of the plot, is to instruct

Castlereagh in the weak points of every man who has to be bribed, or bullied or pressured into voting for the Union. His purpose, in Lever's scheme of things, is to explain the fact that the ascendancy betrayed itself. To do this he must be, pretty nearly, evil personified; but fortunately Lever's interest in the matter is so great that he is moved to create a human being of very nearly epic dimensions; and in the moral test in which they are engaged he ends by finding the player far more interesting than the gentlemen.

But not all the Con Heffernans in the world could make *The Knight of Gwynne* into a serious work of art. Lever simply did not have that sort of thing in him. What he does do is to give this first of the plot-constructed novels of Lever's maturity an unusual readability, which is more than *The Confessions of Con Cregan* or *Roland Cashel* have; though – or perhaps because – they continue the transition from the loosely jointed, rambling, picaresque works of his youth to the considerably tighter and, as they say, better constructed ones he wrote towards the end. And as he wandered over the Continent with servants and family, the whole disorderly household posting on from stage to stage in their own carriage and often being taken for a band of circus people by sober citizens, he turned his attention more and more to "the Irish question", or rather to a series of Irish questions: land tenure, repeal, Fenianism. His interest in these matters was probably motivated by little more than a search for a new sort of "Oirishness" to replace the old. He was gaming away and there was not, in truth, much demand now for elopements and duellings. The Irish question, with all its endless ramifications, had become of interest to anxious, sincere, middle-class, late-Victorian men and women; and Lever, like a host of others, undertook to explain it. Far away from Trinity and the clubs of Dublin though he was, he trots out the clichés: the natural, feudal loyalty of the peasantry, often to an eccentric with a Gaelic name; the wicked agents and middlemen who come between the landlord and those to whom he recognises a feudal obligation.

But a strange thing was happening to him; and by the time "in breaking health and broken spirits" he came to write his last book, *Lord Kilgobbin*, it was fairly evident. Writing during the passage of the first land act and the disestablishment and disendowment of the Church of Ireland, but before Gladstone's Irish policy was fully formed and Balfour's, of course, dreamed of, he is at last able to separate the interests of the landed class from the interests of England and to foresee the betrayal and abandonment by the British policy and politicians of the aristocracy over whom he had thrown, in the long ago, the mantle of his own sort of patriotism, the heroes of which are no longer the expansive duellists who had put on their top-boots and ridden up to Dublin to vote against the Union seventy years before; the object of which, astonishingly enough, is a freedom and betterment which includes the people.

Nothing is more remarkable about this remarkable novel than the sympathetic portrait of the intelligent and articulate "head-centre" of the Fenian brotherhood, Dan Donegan. Lever had always been a political novelist – he had always had the Irish passion for "pure" politics, the ins and outs of it, and how votes are won and lost – but that even he should have become so perspicaceous and analytic is evidence of how political the whole of nineteenth-century Irish literature was: indeed it may not be far-fetched to see the lack of politics in the literature of the twentieth century as a reaction against the endless earlier discussions of the causes of agrarian outrage and Irish discontent. Most of it is repetitious and cliché-ridden. Lever's originality and broadness of view came to him late.

Lord Kilgobbin is undoubtedly a curious book, full of good stuff, including a new kind of satirical, anti-establishment humour – the scene in which the Viceroy recommends his aide to take up a post in Guatemala is not far short of Evelyn Waugh – but unfortunately it is not quite the novel some of its most enthusiastic admirers have claimed it to be. Lever could do nothing by halves. Having decided to write novels of causative and linked event, he entirely over-did it. There is too much plot in *Lord Kilgobbin*; too much "construction" of the most obvious novelistic sort; too much coincidence and all the rest of it. "If I have never disguised from myself", he said, "the ground of any humble success I have attained to as a writer of fiction; if I have always had before me the fact that to movement and action, the stir of incident and a certain light-heartedness and gaiety of temperament, more easy to impart to others than to repress in oneself, I have owed much, if not all, of whatever popularity I have enjoyed; – I have yet felt that it would be in the delineation of very different emotions that I should reap what I would reckon as a real success. Time has but confirmed me in the notion, that any skill I possess lies in the detection of character and the unravelment of that tangled skein which makes up human motives."

But unfortunately it is the unravelment of that tangled skein which the novelist has deliberately tangled up with a view to unravelling it that is the basis of most of the later books. And though some of the characterisation in *Lord Kilgobbin* is, on a sketchbook level anyway, quite brilliant – the Irish adventurer, Joe Attlee, who has elements of both Tim Healy and Oscar Wilde, though neither of them had yet been heard of; the cynical English politician, Lord Danesbury, who reminds one of the philosophical Balfour and the indolent Roseberry, though they too were in the womb of time – event and character, event and motive seem often unrelated and even at cross-purposes. (Of course they sometimes are in life, as the novelists of character-motivated event cannot admit; but in *Lord Kilgobbin* it is the novelist's hand which too obviously plays the part of drift, or circumstance or social destiny or whatever).

Still, it is nice to think that he kept some of the best wine till last and produced it though he was beholden to the British government for the consular job. He ended his days in Trieste on the Adriatic, a post he had received from Lord Derby, who said, "Here is six hundred pounds a year for doing nothing and you are just the man to do it", from which remark one surmises that his lordship may not have thought the writing of novels amounted to a day's work. His last years were ironically saddened by the fact that his son had an unfortunate career in that army which he had imagined as full of scapegrace heroes, and by the boy's death. Also he disliked Trieste, though he wrote *Lord Kilgobbin*, which is high-spirited and optimistic enough, there. He is buried in the British cemetery, near to Winckle-mann the archaeologist. One hopes that James Joyce, who went into voluntary exile in the same city, may have made a pilgrimage or two to his grave. They had, strange to say, quite a lot in common: an unorthodox patriotism; a good deal of contempt for the plot-making process; and, above all, of course, a sense of humour.

WILLIAM ALLINGHAM:
The Lure of London

Since the dawn of time – well, anyway, since Thomas Parnell, who was the friend of Pope and Addison – there have been Irishmen who dreamed of literary careers, and, perhaps more important, literary acquaintance in London; but there can have been few whose longings were so intense as those of William Allingham.

The *Everyman Dictionary of Literary Biography* says that he was born at Ballyshannon, county Donegal; was the son of a banker of English descent; and ultimately settled in London, where he contributed to Leigh Hunt's *Journal*; all of which is true enough except that banker, English descent and even settled in London need to be qualified in various ways and contrive to give an entirely wrong impression if they are not.

Banker in an English context means the Baring-Goulds and the Warburgs. In a Ballyshannon context it means something entirely different. Allingham's father was manager of the local branch of the Provincial Bank; but in the nineteenth century that did not prevent him from being a local business man in his own right, and even owning a ship or two which carried timber and slates to such faraway places as Montreal and the Baltic ports. He would seem to have been of the same class and ilk as Yeats's uncles, the Pollexfens: a Protestant merchant, a figure in a small-town community within a small-town community, probably fairly tight-fisted and with a strong work ethic. But in William's case there does not seem to have been any trickle of inherited money in after years to enable him to become what he wanted to become: a poet among poets in England. And therein, rather than in lack of talent, remoteness or provinciality lay the main obstacle to his dream, a fact which says something for his personal qualities at least.

English descent, however, needs even more qualification than banker does. The Allinghams had been in Ireland since Elizabethan times; and that makes him Irish and the product of Irish conditions. As a Protestant, he would have been at a little distance from "the people"; but as a small-town Protestant, ranking a good deal below gentry, not as far from them as all that; and since he lent his services freely as letter-writer to illiterates and adviser of unfortunates, he acquired a more intimate knowledge of some aspects of Irish life than would have been usual among his social equals. And if "settling in London" meant overcoming physical, circumstantial and financial obstacles, it would, somewhat to Allingham's surprise, involve emotional ones too. The reference book I have quoted gives the impression of having pulled up stakes and got out, just like that: but it isn't quite the truth. When he walked in youth and young manhood by what he would call, in a phrase thousands of his countrymen would come to know, "the winding banks of Erne", or stood on the bridge gazing through the clear water at its speckled brown bed, his mind was full of imaginary literary converse, literary companionship and literary fame. He associated these things with England and not at all with Ireland: with London and not, in any sort of a way, with Dublin. His dream – the dream of converse, of friendship, and even, up to a point, of fame – would come true, in spite of all the obstacles and somewhat to his own surprise. But when it did, he would find himself rather strangely pulled back. His life was a tug of war between London and things to do with Ireland. Not certainly between England and small-town, pastoral Ireland in the nostalgic sense that the poem about the winding banks of Erne suggests, but Ireland all the same. It was a tug of war in which both sides were, in the end, oddly victorious; but then the whole point about Allingham is that he was a writer, a poet, and he had both an actual and a creative life. Still, it was a near-run thing and we must be pleased that he managed it, for the things that were tugging at him could equally easily have cancelled each other out.

In the first life, the actual life, London was apparently victorious. Allingham was lucky beyond even the intensity of his early dreams, though it took him a long time to get what he wanted, partly because of paternal disapproval, partly because of mere circumstance and the actual necessity to earn a living. After going to school at Killeshandra, county Cavan, he went, as his father intended, into the bank; and for eight years he worked as a bank clerk, doing stints in Armagh, Strabane and Eniskillen as well as at home in Ballyshannon. He spent some of his holidays in London, going there first at the age of nineteen and continuing to visit when he could. At first he knew nobody. Then he met Leigh Hunt, a battle-scarred old warrior of wide acquaintance who had been on terms of intimacy with the mythical Byron and Shelley and edited a magazine in which he published young Allingham's poems. Through him he met others, some of them seniors and already towering figures, like Carlyle and Tennyson; others glamorous contemporaries like Coventry Patmore and Dante Gabriel Rossetti. This was the marvellous Rossetti, the young poet *par excellence*; and Allingham knew him and his friends before the fates that attend the most brilliant began to dog his path and brandy and chloral became his refuge and his doom. They were all kind to him – London literary life is kind, or seems kind to an Irishman. More important, they treated him as an equal; so the ironies of his position began to be quite painful. Allingham was now a customs officer. He was stationed in the town of Donegal. He had a salary of eighty pounds a year. And to be a friend of Tennyson's; to spend your few weeks in London; to come back to Donegal and your job as principal coast officer. Well, of course it couldn't last. In 1854, by which time he was thirty and in the Coleraine customs office, he left the service and tried to live as a free-lance in London. He failed. He was not the sort of stuff of which penurious free-lances are made. He had had, as they would say now, respectability and conventionality paternally introjected into him; and he was, as his Irish friends would have said, lucky to get himself re-instated in "the service". But in 1863, when he was thirty-nine and had been back in the Ballyshannon office for some years, he arranged a transfer to the London docks. This time he had a nervous breakdown for which the reasons are not clear. And so there was another spell back home and then another transfer, to Lymington in Hampshire. It seemed to work better. The following year Gladstone quoted from a poem of his in the House of Commons; invited the poet to breakfast; and prevailed upon Palmerston to give him a pension, as he had, years before, prevailed upon Russell to give one to Tennyson and make him the laureate.

As far as the love-affair with England, or, to be more exact, with the world of English letters was concerned, all seemed to be set fair. He was still the intimate of Tennyson and Carlyle, both of whom he worshipped. He became attached to *Fraser's Magazine* and in the course of time succeeded the great J.A. Froude as editor. A shy man, who had been saved from the sort of small-town Irish marriage which would have finished off his dreams for ever, he married an Englishwoman of ability and intelligence, Helen Paterson, the water-colour painter. The gruff Carlyle stood godfather to their child. Yet Ireland was to be his destiny, as perhaps he knew.

The poems by which Allingham had first attracted the

attention of Rossetti and the pre-Raphaelites were not for the most part Irish in subject matter. Indeed they were scarcely anything in subject matter, being in the main vague, dreamy, young man's verses and less than remarkable either for their diction or imagery. In the course of time the Imagists would claim him because of 'Four Ducks On A Pond', which got into the later editions of Palgrave, and which almost, but not quite, solves the problem of what to do with the image. (To this day nobody has quite succeeded in letting it alone.) And in his very first book, in the year 1850, he had in fact published a poem which is an uncanny foretaste of the Celtic Twilight, even to the mention of Yeats's Rosses. This was 'The Fairies':

> High on the hill-top
> The old king sits;
> He is now so old and gray
> He's nigh lost his wits.
> With a bridge of white mist
> Columbkill he crosses,
> On his stately journeys
> From Sleaveleague to Rosses.

Although Saintsbury attacked this in the *Cambridge History* after getting the title wrong (he called it 'Up The Fairy Mountain') as having plagiarised "one of the most beautiful Jacobite ballads" in its first stanza and then failed to live up to it, Quiller-Couch put it into the *Oxford Book of English Verse*, which gave it a spurious appearance of immortality until Helen Gardner came along seventy years later and took it out again. But what is important is that in his time Allingham did not trade on fairies or anything else. He was not, when he first began to attract notice, asking for it as an Irish poet. His interest in local ballads would lead him, right enough, to write the abominable 'Adieu to Ballyshanny' which is in all the Irish anthologies; which every half-literate Irishman knows; and which doesn't at all reflect his feelings about Ballyshannon, a place he was very glad to leave. But though the Irish poems he wrote are collected separately and given prior representation in the first volume of the (heaven help us) six volume edition which began to appear before his death, except for one quite astonishing long poem, totally different from anything else he wrote, you could have known – as many of his friends did know – his work quite well up to the time of its publication and not think of him very much – as many of his friends did not think of him – as an Irish rather than any other sort of a poet. This long poem, *Laurence Bloomfield In Ireland*, is the one from which Gladstone quoted in the House of Commons. It is a verse-novel, which was a form that appealed to the Victorians, but to say that *Aurora Leigh* and *Glenaveril* are child's play compared to Allingham's astonishing poem is no more than the truth. What appealed to Gladstone about it is that it is, in part, a serious examination of the Irish land question; but it is more than that. It is a sombre, varied and realistic picture of the Ireland of Allingham's day and the most succesful use of the heroic couplet in English since George Crabbe. Something happened to Allingham when he began to use this form which perhaps coincided with something that was happening to him mentally at the time – the time immediately preceding his 1863 foray to London – in relation to Ireland. Gone is all the dreamy pre-Raphaelitism of his earlier verses and instead we have precise natural and social observation combined with a degree of controlled emotion ideally suited to the couplet form:

> The cornstacks seen through rusty sycamores,
> Pigs, tattered children, pools at cabin doors,
> Black flats of bog, stone fences loose and rough,
> A thorn-branch in a gap thought gate enough,
> And all the wide and groveless landscape round,
> Moor, stubble, aftermath, or new-ploughed ground . . .
> Or, saddest sight, some ruined cottage-wall,
> The roof-tree cut, the rafters forced to fall
> From gables with domestic smoke embrowned
> Where poverty at least a shelter found . . .
> Th'observant rider passed too many such;
> Let them do more (he thought) who do so much
> Nor, where they've killed a human dwelling place,
> Unburied leave the skeleton's disgrace.

The story is not a highly original one. The young landlord, Laurence Bloomfield, returns to an Ireland of evictions, discontent, outrage and murder. Nor is the message highly original, for ever since Maria Edgeworth's *The Absentee*, writers of all descriptions, including William Carleton, had been blaming agents and middlemen for the state of affairs that prevailed. All would be well, every writer said, if the (usually high-minded) landlord-hero only stayed at home and took matters into his own hands. Bloomfield is torn between what he sees to be his duty and the possible enjoyment of his rents abroad: torn between Ireland and elsewhere, just as Allingham was, elsewhere being, in one sense at least a considerably more glamorous option. Within this framework, though, Allingham offers a sort of total poem about

Ireland: its history, its social stratifications, its religious differences. He was conscious that he was doing something difficult and new, bringing, as Yeats might have put it, the balloon of poetry down to earth and into the confines of thought about everyday issues. In 1860 he wrote to Rossetti: "I am doing something occasionally at a poem on Irish matters, to have two thousand lines or so, and can see my way through it. One part out of three is done. But alas! when all's done, who will like it? Think of the Landlord and Tenant Question in flat decasyllables! Did you ever hear of the Irish coaster that was hailed, 'Smack ahoy! What's your cargo?' 'Timber and fruit!' 'What sort?' 'Besoms and potatoes!' I fear my poem will no better fulfil expectations."

Eventually the two thousand lines became five; and nobody much did like it, except perhaps Gladstone, in spite of its acute social observation, its historical scope, its attempts to be rational about historical entanglements and tragedies which still tempt poets to exploit (while of course disapproving of) the tribal ferocities involved. *The Concise Cambridge History of English Literature* (in its chapter on Anglo-Irish literature) was, in the nineteen-forties at least, still saying of Allingham that "though he was born in Ireland and wrote Irish poems that became popular in Ireland itself" he "was not really an Irish poet. His literary affinities were with the pre-Raphaelites, and he had no marked feeling for Irish thought and speech." And Tennyson was considerably put off by this anti-poetic return to the bogs he felt had detained Allingham long enough: "There you are, with an English name," he said, "English in every way, but you happened to be born in Ireland, therefore you are for it. You don't care a pin about the Grand Empire of England. You ought to be proud surely to be part of it."

Yet, over the years, *Laurence Bloomfield in Ireland* has had its admirers, not least because there is no indulgence in local colour for local colour's sake; because it is full of acute social, historical and psychological insights; because, *pace* the *Cambridge History*, Allingham is a master of natural speech and conversation within his rhyming, decasyllabic bounds. Geoffrey Taylor said that "it is, judged by European standards, a minor classic" and the judgment is a sober one. Allingham knew the difficulties of his task, a "poem on every-day Irish affairs, a new and difficult, and for more than one reason a ticklish literary experiment".

He wrote it between 1860 and 1863 when his longing for England and English converse had reached fever pitch. As we know, his dream came true and he became the respected English man of letters. Ireland continued to pre-occupy him and he meditated a history as well as collecting his ballads. The cliché thing to have done would have been to express an easy nostalgia through poems such as the Ballyshanny piece. Before he died, Katherine Tynan, hoping to please, sent him a clipping from the *Providence Journal* in which a young man called Yeats actually called him the poet of Ballyshannon. "Non-national, how sad", Allingham replied, which suggests second thoughts about his whole career. And in 1885, four years before the end, he wrote to Sir Samual Ferguson, the father figure of the "Irish Literary Revival" in terms which suggest a hope that his name will be associated with Ireland.

But his contribution to Irish literature had already been made: an imaginative immersion from which he emerged shaken, as evidenced by his 1863 breakdown. Nothing else he wrote is worthy of this adult and original conscription of the muse to an everyday task; indeed little else in the literature of the second half of the nineteenth century, English, American or Irish, compares with it. A divided man, whose divisions may, for all we know, have helped him, even before he reached the meridian of his English career, he had already been saved from the fate of so many other minor literary exiles.

GEORGE MOORE:
The Self-Made Modern

If some writers are born, and others are made; then George Moore was both. Few writers of comparable stature have ever allowed themselves to be so governed by studied theories and acquired principles as he was in the composition of the early novels; and yet, once he had mastered other people's ways of doing it and found his own, it is impossible to imagine this voluble, egotistical, eccentric and unpredictable man as other than a writer of highly individual books.

The contrasts are extreme. Whatever the results – and the results are, in at least three instances, quite considerable – there was something more than a little comic in the way he set about applying his French-learned principles and forcing an entrance into English literature, after shrinking rent-rolls and the realisation that he was not destined to be a painter forced this natural *boulevardier* and *bon vivant* back to London in 1880. Everything he did was justified by Zolaesque theory; a lot of what he did would have killed off anybody else's creative impulse straightaway; and he did nothing by halves.

A natural aesthete, he sought out the ugliest and least promising subjects. An impressionist to the core and a lover of all that was fleeting, light and airy, he bent himself nightly to the blue books and the police court reports. In search of material for *A Mummer's Wife* he endured not only a sojourn in Hanley, the ugliest of all the pottery towns, but a stint with a tenth-rate touring company playing French operetta in the dreary Midlands. Everybody knows how he spent hours listening to the maid of all work in the Strand and the laundress in the Temple. Eliza Aria has recorded how he investigated hospital conditions; and Havelock Ellis has told of his interest in the statistics about unmarried mothers.

Yet when George Moore finally achieved his masterpiece he wrote a book which clarified and obeyed his own deepest and most fundamental instincts as a literary artist; was breathtakingly original in form; and, so far from owing much to any contemporary model, anticipated in one way or another most of the masterpieces of the next half-century. And if, moreover, the subject of *Esther Waters* – misfortunate servant girl, of *A Mummer's Wife* – Madame Bovary with tawdry theatrical ambitions, and even of *Evelyn Innes* – rich people with aesthetic pretensions, are too easily defined and too obviously chosen with cold-blooded care, the subject of *Hail and Farewell* is still almost impossible to define or describe. It is certainly not, as Richard Cave seems to think, a history of the Irish Literary Renaissance, for apart from anything else, if it were it would be as dead as mutton. It is certainly not either, as critics with a penchant for cliché have assumed, a record of Dublin doings and gossip. Dublin eccentricities, doings and gossip have always been vastly overestimated as a subject for works of literary art; and in fact its only poor pages are when the "well-known Dublin personalities" and, worse still, "characters" appear. Father Tom Finlay is a plain bore; but Gogarty is a disaster; and we learn to dread the moment when Conan's shadow will fall over the little garden in Ely Place.

Nor is it, in any ordinary sense, an autobiography. Moore was an egotistical man who in the early novels had gone far towards suppressing his own ego entirely and performing not only the feat – rare enough for a male novelist – of entering into a woman's psychology; but that of entering into the life of classes and types known to him only from observation as well. By contrast, of course, and in plain subsidiary intention, *Hail and Farewell* is autobiographical, much of it revealing and confessional to a degree not only rare then, but rare at any time when combined with Moore's insights and interest in the world through which his ego-figure moves.

He tells us a lot that is truly revealing about the timid young man who took up painting partly in order to see the models naked; was fascinated by the unprocurable ladies of St. John's Wood; and vainly envied Lewis Hawkins both his talents and his girls. But if the word "autobiography" has an inevitably self-indulgent ring to it, and if *The Confessions of a Young Man* would have led us to expect posings, pirouettings and self-justifications after the mistakenly Rousseauesque fashion of the 'nineties, nothing could be more refreshing than the novelist's grasp, the placing of the hero as a man among men and women; and the recognitions of other people's identities – both public and private – which distinguish *Hail and Farewell*. Autobiographies do not commonly suggest so much so movingly as Moore's brief advertence to Edward Martyn's relationship with his mother does. We feel for – and respect – few brothers as we feel for and respect the Colonel here. Throughout the early scenes in Paris, with their exactly balanced sense of youth disappointed, youth irrecoverable, and youth wildly fortunate in its time and its place, the interest of Lewis Hawkins is as great as the interest of Moore himself. In a self-contained autobiography we would hear much more and in other forms than the interpolated lecture about the Nouvelle Athènes and the friendships with the Paris great. But *Hail and Farewell* is not an autobiography, though it has autobiographical themes and strands among the many other ones which go to make it up.

Moore's problem after *Evelyn Innes* in fact – perhaps truly after *Esther Waters* – was the perennial one of the Irish prose writer, of Carleton, of Joyce, of Flann O'Brien, of Francis Stuart – the problem of form. He had made ferocious attempts to turn novelist, to externalise, to project, to dissemble, to construct. They were not unsuccessful. *A Mummer's Wife* is better than a French naturalistic novel turned into English has a right to be. *Esther Waters* is a very fine novel indeed; and both books, although in their woodenness and ascetic concentration on the theme they smell of the lamp, have a wide generosity of approach to all misfortunes and a particular generosity of concern for the women who in most circumstances get the worst of it. After *Esther Waters* he remembered his aesthetic obligations; and he experimented with the possibilities of fine writing. The results we know: it might not be much of an exaggeration to say that after *Esther Waters* – after *Evelyn Innes*, anyway, the suspicion that he was done for had occurred to him.

After all, he had tried his best. He had done what no Irishman had ever done before – and, with the exception of the two ladies whose masterpiece, *The Real Charlotte*, had appeared the year after *Esther Waters* – what no Irish person has done since. He had written a first-class, straightforward novel which bears comparison with the masterpieces of other literatures. To do this, however, he had had to suppress a great deal of himself; and he had had, to a degree, to turn English and French: adult and responsible. (His own comments on *Esther Waters* while he was writing it are full of delight at the Englishness of it all.) But having done that, he had still, he must have known, not written a great, much less a unique book. And he had, as he says in *Ave*, run out of material.

Then came the return and the sojourn; and, with whatever interval for reflection, the dawning realisation that he was at last stumbling on a form must have come to him also. Its extreme originality has scarcely been adverted to by criticism yet; but to count up its characteristics is almost to enumerate those of modern literature in general; and whether or no the authors of those works read him in their various ways it anticipates not only *Ulysses* and *At Swim-Two-Birds* but *The Waste Land*, the *Cantos*, Proust (*À La Recherche* began to appear in 1913, the year after *Vale*) and all the English Proustians, big and little, from Waugh to Anthony Powell. Like the form of *Ulysses* and *The Waste Land*, it is non-linear and non-consecutive. It abolishes or transcends time while acknowledging that we are creatures of its passage. It substitutes the laws of memory and poetic association for the laws of logic and narrative. It is concerned with the image as well as with the thought; and sometimes with both as one. While giving the mere moment more value and intensity than it is normally given in prose fiction, it includes everything outside the moment that is admitted as includible by its own laws of connection. It places as much value on the moment of realisation as it does on the moment of conflict; and it unfolds the past with the same degree of suspense and suggestion as other works do the future. In all these respects *Hail and Farewell* anticipates a specifically modern tradition (of which the precursor is admittedly Sterne). In two others it belongs firmly to an Irish one, harking back not only to Sterne but to Maria Edgeworth, Lever, Carleton and a host of others, as well as forward to Joyce and Flann O'Brien: one of its primary modes of embodiment is conversation and one of its most important methods of revelation is to take the comic view.

So natural are the transitions and the departures from one point in time or in space to another that its true inclusiveness only dawns on one after a second or third reading: "A place must be found, I said to myself, in my story for that pack of hounds, for its master, for its whip, and for the marvellous pony, and for a race-meeting, whether at Ballinrobe or Breaghwy or Castlebar. Castlebar for preference". And of course a place was found, though not in the unwritten novel Moore was then discussing, for these things and for much else: for feudal Mayo in the 'sixties, for the life of the Big House, for Oscott, for Montmartre, for Coole Park and Lough Carra, for the September evening under the trees at the corner of Appian Way, for all "past moments that retain the sensual conviction of a present moment"; as well as for Catholicism and Protestantism, nationalism and literature, the religion of art and much else.

And all this, of course, is to leave out the major portraits, done with a tact and delicacy that the novel training must have helped him to achieve. (One speaks of literary tact, of course, which is all that Moore was concerned with, but of which he proves himself again and again, with Hyde, with Yeats, with Edward Martyn, Lady Gregory and others the master.) Nor must we forget the minor characters: Dan Blake, Jim Browne, the Reverend Mahaffey; the old priest who taught him Latin. *Hail and Farewell* is inclusive in the two literary senses that count. First, in its range, its sheer ability to deal with so much of Moore's life and thought and Irish life and thought; and second in its ability to include, to "bring in" what fundamentally mattered to Moore himself and to the secret recesses of his spirit.

Of course, the idea that he was writing a sacred book which would have its effect in redeeming the Irish soul from servility and servitude and opening to it windows upon art and literature is not altogether to be despised. Moore was a man with oddly deep powers of social observation; and with a trenchant, if freakish, degree of concern for the quality as well as the justice of the life around him. But the great Wagnerian climax with its accompanying triumphant bar of music which the whole work comes to towards the end is not because the possibility of a "sacred book" had dawned on the author; but because the possibility of a form had: "I had striven to fashion a story, and then a play, but the artist in me could not be suborned. Davitt came with a project for a newspaper, but he died; and I had begun to lose patience, to lose spirit, and to mutter, I am without hands to smite, and such like, until one day on coming in from the garden, the form which the book should take was revealed to me".

The question has been raised whether it is a form best suited to fact or to fiction; but in one other respect at least this self-conscious literary artist who, abandoning art, came to Ireland on a mission and found a mode of art instead, was a pioneer of some importance. The barriers between art and life; between "fact" and "fiction" were for a variety of reasons about to come down. It is a process that has continued from *Ulysses* through *Black List, Section H*; and it has not ceased yet. In beginning it, as in so much else, Moore was ahead of his time.

EDITH SOMERVILLE AND MARTIN ROSS: Women Fighting Back

I

Edith Somerville first saw her cousin, Violet Martin, on 17th January, 1886. "It was", she wrote in after-life, "as it happens, in church that I saw her first; in our own church, in Castle Townshend . . . It is trite, not to say stupid, to expatiate upon that January Sunday when I first met her; yet it has proved the hinge of my life, the place where my fate, and hers, turned over, and new and unforeseen things happened to both of us."

The date is important. January 1886 was the month in which Gladstone announced his conversion to Home Rule. Loyalists of all shades of opinion had banded together to fight the general election of 1885. Their hopes were high, but they were totally shattered, Home Rulers being returned for every seat outside the bastions of Trinity College and a few North-Eastern counties. Worse, now that the Ballot Act was taking full effect, they were a new kind of Home Ruler. The liberal landlords with Home Rule tendencies elected in the 'seventies had largely given way to shopkeepers, village publicans, tenant farmers, even wage-earners. For more than a decade the ascendancy had suffered shock upon shock. There had been many actual deaths by violence in what were considered treacherous circumstances. What was even more upsetting was the lost illusion of a feudal relationship with their tenants. As Patrick Buckland has put it in the first volume of his history, *Irish Unionism*:

> It is almost impossible to exaggerate the impact of the Land League crisis upon the ascendancy. Such concentrated class antagonism Ireland had scarcely ever known. Agrarian outrage had been lived with, but what was new with the advent of the Land League was that not only "bad" landlords but all landlords were the objects of hatred.

Still, it had been possible, up to now, to speak of agitators, socialists and the underhand influence of Catholic priests. Even

Wilfrid Scawen Blunt had, in a letter to *The Times*, spoken of the Irish as a conservative, feudally-minded people, accidentally thrown in 1880 on the Liberal side. After 1885 no-one could speak like this any longer. Gladstone recognised the fact, welcome or otherwise, and recognised in the 1885 election, "the fixed desire of a nation, clearly and constitutionally expressed". Two weeks after the cousins met outside the little feudal church of Castle Townshend, he formed his third administration with the express purpose of bringing in Home Rule and the first reading of the resulting bill took place without a division on the 13th of April.

Later in the year there would be another outcrop of agrarian violence, often closely associated in the minds of those whose cattle had been maimed or whose houses were fired into with the influence of the new breed of nationalist M.P. By the year's end almost one thousand people were under police protection; two hundred and fifty of them under constant guard.

We can now recognise it as the old colonial story, repeated in Kenya and elsewhere, but the landlord class had been taken horribly by surprise. The illusion that they commanded not only the rents and services but the affection and loyalty of their tenants had gone very deep, the more "idealistic" the landlord the greater being the deception. Sir Walter Scott had given the loyalty of the clansman to his chief a strange romantic appeal. Over and over again in the Irish novel of the nineteenth century the idea that the Irish had attached this deep, inherent sentiment of theirs to the people in the big house is expressed; or, since the facts were so often and so plainly otherwise, it was said that they yearned to, and would, given the chance to do so by the extirpation of middlemen or the dismissal of wicked agents, these eventualities often providing the basis of a touching story with a happy ending.

But the lines of battle were plainly drawn now. There were to be no more such happy endings. The landlord class would live out the rest of its own tenure in a state of siege, more or less violent. Between the late 'nineties and the late nineteen-hundreds there would be a comparatively idyllic interval, or at least what could seem like one if you were selective in what you took note of; but the relentless take-over of the land, assisted by public enactment, spearheaded often by local businessmen of the type that provided the nationalist representation in politics, would continue.

II

Edith Somerville and Violet Martin were women in a male world. It was not a fact they spoke of in the manner in which women often do to-day, but it was a fact nonetheless. The world of the big house was male created. The men, who had won their lands by the sword, or believed they had, belonged to a warrior caste. Thomas Somerville, who built the family home 'Drishane', had made his money in shipping; but Edith's father was a lieutenant-colonel in the Buffs; and her mother was an admiral's daughter. The virtues that the men prized were male virtues: loyalty to the Crown, a tradition and a code; valour in battle; male camaraderie.

Yet throughout the adult lifetimes of the two cousins these defenders of empire seemed strangely unable to defend their own homes, families and lands; even, as they would have thought, the best interests of that corner of the imperial dominions which they called their native country. They were not adept at political combination; and, even if they had been, they would, as they had just found out, have lacked popular support. They were, in many cases, poor businessmen, easily outsmarted or outwitted or cheated by those they thought of as their inferiors. To the bitter cup of feudal disloyalty and the laughter of those inferiors at their most cherished illusions they would, from 1886 on, have to add an even bitterer one: their abandonment by the imperial interest which they had served with such unthinking devotion in so many far-off places and under so many alien skies. The puzzlement and dismay of many at this poor return for service would eventually find expression in the Curragh mutiny of 1914; but the abandonment was then almost complete; to the Machiavellian manouevreings of the hated Gladstone had been added the more wounding disdain of Balfour and even the apparent indifference to their fate of the monarchy itself.

To a strong-minded woman with such fierce unionist convictions as Violet Martin cherished it must have seemed as if the men of her caste were under a strange spell. Nor did her immediate family history reinforce the conviction that they were fitted to snatch any victory out of this strange succession of humiliations and defeats. Family legend said that the Martins of Ross had bankrupted themselves to feed their starving tenants during the Great Famine; but her father, James Martin, was rejected by his ungrateful tenantry in favour of the Home Rule candidate – admittedly, a gentleman – in the election of 1872. Burdened by debt and possibly broken-hearted, he died soon after. Her brother Robert shut up the great house by the Galway lake and moved to London where he pursued a not too distinguished journalistic career. Violet and her other sisters and brothers were taken to Dublin by their mother and lived there in circumstances which were in strong contrast to the freedom and graciousness of big house life. When, sixteen years later, the big house was re-occupied by the family which had built it and lived in it for so long, it was Violet who did most of the work. "From her mother had come the initiative", Edith Somerville wrote, "but it was Martin who saved Ross . . . There was everything to be done, inside and outside that old house, and no one to do it but one fragile, indomitable girl . . . even more than the laying waste of Ross House and gardens I believe it was the torture of the thought that the Ross people might feel that the Martins had failed them, and that the 'Big House' was no longer the City of Refuge for its dependants in the day of trouble, that chiefly spurred Martin on, in her long and gallant fight with every sort of difficulty, that summer, when she and her mother began to face the music again at Ross."

III

The binding theme of the two best-known novels of Somerville and Ross is the attempt by a strong-minded woman to reverse or control circumstance; to acquire or defend property; to improve or enhance her own or her family's social position. Charlotte Mullen in *The Real Charlotte* has neither birth, nor breeding, nor, to begin with at least, money. Nor has she any of the "natural" weapons of her sex: grace, charm or good looks. A certain rough wit and readiness at repartee ensure her the form of acceptance as a "character" that is always available in Ireland, whatever the social milieu; but her comparative literacy and her undoubted intelligence give rise, if anything, to suspicion. A land-agent's daughter who inherits the property of the aunt with whom she has lived as a poor relation, she occupies an uneasy position in the hierarchies of Protestantism in and around the town of Lismoyle. Tally-Ho Lodge is far below Bruff Castle, the home of the Dysart family and the centre of everybody's social ambitions. But it is not so far below Bruff Castle as it is above the hovels of the fish-women to whom Charlotte lends money at exorbitant interest.

Charlotte has many schemes, but the instrument of one of them is to be her nineteen-year-old orphan cousin Francie Fitzpatrick, a common but pretty girl from Dublin. If she can be thrown together with Christopher Dysart in suitable circumstances a match may result. The prospects for Charlotte of such an alliance would be dazzling. What ruins the scheme are Christopher's ambiguous, gentlemanly qualities and Francie's all too unambiguous reaction to the male attractiveness of one of the officers of the garrison, Captain Hawkins. Christopher is a Hamlet *de nos jours*, with a streak of intelligent cynicism just strong enough to unfit him for everything in the big world, including the career in the diplomatic service he is supposed to be pursuing, and a dash of artistic sensibility just too weak to make an artist of him. Conor Cruise O'Brien, in his essay on Somerville and Ross in *Writers and Politics*, has seen the attitude of the authors to the Dysarts as reflecting a snobbery which gives a coldness to the book. Francie, he says, is "not well-bred, and therefore not quite human". The Dysarts are a "highly idealised ascendancy family". It is a strange judgment, for Christopher is a prig, his father a lunatic at large and his mother a nincompoop. Francie, on the other hand, is vibrant with youth and the desire for life, a miraculously convincing portrait of a young woman on whom biology has conferred a radiance which far outshines her vulgarity and ignorance. Common, in the pejorative, merely social sense she may be. If she is commonplace, then life itself is commonplace and a bore; but, though it often seems so to Christopher, the authors know otherwise.

And the case with Charlotte is something likewise. This ugly, "thick-set" woman, scheming with Lambert the agent for possession of Gorthnamuckla, a half-ruined "little big house" and its lands; plotting her own social advancement through Francie; ceaselessly and dangerously active among the semi-dormant inhabitants of a torpid pool, seems to Dr. O'Brien to be "evil". It is a suggestion which reminds us that he once wrote a book about the Catholic novel which committed him to a sympathetic understanding of the notion that human beings can be the instruments of supernatural purposes, can, as it were, take on, from above or below, a goodness or badness beyond the human scale.

Fortunately, however, the authors of *The Real Charlotte* held a more rational view of the world we live in. Charlotte is a graceless, greedy, unscrupulous, secretive and ambitious woman. She plots her own advantage in a scheme of things in which the Dysarts have already so many advantages as to have no necessity to plot; and, if the principle of the world is energy, she is superior to them, as indeed she knows herself to be. To believe that they are superior to her in any mode of conduct or activity except those dependent on prior possession, is to convict oneself of snobbery.

And accordingly the tragedy of the book is hers and Francie's. There are flickerings of tragedy in Christopher Dysart's situation: he could, after all, had he been a more determined young man, and capable of knowing what he wanted, have taken for bride, almost as of right, a beautiful nineteen-year-old who had evoked in him a response to life that little else seemed likely to do. The alternative, what he probably does take outside the confines of the book, is amply summed up by the portrait of the societally acceptable Miss Hope-Drummond, who is languidly setting her cap at him.

But Francie's enormous, if latent, sexual drive is focussed on the worthless, philandering Captain Hawkins. She neither properly understands nor cares about the rigid social conventions of Lismoyle society. She is not as concerned with her own advantage as everybody naturally assumes her to be. She misses her chance.

And, strangely enough, Charlotte's schemes also go partly awry because even ugly, masculine-seeming women are capable of passion: in her case directed at another worthless male weakling, the Dysarts' self-centred and dishonest agent, Roddy Lambert. Her desire to possess this vulgar oaf, who is, because of his wife's money and position fractionally higher in the social scale than herself, but as low or lower in any possible human one, involves her in several miscalculations. Since the book is concerned with triangular relationships which cannot be resolved, misunderstandings, ludicrously ill-founded loves and ambitions, it is possible to see it as comedy; and indeed it has, often enough, been so described. In fact it is written with a depth of feeling and a tenderness towards the unavailing in human love, particularly where Francie is concerned, that give it an extraordinary quality; but its underlying theme is the defeat of two women, both of whom in one way or another represent the life-force, by societal convention and coldness.

The theme of *The Big House of Inver* is also the defeat of a woman, Shibby Pindy or Prendeville, whose ambition is, in the scheme of things, impossible of realisation. The book was published in 1925; but its conception went back to 1912; and it seems only right to regard it as a joint work, particularly since Edith Somerville wished it to be thought of as such.

The big Queen Anne house of the title had been built by Robert Prendeville, a smuggling Galway landowner, whose handsome son, Beauty Kit, marries a great prize but dies of the smallpox. After his death his aristocratic wife shuts herself up in the big house and there lives

> for long, lonely years, refusing, in arrogance, to know, or to let her children know, her neighbours, freezing herself into, as it were, an iceberg of pride, living to see, at last, her only son, Nicholas, marry the daughter of one of the Inver gamekeepers, and her two daughters, Isabella and Nesta, go off with two of her own grooms.
>
> The glories and greatness of Inver therewith suffered downfall. Five successive generations of mainly half-bred and wholly profligate Prendevilles rioted out their short lives in the Big House, living with country women, fighting, drinking, gambling.

In the sixth generation comes Captain Jas, whose army career ends in disgrace; whose dissipations are, like Lord Kilgobbin's, such that he finds the company of village toadies more congenial than that of his equals; and who, after the fashion of his kind, fathers a daughter, Isabella or Shibby, on a village girl who dies in child-bed. Partly in order to dish a cousin who expects to inherit, Captain Jas marries, at sixty-three, a respectable, but penniless and acquiescent young woman from the neighbouring town. The fruit of this late union is Christopher, a dazzlingly handsome young man who resembles his ancestor, Beauty Kit, and inherits much of the family's tendency to drift and dissipation.

Shibby and this seventh generation Kit, are therefore half-brother and sister, though there are forty years between them. When the story properly begins the big house facing the sea is shuttered and empty. Kit and his father live in the old Norman tower with Shibby as house-keeper and unacknowledged member of the family. The demesne has been acquired, along with much of the land, by the Weldons, who are the Prendeville's agents. It has become Shibby's passion to restore her beloved, beautiful half-brother to his inheritance; and to that end, though she would prefer a more aristocratic match, even another Lady Isabella had such been suitable, she plots a marriage with the Weldon's daughter, Peggy.

She is defeated in the end because Kit has too much of the Prendevilles as well as something of the peasant in him. He too has become carelessly involved with a village girl, Maggie Connor; she becomes pregnant, and his attempts to cast her off are complicated by her madness. There is a curious echo here of the partnership's first book, *An Irish Cousin*, in which a mad peasant girl had played a mysterious and never quite explained part in the general Gothic atmosphere: and of *The Silver Fox* in which Maria Quin's grief for her brother who has been killed by the hunt vents itself in curses on the uncaring riders. The demented figure of Maggie Connor flits in and out of the book, cursing Kit and the Prendevilles; and we cannot but feel that there is something in this recurrent theme of the ascendancy's superstitious fear of the "natives" whom they had wronged; who spoke a mysterious language and had mysterious powers pertaining to their ancient possession of the soil, something of the Anglo-Indian and African settlers' fear of the native magic. Finally Maggie Connor's drunken brother Jimmy waylays Peggy Weldon and tells her that Kit has fathered a child on his sister. In her confusion her parents succeed in getting her to accept an offer of marriage from a wealthy English bore, Sir Harold Burbank; but Captain Jas and Kit have already betrayed Shibby by selling the big house to him behind her back. Her breaking is in proportion to her strength and single-mindedness, which far exceed those of the men of the Prendeville line which she has tried to restore.

Between the publication of *The Silver Fox* and their next major novel, *Mount Music*, in 1919, the friends published three volumes of the perennially popular *Irish R.M.* stories, the first appearing in 1899. Again the date is important for extraneous reasons. These were the years of the establishment of county councils, the Congested Districts Board, of the Wyndham Land Acts, of Balfour's decision to kill Home Rule by kindness; and, though self-government began to become a serious question again when the Liberals raised it in 1912, with a certain amount of acquiescence in defeat and in the fairly good bargain they had made, the ascendancy could for a while view Ireland again in the way in which they had always wanted to view it, and as much Irish literature has succeeded in viewing it in flagrant defiance of all the facts: that is, as a sort of comic Arcadia, where confusion and misrule are rife but nobody comes to much harm except in a comic, knockabout way. It is a view that is reflected in much of the minor literature of the time, notably the novels of George A. Birmingham, the stories of Lynn Doyle and the poems of Percy French; and it has its attractions for minor writers even to-day.

Which is not to say that the *R.M.* stories do not have their own kind of realism. They contain more peasant characters than anything else the authors wrote. The observation is exact and the ear for dialogue superb. Patrick Kavanagh used to say that Somerville and Ross had a better ear for Irish dialogue than anybody except James Joyce; and something of its quality is summed up in the answer the engine driver in 'Poisson D'Avril' gives to the warning about the local train's delay on the line, since "the goods" is coming behind: "Let her come. She'll meet her match."

In 1919, four years after Violet Martin's death, *Mount Music* appeared. Again the surviving author claimed that, in its genesis and its early drafts, it owed much to her friend; and again it seems only fair to grant the wish that it should, in some sense or other, be regarded as a collaboration. The main part and the climax of the story is set in 1907, a matter of some importance because between 1903 and 1909 tenant purchase was an option, but it was not yet compulsory for landlords to sell, and the Irish Party was still factionalised, the re-unification achieved under John Redmond not having been the success anticipated in 1900. The unusual precision of the dating is necessary because a good deal hinges on these facts.

Again the most interesting, and, with one exception, in all senses the strongest character is a woman; this time, for a change, a young woman, Christian Talbot-Lowry. Her father, a martial hero of Indian and Afghan conflicts, is the owner of Mount Music, the big house of the title. In spite of the fact that his wife, the daughter of an English earl, had brought twenty thousand golden sovereigns with her to Ireland, his estate is heavily mortgaged. He exists on credit, but sale to the tenants under the government scheme would leave him with neither ancestral home nor ready money, an outcome that, with weak obstinacy, he refuses to contemplate, though the refusal to sell has made him unpopular to the extent that obstacles are put in the way of the hunt and a horse that Christian is riding is killed after a man armed with a hay-knife suddenly appears at a bank it is jumping.

The attitudes of this stubborn "pterodactyl", as the authors call him, are contrasted with those of his young cousin and neighbour Larry Coppinger, of Coppinger's Court. The son of another Indian army hero who married a member of an ancient Catholic family in the North of England, Larry has been brought up in his mother's communion. Furthermore he has read *The Spirit of the Nation* and is able to quote Thomas Davis. Worse (from Dick Talbot-Lowry's point of view anyway) he has set a bad example by selling to his tenants. And to cap all he decides to stand as a nationalist candidate.

In some ways he is Christopher Dysart all over again: a dilettante in art, politics and love. He paints sporadically and without much determination. His share of the spirit of the nation is scarcely enough to carry him through the sordidities of a by-election campaign; and in any case he chooses the wrong faction and is defeated. When he comes up against Talbot-Lowry's opposition to his engagement to Christian he gives in without a struggle. And on the re-bound he allows himself to become, engaged, almost against his will, to Tishy Mangan, the daughter of the local doctor, who is a prominent small-town politician with immense ambitions.

Dr. O'Brien sees Mangan as evil too: at least he speaks of a "daemonic force in a credible character"; but if that is the case there must have been a lot of daemonism around in 1907. The worst we can say of him is that he has secretly been buying up the mortgages on Mount Music; that he has ambitions beyond her social station for his daughter; and that he confuses her social advancement with her happiness. The best is that he is the strongest-minded male in the book.

There is a contrived happy ending, brought about by Tishy's elopement with the fellow she really loves and by the usual novelist's device of killing off one of the characters, in this case the daemonic Dr. Mangan. Christian gets her Larry, with what ultimate result in happiness we know not. Maybe she had what marriage councillors call "strength enough for two".

IV

The killing off of Dr. Mangan is a not untypical device. Somerville and Ross were not averse to doing in a character to round off a book. Their most entrancing and successful creation, Francie Fitzpatrick, is killed off at the end of *The Real Charlotte*, after Roddy Lambert's wife has already been got out of the way. Captain Jas dies amid the flames of the big house of Inver. They were novelists and they wrote the novel as it is written. At a crucial stage of *The Real Charlotte* Francie accidentally drops a letter and a photograph of Captain Hawkins on the floor in front of Christopher Dysart; and a great deal is made to hinge on Charlotte Mullen's discovery of Lambert's cheques and account books. They tell a story, often the sort of story in which the reader agonises for the outcome. Were it not for Dr. O'Brien's testimony that he finds the class convention comes between her and our pity, it would be difficult to imagine a reader who did not agonise for the fate of poor Francie Fitzpatrick.

But this ability of theirs to make a causative narrative construction hinges on more than a willingness to make unblushing use of passable chance or coincidence. The novel as it is written needs people who can go up or down the social ladder, who are anxious for social advancement or the retention of their position but conscious of social convention. There has to be the possibility not only of ruin but of lesser punishments, such as disgrace and ostracisation, often visited on the improperly ambitious.

As ascendancy writers Somerville and Ross had the advantage of having rigid social conventions to deal with. They also had wealth as a subject and the possibility of quite large-scale reversals and advancements of family fortune. They had a keen sense of social position and property, with what they thought of as its traditions, was an important theme to them. It has not been so to other Irish writers who were more infected by the general atmosphere which I have called in the chapter on William Carleton one of near-anarchic "sloth, cheer and despair." Of course in literature they were traditionalists too. For all these reasons they wrote novels, not fictive constructions like Joyce, Flann O'Brien and Beckett; imaginative transpositions of circumstance like Francis Stuart or George Moore, chronicles such as *Castle Rackrent*, or mélanges of anecdote such as Lever and Carleton delighted in. They wrote extended anecdotes in the three *R.M.* volumes all right; but in *The Real Charlotte* they wrote the only great Irish novel that is really and truly a novel and employs all the novelist's devices shamelessly but with finesse.

You can say that this lessens it if you like, but we must judge by results. I have spoken of their major, or binding theme; but there are riches and to spare within it and released by it, as one theme is released by another in great literature. It is an enormously sharp-witted and perceptive social drama, with tragic results for at least two of the participants to some extent dependent on the arbitrary conventions of the social code. It contains two of the most convincing and penetrating portraits of women in all literature, and in Francie's case one of the most enchanting. In Francie's marriage to Lambert, as in Peggy Weldon's and, to a lesser degree, Tishy Mangan's parentally inspired engagements, the situation of women who marry or become engaged under social and economic pressure evokes in the authors a deep, sympathetic response, which is part of their vision of the struggle between the life-force, in its often distorted forms, and its enemies in their often more acceptable ones.

But besides these things there are throughout it, as throughout the rest of their work, more evocative descriptions of the Irish landscape in its various moods than anyone else has written. And above all, perhaps, there is also, in its very depths, a heartbreaking awareness of the tiny chances and mischances, the moments of misapprehension and indecision, on which the huge, eternal destinies of lovers hang.

What actual experiences of these matters the authors may

have had, we do not really know. From the accounts of their relationship and writing methods they gave there must have been a deep undercurrent of psychic sympathy between them. Let us hope, for their sakes, that there was something more, at least in the avowal. But, whether or no, they were still probably blessed beyond the ordinary.

WILLIAM BUTLER YEATS:
Containing Contradictions

W.B. Yeats was born one hundred and seventeen years ago. Up to this point it would have been plausible to assert that by the common consent of fellow-practitioners and critics alike he was the greatest poet of any nationality to write the English language in the twentieth century. But there are now some signs of a long overdue reaction against that view of him.

Academics and others who feel they have a vested interest in Yeats may well be disturbed; and it may or may not be of comfort to them to reflect that, like the mid-Victorian reaction against Wordsworth which Matthew Arnold sought to correct, this one, when it comes, will probably be for the wrong reasons, for the attackers are already choosing ground, political and other, on which Yeats is not really vulnerable.

Of course he has partly retained his eminence for the same reason as Eliot – no poet of comparable ability has yet arisen (or at least secured sufficient notice) to supplant either of them, as Arnold said Tennyson had supplanted Wordsworth. Whether this augurs a permanent decline or not is hard to say. It may equally suggest an astonishing level of achievement in the second, third and fourth decade of this century. As usual, we must look into our own hearts when we speak of what is wrong with the world.

Among other things W.B. Yeats was of course the dominating figure in the Irish revival and we here in Ireland are all supposed, such as we are, to have been influenced by him. Indeed hardly a day passes but some critic speaks of the terrible burden the contemporary Irish poet suffers under: the necessity and the difficulty of struggling free from that influence.

I wonder. Speaking, in all modesty, as one who began to write, or at least to publish poetry in the late 'forties, I can only say that I never felt it. During the formative years the great body of his work was almost unknown to some of us. All we knew were early selections and, worse still, early anthology pieces, whose appeal was, to say the least, strictly limited. This was partly due to the fact that Messrs. Macmillan pursued a strange policy with their paper ration during the war years and after which meant that his *Collected Poems* did not appear again until 1950; and if verbal and technical influences do not take early enough they do not take at all.

What I admire now technically is his insistence on a proper and unmistakable prose style and syntax in the verse, so that the strongly marked rhythms of the sentence and the equally strong rhythm of the verse run counter to each other; are, in a sense, each other's opposite; and finally strengthen each other by their opposition – as, in Yeats's scheme of things, do all opposites whatsoever. What I deplore is the throwing around of big lines as if the drama was always in its last act. I think every poet should have a big line at his command, but that like a Sunday punch or a miler's kick it should be kept in reserve until it can change the nature of the proceedings. To say this, however, may be merely to admit that one is Irish, that one has a weakness for rhetoric and, if one has any sense, a dread of it.

That Yeats should be or should have been the greatest poet of our time at all, though, is remarkable on several grounds. It is odd first of all because he was born slap in the middle of the reign of Queen Victoria and a good judge would probably have opined round about 1905 that he had shot his bolt. It is peculiar because he was imaginatively preoccupied with the passions and regrets of a small, comparatively backward country which he would have had look backward rather than forward. And it is surprising because in an age when much of the best poetry written was an expression of disgust or despair, an abandonment of what was felt to be the heroic lie, Yeats wrote heroic poetry which believes in heroism and celebrates it. Analogously in an age when art began to explore certain forms of apparent ugliness for the first time, and to extract a great reward from them, Yeats maintained a rather old-fashioned belief in beauty. "I say again against all the faggots", he wrote in 1937 (he meant all the dry old sticks), "that it is our duty to paint, or describe, desirable people, places, states of mind." But indeed the ways in which he was apparently out of date in his own time are almost endless.

Almost alone among the poets of this age Yeats believed in tragedy, the dark fruition of the individual will. He celebrated character in action and refused to contemplate man as the victim of determinist forces outside his control. He found the First World War and its poet Wilfrid Owen uninteresting. Somebody had driven his car on the wrong side of the road again and that was all, he said. In an age of alleged scrupulosity as to the use of reason (Bertrand Russell et al.) he, to a large extent, threw reason out of the window. "You can refute Hegel", he wrote on his death-bed (to a lady called Lady Elizabeth Pelham), "but not the Saint or the Song of Sixpence." And quoting William Blake, he said in 1937 (thus repeating himself after an interval of forty years), "argument, theory, erudition, observation are merely 'little devils' who fight for themselves."

It is also of course notorious that in his political attitudes he ran counter to many of the major currents of his day, basing his hatred of contemporary society not on an impatient hope for the future, but on the vision of a dying and probably never-existent aristocratic past, while it has recently been called to our attention again that there appears to be a certain glorification of violence in his work. The list of attitudes to which we could object is indeed long; and if poets were to be judged on the head of such matters and on nothing else we would find it hard to account for our admiration of Yeats, supposing we do admire him and supposing also (which is perhaps more important) that we could pin him down; but in fact the greatness of Yeats resides as much as anywhere else in his wonderful ambiguity and his unending power of reversal. He can turn anything on its head and can usually be trusted to do so. If in the case of Dr. Johnson's friend the difficulty about being a philosopher was that "cheerfulness was always breaking in", the same is true of Yeats only, as people used to say, with knobs on; for not only cheerfulness, but frequently despair and a host of other things can usually be counted on to arrive and break in just when his philosophy is about to make him ridiculous.

That Yeats was Protean and self-contradictory has been observed often enough before, though his father's portraits of him, which reveal that there were about seventeen different Yeatses, all different from each other, and all different too from the dreary, dreamy Augustus John figure most people are used to, remain a somewhat neglected source of information about this. It has been noted also (and of course we have the authority of John Keats for it) that to be Protean and self-contradictory is no bad thing for a poet provided he can survive or contain the state. Amongst other things, this means, where a romantic like Yeats is concerned, being less of a romantic and more in love with the classical synthesis than might appear at first, and also of course having a sufficiency of talent.

But in the whole history of literature there can scarcely ever have been a poet so wonderfully and fruitfully self-contradictory as Yeats. If he sang of war, no other poet who did (and few who didn't) have had such a love of civic harmony and such a deep sense of its true possibilities. In him heroic assertion is constantly accompanied and undermined by the most revealing sort of confession. The quality of the rhetoric is (let us gratefully acknowledge) often totally altered by the use of brilliantly effective colloquialisms. Above all perhaps, the tragic ecstasy is counter-balanced by tragic pain: if he is the great poet of many different and surprising things, loneliness, misunderstanding and shame should not be overlooked among them.

What critics have to a large extent failed to remark on, though, are Yeats's extraordinary powers of reconcilement: the fact that his whole process was dialectic and that out of his contradictions and collisions of opposites – the real and the ideal, time and eternity, art and reality, body and soul, the heroic and the actual, the man and his mask – a third thing was so often and so surprisingly born. Every graduate knows that he believed in aristocracy and that he hated Demos. The not-so-blinding discovery has also been made that this consorted a bit ill with a belief that the folk were somehow the residuum of all wisdom and indeed of all poetry. What has not been adverted to is that out of this apparent contradiction emerged a belief in political unity of being and unity of culture which is neither aristocratic nor democratic but a different thing from either, although born of both.

The reaction against Yeats which is even now building up will be on what might broadly and crudely be called political grounds. It will fail first because Yeats's vision of how things might be, the civic harmony, the civic purpose that he sang is no more like Hitler's or Mussolini's than it is like Melchizedek's. And it is not a matter of degree. It is not that he would have murdered six Jews whereas Hitler murdered six million. His imagined – his thirsted for – social order is not like theirs at all; and it is not even like Metternich's either: though one could make a rather good case for the fact that it is somewhat like Karl Marx's. Like Marx, Yeats wanted an end to the cleavage between the individual life and the community life. Like Marx, Yeats hated a social order which stunted man's faculties and capacity for joy, whether the man was artist or artisan: indeed as an old disciple of William Morris's he rather wanted everybody to be both artist and artisan. One of his weaknesses is a vision of aristocratic society as being a society of whole men, not another way of arranging the division of labour. Another and more important one is that, like most conservatives of our era – like Eliot, Pound and Wyndham Lewis – he didn't realise that to support the conservative interest is simply to support the money power, lock, stock and barrel. The Prince D'Aquitaine is not weeping by the *tour abolie*. He is on the board of the Chase Manhattan Bank; and the generals and admirals who have seized power anywhere in his name or in the name of the conservative interest have been merely tools of the money power also. So, since Yeats hated the money power, "the neon signs, the heterogeneous architecture" that he saw from O'Connell Bridge, he is in some of his prose statements simply convicting himself of ignorance of what is going on in the world. But that is not a capital charge. And no one who has really read Marx could object to the best of his political poems – 'The Fisherman' for example, since if they were reduced to slogans, they would come out roughly as "Art for the People and the People for Art" and that is what Marx wanted too. The pity really is that narrow scholiasts who do not seem to care very much for poetry anyway, and who think along prose lines – that is, in a way that, unlike Yeats's poetic way, cannot contain its own contradictions – should have been so much in charge of the argument to date. The consolation is that they have about as much chance of damaging Yeats as they have of writing an equivalently exciting poetry themselves.

A more promising ground for those who are joining the reaction against him might be one which has been enunciated by Francis Stuart. This is that there is in Yeats's work a series of dramatic confrontations which are phoney because they are too carefully controlled. The charge is not so much that the hero of these confrontations never really gets hurt, whether in love or in war, for that might be a matter of lucky chance, but that he never really intended to get hurt in a game which was from the outset very carefully rigged.

These are the grounds on which Stuart has been objecting to Yeats, or at least Yeats adulation, for some time past; and significantly enough they were the grounds on which Patrick Kavanagh also objected in one of the last poems he wrote:

> Yeats it was easy for you to be frank
> (With your sixty years and loves like Robert Graves)
> It was thin and in fact you never put the tank
> On a race. A cautious man whom no sin depraves . . . .

The charge would of course be of no importance as far as the poetry is concerned (however it might affect our attitude to the man) except that one of the great movements of our time has been a sort of breaking down of the barriers between and an intermingling of art and life; and that Yeats, by notoriously making himself a protagonist in his own mythology – as a lover, as poet, as rebel, as risk-taker, as anti-philistine – invites a sort of biographical response which is inseparable, and which he means to be inseparable, from the aesthetic one.

The question has an added difficulty because much of the time Yeats is adopting the old bardic role; and, as we know, the bard did not go into battle himself. He sat his horse where he could witness the fray and he sang the bravery of those who took part. So Yeats sings the bravery and bearing of a long line of heroes, from Cuchulainn to Robert Gregory, and there is certainly nothing in the history of the art he practised which suggests that his song is invalid unless he descends and takes part, as Papa Hem thought that even the novelist had to do.

Nevertheless, for much of the time Yeats does claim that the ultimate "I" of the poems was in the firing line as well; and he claims that the truths he enunciates were a product of his experiences there.

> Know that when all words are said
> And a man is fighting mad
> Something drops from eyes long blind,
> He completes his partial mind,
> For an instant stands at ease
> Laughs aloud, his heart at peace.

Though it will be noted that in the poem in question there is an immediate sort of reservation:

> Even the wisest man grows tense
> With some sort of violence
> Before he can accomplish fate,
> Know his work or choose his mate.

The really wise man does not listen to Mitchel's prayer perhaps. But the proper defence for those who believe Yeats to deserve his position of pre-eminence is probably two-pronged. First, Yeats really did fall in love with Maud Gonne, hopelessly and irrevocably. He did live *la vie de poète* and endure, for many long years, the poverty that went with it. He did oppose the majority on a number of questions: indeed he opposed the liberal majority, which, during the controversy about Bishop Colenso and the number of pigeons the priest ate in *Leviticus*, Matthew Arnold said was the most dangerous thing of all to do. And it really wasn't his fault if, in any of these things, he didn't get more hurt; any more than it was his fault that he had, in the matter of poetic reputation anyway, an early success and never dropped out of critical favour thereafter. We can't always hold that against people: it would rule out too many.

But secondly it can be said that, sadly or otherwise, it is in part at least the artist's duty to hold back. It may be more fun to be D'Annunzio. It may even, for a while, be more fun to be Dowson. But it is better to write the poems.

JOHN MILLINGTON SYNGE:
Apart from Anthropology

The creative process thrives on ambiguities and indeed apparent contradictions. Criticism is often surprisingly less happy with them afterwards. In the case of John Millinton Synge certain ambiguities which were at the mainspring of his creative urge have had an unsettling effect on criticism; and made him the victim of confusions about the relationship of his life to his art – and of Irish life to his art – which still prevent us from assessing his achievement dispassionately and perhaps celebrating it as we should.

He has not on the whole been well served by his critics, and perhaps even less so by his partisans. He had the misfortune first of all to have a man of supreme genius as an ally and indeed as an impresario, making as is usual an impresario's inaccurate claims. Yeats was a great theorist of art and artistry but he wrote criticism only in snatches and as an addendum to theory. Of the three essays included in *The Cutting of an Agate*, the first, the preface to *The Well of the Saints*, reminds us of the famous exhortation to "Go to the Aran Islands. Live there as if you were one of the people themselves; express a life that has never found expression" – and we are back with Synge as the anthropologist-naturalist and all the dreary quarrels, from the *Playboy* row down to the present day, about his accuracy in the plays as a describer of folk-life and Irish peasant character, the endless arguments about whether he was, on the one hand, traducer, or, on the other, idealiser. In the same essay Yeats goes on to say:

> He went to Aran and became a part of its life, living upon salt fish and eggs, talking Irish for the most part, but listening also to the beautiful English which has grown up in the Irish speaking districts, and takes its vocabulary from the time of Malory and of the translators of the Bible, but its idiom and its vivid metaphor from Irish. When Mr. Synge began to write in this language, Lady Gregory had already

> used it finely in her translations of Dr. Hyde's lyrics and plays, or of old Irish literature, but she had listened with different ears.

This too perpetuates argument and, worse, confusion. "Kiltartan" is still, quite properly, a dirty word in certain circles; and although Yeats, with his usual percipience, almost cuts out the confusions he has already raised when he adds, "He made his own selection of word and phrase, choosing what would express his own personality", he has still said enough to invite, in the course of time, retorts such as that of the strictly urban-minded Myles na Gopaleen who declared:

> A lifetime of cogitation has convinced me that in this Anglo-Irish literature of ours (which for the most part is neither Anglo, Irish, nor literature) nothing in the whole galaxy of fake is comparable with Synge . . . The trouble probably began with Lever and Lover. But I always think that in Synge we have the virus isolated and recognisable . . . It is not that Synge made people less worthy or nastier, or even better than they are, but he brought forward amusing clowns talking a sub-language of their own and bade us take them very seriously. There was no harm done there, because we have long had the name of having heads on us. But when the counterfeit bauble began to be admired outside of Ireland by reason of its oddity and "charm", it soon became part of the literary credo here that Synge was a poet . . . a bit of a genius indeed . . . And now the curse has come upon us, because I personally have met in the streets of Ireland persons who are clearly out of Synge's plays. They talk and dress like that and damn the drink they'll swally but the mug of porter in the long nights after Samhain.

What Myles is saying is slightly different from what Oscar Wilde said: according to Myles, life imitates bad art; but it is noteworthy that Synge is also getting the blame for the new sort of intellectual stage Irishness which undoubtedly has been the bane of much of our literature since independence. In effect, Myles says, Synge raised the tone of stage-Irishism, and made it acceptable in more or less nationalist literary circles. Nationalism, or at least the more nationalistic kind of writer, having attacked the Synge-song to begin with, ended by apparently adopting it. The appeal of the picturesque triumphed over the ideal of purity; an ideal strangeness was more important than an ideal sexlessness.

This is perhaps why the *Playboy* riots now seem so far away. Synge's brief moment (1902 to 1909) coincided with the rebirth of a kind of nationalism which was guilty of more distortions in the interests of the ideal than he was in the interests of anything; but, if it is now a long time in fact, it is an even longer stretch in terms of fashion since Arthur Griffith attacked the *Playboy* as a libel on Irish womanhood and five hundred policemen were needed to keep order within and without the theatre.

But the row was one after Yeats's own heart; and he continued to rub it in. In the third essay in *The Cutting of an Agate*, 'J.M. Synge and the Ireland of his Time', the poet who was to found a whole aesthetic on the idea of art as the creation of exalted, noble images for contemplation, claimed that the "lyric beauty", the "violent laughter" and etcetera of the *Playboy* were all taken straight out of peasant Ireland. At the time this was written he was annoying the peasants and their literary embodiers and spokesmen further, but of course, given that they were to pin their faith also to the idea of exalted, noble images, even if mostly in the somewhat degraded form of the picturesque, it would not be long until they came his way. Twenty years after that essay, Daniel Corkery, in what was long a seminal book, *Synge and Anglo-Irish Literature*, was to argue also that Synge's importance was the depth of his knowledge of the people and to declare flatly:

> Here, by one stroke, to show how he stands apart from all his fellow writers, it is but necessary to state, that he, an ascendancy man, went into the huts of the people and lived with them.

"An ascendancy man". He takes back what he gives; but what he gives has proved fatal enough also. Today, by a supreme historical irony, Synge's defenders are among the lovers of the peasant-picturesque, the remnants of the old Abbey and Radio Eireann gang, the lineal descendants of the nationalists of 1907 (the only difference being that they have substituted one kind of noble savage for another): his enemies among the cosmopolitans, the urbanites, the sophisticates like Myles. The charge of being an ascendancy man who distorted and condescended by reason of that fact has been dropped by one side and revived by the other. It is a sentimental literary idealisation which is now charged against him, not a libel or a travesty.

Yet that he was "an ascendancy man" is undeniable: the point to be made, if any point must, being that this particular ambiguity or contradiction was more important to him as a man turning his life-experiences, contradictions and ambiguities into art, than it is to us. Synge was in fact sprung from the narrowest, most bigoted, bible-thumping, proselytising, peasant-despising while yet peasant-exploiting kind of Protestant, ascendancy, landlord stock. Yet he fell in love with the Catholic "natives". He tramped the roads of Wicklow and West Kerry; he went to the islands; he learnt the language; he listened at chinks in the floor-boards. And he wrote *The Tinker's Wedding, The Well of the Saints* and *The Playboy of the Western World*, "travesties" according to the most fervent and patriotic of the natives then. Marvellous illuminations of a life undreamed-of according to urban sophisticates. The irony being, of course, that it is the urban sophisticates who accuse him of ridiculous distortions and indeed idealisations now; while it is the most peasant-minded and patriotic (in the literary sense anyway) who stick by him, believing (correctly as it happens) that their own importance depends entirely on whether the poetic peasant exists and whether the contemplation of his life has marvellous illuminations to offer the rest of us.

It is therefore Synge's misfortune that his secondary, or what might even be called his background, subject, the life of the Gaelic West, still obscures what is perhaps his real subject, his real achievement and his claim to lasting fame. Of course there is no doubt that it was his entrancement with the people of Aran, of the Wicklow glens, and of West Kerry that set fire to his imagination and released his real theme. True creation, art as opposed to any other kind of statement, is a matter of embodiment. And there can be no doubt in the mind of anyone who reads those sad, yet celebratory and noble books, *The Aran Islands* and *In Wicklow and West Kerry*, in which a dying man contemplates with the brooding intensity of genius the remnants of an immemorial but already dying culture, that Synge found himself and found embodiments for his real theme in the poor, barren and beautiful places of Ireland. In passage after passage he reveals not only insight, but his love and his personal emotion. Thus, on Inishmaan after a night of storm, he writes:

> The continual passing in this island between the misery of last night and the splendour of today, seems to create an affinity between the moods of these people and the moods of varying rapture and dismay that are frequent in artists, and in certain forms of alienation. Yet it is in the intonation of a few sentences or some old fragment of melody that I catch the real spirit of the island.

In West Kerry, near Dunquin, he watches the people wending their way to Mass on a Sunday morning,

> the men in homespun and the women wearing blue cloaks, or, more often, black shawls twisted over their heads. This procession along the olive bogs, between the mountains and the sea, on this grey day of autumn, seemed to wring me with the pang of emotion one meets everywhere in Ireland – an emotion that is partly local and patriotic, and partly a share of the desolation that is mixed everywhere with the supreme beauty of the world.

And he had, whatever simple people may have said afterwards under pressure from Dublin enemies retailing stories of scandalous plays performed far away, the gift of friendship and sympathy; with the young, with the very old, and – perhaps this is the most significant thing of all – with the women. Over and over again he speaks of the beauty of the island women in their red dresses against the bare rock, of their singularly beautiful faces, of their openness, frankness, and simplicity.

As an anthropologist-naturalist, then, or whatever it may be proper to call him, Synge was, in the prose books at least, not an inconsiderable observer, though naturally he saw all that he did see through the light of his own predestined imagination. But critics who have concentrated, as for extraneous political and other reasons they have, on the contradictions inherent in the spectacle of this scion of the ascendancy as the writer of peasant plays are wasting everybody's time. Whatever Synge may have said during the stress of the *Playboy* riots, however sedulously critics, including Robin Skelton in *The Writings of J.M. Synge*, may search for the origins of his plots in his experiences in the West of Ireland and in Wicklow, these are not primarily naturalistic plays. The mob who gleefully hooted "Lynchehaun" at the author in the Abbey were right. (Synge had tried to justify the probability of his play by reference to a dubiously existent murderer of that name who he said had been hidden by the people of Erris.) It illuminates matters here to remember that Synge lived in the era when the "problem play" was dominant. Naturalistic drama with a social theme was the accepted mode. People expected it and they looked for it. It therefore also illuminates matters to remember the surprising fact that Synge and Chekhov were almost contemporaries. Chekhov was of course interested in what was happening to the Russian soul; he was interested in the Russian character; he was interested in social change. Synge had all these interests too, so far as the people of the West were concerned, but both were vastly more interested in primary themes of their own. Synge had really only one, and he was probably prepared to throw naturalism and social accuracy overboard to some extent at least to get it. What was it?

When we realise what it is, when we "isolate" it from the other questions, we go far to restore Synge to his proper place among writers of any nationality; and that it is a high one the present writer has no doubt.

Unfortunately, however, when we make the attempt we come up against further contradictions and ambiguities in the relationship of the man to his work which have been and are the source of critical confusions also, for critics have touched on these too, and again mostly as if they somehow invalidate the work, when in fact they may illuminate it. At least from 1897 on, Synge was a sick, indeed, to be brutal about it, a dying man. Yet the work glorifies health, vitality, licence, vigour. Further, he was reserved, introspective, almost silent in most sorts of company. Yeats described him as being one of those sorts of artists who

> have little personality, as far as the casual eye can see, little personal will, but fiery and brooding imagination. I cannot imagine him anxious to impress or convince in any company, or saying more than was sufficient to keep the talk circling.

Yet the plays are full of talkers, spellbinders, liars, eloquent chancers of all descriptions. (Christy Mahon is by no means the only one.) Furthermore, as Skelton and before him Greene and Edward M. Stephens in the official biography made clear – Maurice Bourgeois was the first to hint at it – Synge was an unhappy lover who had had at least two serious rejections of affection before he began his final relationship with the Abbey actress Molly Allgood. The first and most serious of these, by Cherry Matheson, was on religious grounds. Synge had declared himself an atheist, and she, the daughter of a leader of the Plymouth Brethren, regarded this, however she may have felt about him, as an insuperable obstacle. When finally, only four years before his death, he met the nineteen-year-old Molly, he had the good or ill fortune to find the sort of girl who kept a man in uncertainties of all descriptions. The portrait by John B. Yeats in the Dublin National Gallery which Skelton reproduces and the photograph which also appears in his book show her for what she was: a beautiful, high-spirited, intelligent girl, full of vitality, but wilful and stubborn to a degree. Pegeen Mike of *The*

Playboy in fact.

In *J.M. Synge and his World* Skelton quotes a passage from a draft of Synge's first and until recently unpublished play, *When the Moon has Set*:

> My life has gone to ruin because I misunderstood love and because I was scrupulous when I should have been strong. I treated women as if they were gods and they treated me as if I might be damned for their amusement . . . If you love a woman subdue her.

And when one reads all the plays together, one is struck by a strange fact. Synge has really only one primary theme: the ironies, and in particular the verbal ironies, of the relationships of men and women. To make this assertion is certainly not to demean him, for the theme is, to say the least, an important one. To add that, apart from Shakespeare in certain of the comedies, he is the greatest dramatist to have handled it in the English language is to do no more than give him his due.

His first play, *Riders to the Sea*, is something of an aberration in the corpus of his work. Skelton praises it for its mythic elements; and it has been held up to admiration as classical tragedy in miniature. Criticism is generally pleased to have such matters to discuss, but the truth is that *Riders to the Sea* is a contrived solemnity by a writer who had not yet found himself. Even so there are glimmerings of his themes, albeit "tragic" rather than comic ones, for the point is the relationship of the women who wait and mourn with the men whose devouring mistress is the sea.

In *The Shadow of the Glen*, written more or less concurrently, and *The Tinker's Wedding* his primary subject is clearer to his audience, as it was perhaps to himself also, and from now until the end, even in the tragic *Deirdre*, he will not relinquish it. In *The Shadow of the Glen* Nora picks Michael to supplant her ageing husband with a degree of clear-sightedness and a degree of contempt, simply, she claims, because he is a man, passable and available; and because, like her husband, he has money. At the same time she pays him the oblique compliment of a claim that her standards in men are high:

> . . . if it's a power of men I'm after knowing they were fine men, for I was a hard child to please, and a hard girl to please, and it's a hard woman I am to please this day, Michael Dara, and it's no lie I'm telling you.

After all of which she goes off with the tramp, leaving both an embittered husband and a bewildered Michael behind her, and advancing as her reason one worthy of a later heroine in the statement that the tramp has, after all, "a fine bit of talk".

The long-debated question, also raised by the conduct of later heroines, as to whether women or men have more regard for convention, and respect for the bonds of marriage, is the central theme of *The Tinker's Wedding*. Of course Sarah wants marriage, even though, as her husband reminds her, she has been going beside him a long time and reared a lot of children. Of course Michael is, being a man, resistant to the idea. So far Synge does not differ from the consensus of male writers on the theme.

But Sarah also wants a continued freedom to assure herself that her powers of attraction are not lost, a need which the majority of male writers have, from the dawn of time, attributed unhesitatingly to the male. And in the end it is her primal realism, not Michael's, which prevails over the marriage idea and dismisses it and the respectability which goes with it as less important than the price to be paid.

But neither *The Shadow of the Glen* nor *The Tinker's Wedding* are truly more than curtain-raisers; and it is on the two great plays that followed that Synge's reputation must finally rest. *The Well of the Saints* mixes so many elements – the eternal conflict of illusion and reality, wish and fulfilment; the meaninglessness of human existence compared with the human being's capacity to feel and to suffer; the contrast between the riches of absolute poverty and the deprivations of partial possession – that it is easy to miss its central truth. Blind or otherwise, deluded about each other or not, Martin and Mary Doul have found the love that springs from mutual need: perhaps, the play seems almost to suggest, the only love there is. But it is in the nature of the male to dream of conquest; and in that of the female to despise what she possesses on the grounds that it is less than all she might have had. Martin, restored to sight, finds only mockery and cruelty in the eyes of the girl who has seemed to encourage him. Mary in the end comforts herself with the thought that there are white-haired old women whom the young men never tire of looking at. But the last word is the Saint's; and although it appears to be about the old couple's choice of blindness, we are meant to feel the ironic implication, that it is about the emotional irrevocability of their choice of each other; "They have chosen their lot, and the Lord have mercy on their souls."

The Well of the Saints abounds in ironies; in *The Playboy of the Western World* they are piled one on top of another in superb succession, and they are almost all related to what males have agreed among themselves to call the contrariness, the unpredictability, and the caprices of women. Never mind that the ultimate fraud is Christy, the greater crime, in the eyes of the ordinary male, is Pegeen's preference for him. The plot is too well known to need discussion: suffice it to say that neither Synge's preface, the anthropological school of criticism, the five hundred policemen, nor Yeats's idealisation of the peasantry can conceal the fact that the play is about the effect on women – on Pegeen Mike, the Widow Quin, and the famous drift of girls standing in their infamous shifts – of a man's fraudulent reputation for being a dangerous rogue; and that Pegeen Mike is one of the great feminine creations of dramatic literature, romantic, realist, obstinate, and tender all at once, while the Widow Quin is among the most memorable of women cynics. The fact that Christy, though a timid fraud, rises to genuine heights of daring and boldness while under the eyes of the girl he has beguiled is one of the ironies of the male's role, but the final master stroke concerns the woman's attitude, and it comes in the very last line. Pegeen has scorned and even hated him for the fraud he is discovered to be and the fool he has made of her, yet she cries out at the end: "Oh, my grief I've lost him surely. I've lost the only Playboy of the Western World." He had, after all, the fine talk.

Deirdre of the Sorrows was written in the last year of Synge's life, when he probably knew he was dying, but when his relationship with Molly may have been, strangely enough, at its happiest. The usual misconceptions surround it. It is in no sense a classical tragedy (unless Conchubor, not Naisi, is the tragic hero) and the syntax is certainly not anglicised Irish. It is in fact, like all the others, a play about the unbiddability of the female heart, and its two highest moments are revelations of female psychology. One is Deirdre's reaction when she overhears her lover discussing with Fergus the possibility that they might grow tired of each other; the other is when, without hope of ever making amends, she reviles him for going off to die with his brothers and is immediately stricken by remorse for what can never be unsaid.

There are in fact few writers to equal this somewhat unsuccessful lover as an inventor of women and an observer of the situations they contrive to create out of what seems to male eyes mere caprice and wilfulness. That this "ascendancy" writer succeeded in fashioning partly out of Irish syntactical modes and stored phrases a language to fit his own vision is part of his achievement, though it is largely fruitless to argue how much he owed to either memory or Irish. That he also decided to set his stories in the habitations of simple people where the mere sophistications of society would not occlude his vision or obscure their psychology we owe partly to his love for the bare and barren places of Ireland, but even more, in all probability, to the deep interior instincts of a great artist.

It would, on the face of it, seem that the comic misconceptions inherent in the relationship of men and women appeal to Irish writers more than to others. Congreve, Sheridan, Wilde and Shaw, all more or less compatriots of Synge, had after all, been before him with the theme. But their interest had been as much in the societal misconceptions as in the psychological, the one sort admittedly feeding off the other, but the main burden of the comedy, with its societal archetypes, being in the interaction of the two. Synge sought out the primitive so that he could be free from these conventions and bring men and women face to face in a world where five pounds or a tin can were as important as a peerage or a great name. If, in doing so, he overlooked the strength of convention in his apparently primitive social milieux the fact is simply one further proof that he had, as an artist, a purpose other than the anthropological. That purpose was to expose the equivocations, the comic and tragic humiliations, "the moods of varying rapture and dismay", the sheer bewilderment inherent in the relationships of men and women. It is done of course partly through male eyes: there would be no comedy if there were no dismayed or bewildered men. But whatever may be said about Wilde or Shaw, Synge is streets ahead of Congreve or Sheridan when it comes to understanding women and the springs of what the male merely sees as unpredictable and erratic behaviour. It is not, strangely enough, the successful lovers who know what Synge knew about women. And it is part of the triumph of the man as well as the artist that he feels with them, rejoices with them and laughs with them rather than with the almost always simpler, stupider and slower-witted males of his plays. Synge, the man, may have had a hard time of it with Molly; but he achieved as an artist the coolness of vision which is essential to comedy; and beneath all the comedy the underlying emotion is a veneration for the life-enhancing, convention-defying subtleties of feminine psychology which is rare enough in any literature; but which, taking Joyce and Yeats – not to mention Shaw – into account is, whether surprisingly or not, perhaps less rare in Irish literature than in some others.

JAMES JOYCE:
The Advent of Bloom

I

It has become the fashion to assume, when discussing what *Ulysses* is about, that it is about its own technique. Of course many books are primarily concerned with their own technique. The majority of dramatically constructed novels, whose action consists of an organised, interlocking, self-sustaining, artificially contrived sequence of events, are not so much about life as about their own dramatic technique. But *Ulysses* is not so constructed. There is drama in its action as there is drama in every day, but event does not factitiously control or create the nature of further event as it does in most fiction; and if *Ulysses* can be said to have a plot, its plot is formless and does not give form to the book – it is not shaped to produce a series of dramatic sensations for purposes aesthetic or otherwise; it has no conclusion in event, only a termination in time; it is not resolved by a neat regroupment of the characters in their sexual relationships, nor by mayhem on Joyce's part, since nobody dies, or commits suicide, or is murdered to bring the book to a close.

However, it would seem that this mere absence of a complicated, technical machinery of dramatic causation has given rise to the impression that the form the book does have conceals vast mysteries and profundities of intention. The propagators of this idea belong mostly to the nowadays dominant school of academic, pseudo-scientific, semeiological and hermeneutical criticism, and, however much their "interpretations" may differ, in their general agreement about methods of interpretation they now form a majority bloc of opinion and are so active as to render Joyce the outstanding victim of these methods.

It has long been notorious (though many early readers remained understandably oblivious of the fact) that *Ulysses* is partly organised round an elaborate system of correspondences and basic motifs. Each section corresponds more or less to an episode in the *Odyssey*; some employ multiple references to a particular colour; all but one to a particular organ of the body; each has a basic "symbol", though the actual meaning of the word in this context may puzzle some of us. There exists even a famous "schema" which Joyce drew up illustrating all this and presented to Herbert Gorman, though he subsequently objected very strenuously to its publication.

The common demand for esoteric meanings in *Ulysses* has fed voraciously on the details of the "schema", on the Homeric and other parallels and on Joyce's multiplicity of allusion and reference: it has been assumed that, hidden within this labyrinth, is the key to what he "meant", what the book is really "about". And not only have the basic analogies and correspondences been so enucleated and construed, but, not content with what is admittedly there, the higher criticism has turned each page into a jungle of symbol and reference, so that in the interests of semeiology, and on the most dubious grounds, the ordinary physical, substantive reality, the living world of the book has been almost entirely denatured. The function of the various techniques of narration employed (catechism, narcissism, incubism, etc., to use Joyce's own amusing terminology) has been wistfully debated as a key to the meaning of the whole; the action itself has been held to have symbolic or allegorical significances (the difference is not always clear to the unenthusiastic mind) which go far to rob it of any simple human significance at all. Thus the taking of a cup of cocoa becomes, because cocoa is "mass-produced", "the sacrifice of the Mass". Galileo-Bloom gets into bed with Venus, both goddess and planet; and in the Ascot Gold Cup, Sceptre, "the phallic favourite, loses to Throwaway, the outsider who represents infertility". Such circumlocuities of intention on Joyce's part are not quite inconceivable, of course, but one is entitled to ask whether, if Sir William Bass's great mare had recovered from the effects of winning four classics in 1902 and had won the Gold Cup of 1904, the symbolism would have been reversed. Or would Joyce have left the race out altogether? If he had, his picture of Dublin on the day of such an event would be remarkably incomplete.

Besides the Homeric parallels, the colours, the organs of the body and the basic symbol of each episode, there are what might be called other extensions of the situation: biblical, biographical, historical, classical, etc. Thus Bloom is not only Ulysses, but he is also Shakespeare; he is sometimes, apparently, Christ; and, in my own opinion, he is definitely the Holy Ghost. And there are certain recurrent images, phrases and themes such as, besides the aforementioned Gold Cup race, Mr. Deasy's letter, the jingle of Boylan's sidecar and Bloom's bed, the blind piano tuner, etc. With the possible exception of Nosey Flynn's snuffle these have naturally been accorded the status of significant symbols. In

James Joyce: His Way of Interpreting the Contemporary World William Y. Tindall offers the following explanation of what lies behind the innocent-seeming foot and mouth disease:

> Continual allusions to cattle and their disorders [in fact the foot and mouth disease, often a feature of the Irish scene, is the only one mentioned] establish the foot and mouth disease, the subject of Mr. Deasy's letter to the press, as a significant theme. In the maternity hospital, cattle serve as an obvious symbol of fertility, and foot and mouth disease, the trouble with cows [foot and mouth disease affects also bullocks, which of course are sterile anyway], becomes a symbol of infertility and Dublin's distemper. That foot and mouth also function on a Freudian level (foot as male and mouth as female) corroborates their meaning in this context. As "bullock befriendingbard" Stephen champions fertility or art against the sterility all round him.

Most of the exegesis concerned simply shows the higher criticism of to-day to be the old Browning Society in disguise: great writers have great messages which need deciphering and a great work has a great inner meaning which can operate on us in paraphrase. The judicious interpretation of symbol and correspondence can prove *Ulysses* to be "important" in terms of its inner "message" or "meaning", neo-Thomist, neo-Freudian, mythopoeic, metempsychotic or what not. It has proved perfectly easy to reduce it to the merest and dullest of allegory. Thus besides the neo-Freudian interpretation of the use that is made of "cattle and their disorders" may be put J. Mitchell Morse's neo-theological interpretation of an incident in the cabman's shelter in *The Sympathetic Alien: James Joyce and Catholicism*. Stephen, we are told, "rejects the inefficacious sacrament of the cabmen's shelter ('something in the shape of solid food – a bun or so it seemed' and 'what was temporarily supposed to be called coffee')" and this incident is the climax of the book because, though he "does have many social sins on his conscience – almost the whole catalogue of *ayanbite of Inwyt*... he is absolved from them by... refusing to take communion. That is the act of renunciation that purifies and frees the artist in him." What happened in fact was that Bloom ventured "to plausibly suggest to break the ice" a cup of coffee and a roll for Stephen. When they were brought he was preoccupied with his theory that the proprietor of the stall was Skin-the-Goat, the famous assassin of Lord Frederick Cavendish, so he silently pushed the cup of "what was temporarily supposed to be called coffee" and the "rather antediluvian speciman of a bun" over to his companion. Some ten pages later he breaks off a discourse on Bacon's authorship of the plays of Shakespeare to say – "Can't you drink that coffee by the way? Let me stir it and take a piece of that bun. It's like one of our skipper's bricks disguised. Still, no one can give what he hasn't got. Try a bit." Couldn't Stephen be contrived to get out his mental organs, for the moment refusing to dictate further!

This "reading" of Mitchell Morse is illuminating in several respects. First, the reluctance to take the matter further: why, if the bun is the host, is it "like one of our skipper's bricks disguised" (the sailor who was on the *Rosevean* "from Bridgewater with bricks")? If this game is started it should be kept up on the assumption that Joyce was consistent. Second, the puzzling refusal to explain why, when on the very next page he is urged "to have a shot at it now" Stephen does take "a sip of the offending beverage". And if the offending beverage, the coffee of the cabman's shelter, is part of the sacrifice of the Mass, what becomes of the other explainer's "mass-produced" cocoa, which Stephen and Bloom share a little later in Eccles Street? Where the one eminent exegetist sees Stephen refusing to participate in the sacrifice of the Mass in the cabman's shelter, the other sees Stephen and Bloom celebrating it a little later on in Eccles Street. The untutored reader, who may well find a sufficient delight in either episode without the aid of such hermeneutics, will doubtless feel that it is not in fact incumbent on him to decide whether it is the coffee or the cocoa which is the blood of Christ; but it is perhaps worth remarking that there may be some confusion on somebody's part, whether Joyce's or his critics', as to what precisely is a symbol.

A symbol is presumably something that, when contemplated, will reveal mysterious depths of meaning; and it will, presumably, have some aura of suggestion about it to begin with. The mass-produced cocoa, and the temporarily-agreed-on coffee, may be signs or emblems; *Ulysses* may be a work of boring algebra; but although the proponent of the cocoa suggests that it was while existing on that humble beverage in Paris that Joyce came to value it, there would still seem to be certain inescapable aesthetic difficulties about erecting it into a symbol. In other words, if this is the kind of thing *Ulysses* is about, the ordinary apparatus of aesthetic perception, however alert and sensitive, will not do; what is needed to "find out what it is about" is a curiosity like a process server's. The semeiologists and exegetists universally fail to see that any attempt to approach a work of art through a series of acts of mere intellectual comprehension is stultifying. There is a joy in apprehension, but this laborious deciphering is not it, and has only the effect of reducing the world of *Ulysses* to some monstrous enchanted fairyland where everything turns out to be masquerading as something else. Those who are adept at telling us what Joyce was up to are singularly unable to give us any valid and satisfying *aesthetic* reason why he should be up to it; if this is what he was up to, his mind was that of a puzzle setter, not that of a great literary artist. As Pound says about the Homeric parallels, "any blockhead can trace them", but not any blockhead can give us a convincing aesthetic reason why they should be there.

The Homeric framework is in fact pretty loose: the chronology of the *Odyssey* is not followed at all, and Joyce is more than arbitrary in deciding what he will or will not use. It remains obscure why some episodes should have basic colour motifs and others none; and why the first three should have no organ of the body motif. That the symbol of the Lotus Eater's episode (the one in which Bloom buys the soap, goes into the church and thinks about his bath) should be the Eucharist, may be an ironic comment about the effect of that sacrament on the faithful; but since the Eolus or Cave of the Winds episode takes place in a newspaper office, and that of the Sirens in the bar of a hotel, it cannot be held to be either very esoteric or very significant that the symbol of the one should be an editor, and of the other, barmaids.

The commonest explanation of the Homeric parallels is that they are an elaborate ironic device designed to exhibit the decay of Western civilisation and the emptiness and spiritual barrenness of the bourgeois, urban civilisation with which Joyce is supposed to be concerned. That he did exploit his framework for ironic purposes is undoubtedly true, but a certain elephantine coarseness of irony would be implied if the whole thing were simply a huge long joke at the expense of Dublin, the twentieth century and Leopold Bloom. What irony there is may be directed both ways. If the adventures of the real Ulysses cast a dubious light on Bloom, Bloom in his turn casts an ambiguous light on his forerunner. Joyce believed that a great deal of life had never got into heroic literature. But in general his ironic effects are subtler than any that could be produced by mere comparisons, either way. Nor has it been demonstrated that he brooded as much about the decline of the West as some critics, themselves addicted to certain views about that phenomenon, would have us believe. Dublin was not then, any more than it is now, typical of "modern urban civilisation" and, whatever the characters of *Ulysses* may be, they are not "modern industrial man", or even modern urban man, or typical middle-class man or anything else. Bloom, in spite of his nine hundred pounds' worth of Canadian scrip, is scarcely respectable enough to stand in for the bourgeoisie. Of his companions at the funeral, Martin Cunningham, the most eminent, has a wife who pawns the furniture every Saturday; Tom Kernan is a habitual drunkard who has been seriously injured when falling down the lavatory steps of a public house; Simon Dedalus is a jobless bankrupt whose only occupation is the praising of his own past; Jack Power keeps a barmaid under mysterious circumstances. The deceased himself has recently lost his job through that failing which is, according to Simon Dedalus, who ought to know, "many a good man's fault". And of Simon Dedalus's friends and companions of the afternoon session in the Ormonde, neither Bob Cowley, who has two bailiffs "prowling round the house trying to effect an entrance", nor Ben Dollard of the *basso profundo*, a wealthy businessman who has been reduced by Bass's Number One Ale to living in a doss-house, could be taken as representative material for a thesis on bourgeois material civilisation unless that thesis were a temperance tract: any more surely than could jingle jaunty Blazes Boylan; Lenehan ("that toucher") who earns a dubious living on the fringes of racing journalism; J. J. O'Molloy ("Gambling. Debts of honour. Reaping the whirlwind"); the Citizen ("waiting for what would drop from the sky in the way of a drink"), Hynes ("a decent fellow when he has it but sure like that he never does"), the editor of the *Freeman* himself ("a sad case... incipient jigs"); or indeed any of the characters, from McCoy, Nosey Flynn and The Nameless One down to "the former Gumley", reduced by drink to the status of night watchman, or Corley who borrows half a crown from Stephen for a kip for the night. If this is the plight of modern urban middle-class man it is indeed a parlous one; if this material is an epitome of the state of modern urban civilisation, the said civilisation's ills are odder (though perhaps simpler) than one had thought.

But a common misconception about *Ulysses* is that its characters are a cross-section of middle – or lower-middle – class Dublin. They are in fact splendidly typical of a certain kind of Dubliner, but not even in a city so small as Dublin could they all, or nearly all, be so well acquainted with each other unless they had a bond or an activity in common. That activity is song. With the exception of Stephen's medical friends practically every character is connected with that world of semi-professional, semi-amateur concert and operatic singing which flourished in Dublin, a city then, and to a much lesser degree still, devoted to vocal music, a world still, though moribund, by no means defunct. In habit and in speech they are also typical members of the drinking classes; but it is as well, where generalisations are concerned, and to get the picture of Dublin straight, to remember that they know each other largely because they belong to a particular circle whose bond was song. Joyce and his parents belonged to this and, apart from the students, Father Conmee and the company in the library, it furnishes the cast of the book.

Not very oddly perhaps, Ezra Pound and T. S. Eliot both came quite early on to much the same conclusion about the Homeric parallels; Pound when he said that "these correspondences are part of Joyce's mediaevalism, and are chiefly his own affair, a scaffold, a means of construction, justified by the result, and justifiable by it only"; and Eliot, in his review of *Ulysses* in *The Dial*, November 1923, when he concluded that the mythical extensions were "a way of controlling, of ordering, of giving a shape and a significance to the immense panorama of futility and anarchy which is contemporary history". There is a difference between the two descriptions, but in one respect they are the same: the Homeric parallels, like much else, are a constructive and controlling device. Like much else they have perhaps achieved an exaggerated importance because Joyce insisted on talking about his work only in terms of the structural devices that sustained it. In an examination of Joyce's working methods, *The Art of James Joyce*, an intelligent scholar, A. Walton Litz, points out that "the many Homeric parallels not included in the final text of *Ulysses* are significant, since they illustrate how much more important the Homeric background was for Joyce than it is to the reader". He goes on to show that the elaborate correspondences of the "schema" are absent from the early versions of the book and he justly adds:

> In his attempt to bring the effects of poetry to the novel, to "internalise" the narration and record various levels of consciousness, Joyce needed as many formal orders as possible to encompass and control his work. And as conventional representation decreased in importance toward the end of *Ulysses*, the need for other patterns increased. The multiple designs Joyce wove into *Ulysses* provide a stable scaffold for the reader, but the "support" they gave to Joyce may have been even greater. Most criticism of *Ulysses* is founded on the assumption that the essential life of the novel lies in the elaborate scheme of correspondences which Joyce revealed to his early commentators; but anyone who has examined his worksheets will realise that many of the correspondences represented for Joyce a kind of "neutral" order. They provided frames which

> could control his diverse materials without merging into them. Deprived of the traditional orders of home, country and religion, Joyce had a desperate and rather untidy passion for order of any kind. All sorts of mechanical systems are used on the note-sheets to organise the diverse elements . . . there are many more Homeric references on the *Ulysses* note-sheets than ever made their way into the text, and we are forced to conclude that the parallel with the *Odyssey* was more useful to Joyce during the process of composition than it is to us while we read the book. Time and again he spoke of the comfort he derived from the narrative order of the *Odyssey*: it provided him – in his own words – with fixed "ports of call". The major parallels between the wanderings of Mr. Bloom and those of *Ulysses* are an important dimension of the novel, but in working out the trivial details of the Homeric correspondence Joyce was exploring his own materials, not preparing clues for future readers.

Of course, Joyce used his controlling patterns, as any form may be used, to find further illuminations of his material. Part of the function of form, for the writer, is that it is itself suggestive. Both the Homeric parallels and the less important correspondences provided Joyce with new ironies and insights as he went along – the use that he makes of the organs of the body, the human heart in the funeral sequence for example. A fruitful technique is itself creative, an organism which will not only help to control, but to develop and to extend the limits of vision, and Joyce's structural devices, the *Odyssey* and the other correspondences, do this. To say that they remain primarily technical devices is not to demean them. The imagination will not function without a framework of some sort. Joyce was dispensing, among other things, with plot in the ordinary sense of the word, the mechanism, the sustaining device that provides the reason for the existence of the majority of novels and the form for nearly all of them, which largely decides when they should begin, how they should progress and when they should end, and dictates to a considerable extent what objects should be mentioned, what scenes described, what characters introduced. He had to find his "ports of call"; he had to find, indeed he did find, a framework which would not only control his material and give it unity, but provide the all-important scaffold for the imagination as well. Nor indeed should it be forgotten that in every use of form as well as in every extension of allusion there is an element of play, that element of play which paradoxically deepens the being of a work of art and without which the composition of works of art on the scale of *Ulysses* would scarcely be possible.

II

The attempt to reduce the physical reality of the world of *Ulysses* to a series of hieroglyphs ignores the references to symbolic or metaphysical intentions in art which Joyce himself made. There is a curious passage in *Stephen Hero* in which we are told that Stephen "even thought of explaining the audacities of his verse as symbolical allusions. It was hard for him to compel his head to preserve the strict temperature of classicism." And in *A Portrait of the Artist as a Young Man*, Stephen specifically rejects in so many words an aesthetic based on symbolism (and incidentally formulates a post-Cézanne aesthetic of great exactness). Speaking of Aquinas's use of the word *claritas* he admits that it had baffled him for a long time and goes on:

> It would lead you to believe he had in mind symbolism or idealism, the supreme quality of beauty being a light from some other world, the idea of which the matter is but the shadow, the reality of which it is but the symbol . . . the artistic discovery and representation of the divine purpose in anything or a force of generalisation which would make the aesthetic image a universal one, make it outshine its proper conditions. But that is literary talk . . . . When you have apprehended that basket as one thing and have then analysed it according to its form and apprehended it as a thing you make the only synthesis which is logically and esthetically permissible. You see that it is that thing which it is and no other thing. The radiance of which he speaks is the scholastic *quidditas*, the *whatness* of a thing.

Nor would the treatment meted out to George Russell and his theory that "art has to reveal to us ideas, formless spiritual essences" in *Ulysses* suggest that Joyce's purposes were symbolic, at least in so far as that word suggests a metaphysical intent, or that any great change of mind had taken place between the writing of the *Portrait* and the writing of *Ulysses*.

It has been suggested that in the use of Homer, Joyce desired to give his work epic dimensions; and that in his use of physiology and the arts, etc., his purpose was primarily encyclopaedic, that he wished *Ulysses* to enclose as many human preoccupations and to include as much erudition and general information as possible. This latter would also be an idea hard to justify on mere aesthetic grounds; but there is no doubt that the complicated interplay between his material and its intentional extensions of reference does enlarge *Ulysses* in the sense of increasing the universality of the action. But this would have been a dangerous game to play if the action were not substantially and hypostatically real to begin with. Most Joyce criticism tends to rob the ordinary surface reality of the book of this substantive realism.

Many of the "significant themes", the recurring motifs, are perfectly natural and important details whose justification and necessity are plain. The names of Dublin landmarks which the characters have to pass and re-pass have been credited with obscure symbolical depths as if Joyce had made up the whole city out of his head: if he had picked other landmarks one supposes that they would have been turned to good purpose by the commentators also. What Professor Tindall calls "continual allusions to cattle and their disorders", meaning the foot and mouth disease, are not necessarily intended as pointers to a Freudian symbol, and an ineffably clumsy one at that. They constitute apt natural detail, a source of some superb comedy, and an element in the comic technique by which such figures as Mr. Deasy and the editor ("J.J. O'Molloy, about to follow him in, said quietly to Stephen: I hope you will live to see it published.") are made real. Above all it is a perfect piece of grotesquery with which to shackle Stephen and it contributes a good deal to our knowledge of him: he takes an amount of trouble over the letter and risks a little humiliation; he blushes when he hands it over. In his own mind it is an ironic reminder of his situation, the "bullockbefriending bard" who is reminded by Lynch that so far only a "capful of light odes can call your genius father"; and in the reader's consciousness it may stand not as a symbol but simply as an associational reminder of his wasteful, uncreative days. It will be seen that in interpreting it as a symbol for Stephen's championship of fertility or art against the sterility all round him, Professor Tindall has not only indulged himself in totally unwarrantable Freudian assumptions but has actually gone directly contrary to the plain reading of the text as well. Like all the other recurring themes, echoing, re-echoing and re-appearing in various places at various hours of the day, it contributes to the unity and to the living texture of the whole book and to our feeling for the city and its common preoccupations. And like some others, the Gold Cup for example, which is first in the debatable future and then in the irrevocable past, it serves beautifully to remind us of the actual passage of the day. When late at night in the coffee stall we find that the letter is actually in the paper with Bloom "a bit flabbergasted at Myles Crawford's after all managing the thing", the whole long day is thrown into perspective behind us. And these repetitions also serve to remind us of the people who are off-stage and of other specific moments in time; they are part of our developing consciousness and knowledge of the people and the milieu of the book.

Judging from the work of some of his commentators, to attempt to seek secondary, hermeneutic purposes on Joyce's part is often to miss the real nature of his achievement. To anyone who knows Dublin, the recurring theme of the Ascot Gold Cup will seem perfectly natural and right; and it is certainly very illuminating. It serves to emphasise Bloom's isolation among his fellow citizens and their suspicions of him (they have it both ways: he is accused not only of being a "whiteyed kaffir . . . that never backed a horse in anger in his life" but of secretly backing the winner and "then sloping off with his five quid without putting up a pint of stuff like a man"). It increases Bloom's stature (he and Davy Byrne, the moral publican, are above such frivolities, but he condemns nobody else for indulging in them). There may or may not be a pun to connect Bloom's masturbation on the strand and his abandonment of his wife to Mulligan with the names of the winner and the much-backed Sceptre, but in that case why does Mulligan himself back Sceptre? The Gold Cup is abundantly justified by the light it throws on Bloom; it would be justified anyway even by the light it throws on Nosey Flynn, Davy Byrne and company in Barney Kiernan's. And it would be more than worth its weight in gold were it only for the fact that it is the cause of such consummate abuse of Bloom. The commentators speak as if the ability to invent the pun were more remarkable than the ability to invent the comedy. If the pun does exist, it is not a very remarkable stroke aesthetically, though it may exhibit Joyce's cleverness; on the other hand the human use that is made of the Gold Cup is superb.

Those who are intent on turning *Ulysses* into mere anagram and allegory are perhaps so because they are incapable of appreciating the "profane joy" with which ordinary mundanities are invested in it. Perhaps too they are unsympathetic towards the kind of life which in large part it portrays; incapable of savouring, for example, the citizen's language as Joyce himself savours it, to some extent even uninterested in the primary satisfactions we derive from language and the representation of life. Whatever Joyce's secondary purposes may have been, whatever eleborations of technique and allusion he indulges in, that is not where the true greatness of the book lies. Mr. Bloom may be Shakespeare; what is important to us is that he is Bloom. The fact that he is not only Odysseus but Shakespeare and Sinbad the sailor as well, does not account for his fascination: as if Joyce's talents lay in the ability to invent more and more "meaningful" parallels. Nor is the worth of the book to be suggested by explaining what it is really "about", as if Joyce was a nostrum vendor, a mystic or a philosopher. What the book is "about" may be important in the sense that every writer may have to be judged by the *quality* of his vision as well as by his ability to express it, though this is a debatable point which would require a lot of definition. It is irrelevant, if we mean by what it is "about" a mere attitude hidden in the hermeneutics which, if discovered, would only have the force of an attitude and not the force of art. To speak of the quality of a man's vision is not to speak of the worth of his mere, paraphrasable opinions about history or religion or our place in the cosmos: an ideology which could be discovered and exclaimed over like that of any other fashionable sage. Every recorded statement we have exhibits Joyce's total contempt for abstract ideas, his cheerful and not at all hag-ridden scepticism about religion, his indifference to the profundities of the new psychology. A good deal of confusion exists about the nature of his vision; he has been accused of everything from sentimentality, to indifference, to rage; but before asking what his book is about it is equally, if not more, important to enquire into the almost totally neglected question of what in fact it is.

III

What it is can perhaps be seen more clearly by a preliminary examination of what it is not. It is to begin with unlike almost any other novel ever written. Almost all other novels are patterned dramatically. They are concerned not only with a situation, but with a situation that unfolds itself, a plot which progresses through a chain of causation, often involving coincidence, frequently violence or at least death. Life in such books is to a greater or lesser degree subordinated to event. We get little or no static living, but only those events which contribute more or less to the main stream. Irrelevancies may be included but they are usually said to have had some influence on the behaviour of the characters in the crises of event. Life has to be contained within the pattern of event; it is therefore neater and smaller than real living. The events, being patterned, are also neater than the events in life, which have usually no pattern. Plot events are causative, being explainable in terms of each other, whereas events in life are frequently isolated and inexplicable, or, if explicable, they are so only in terms of an infinite conglomeration of factors which would stretch outside the book. The events out of which the pattern of event is made are both more clear-cut and more probable than the events in life, though the pattern as a whole is usually highly improbable.

The justification for this patterning in most serious works is presumably more than the amusement of the reader with a good story, the satisfaction of his aroused curiosity, or the gratification of his delight in violence or intrigue. The justification, if there is one, must rest both on the negative claim that much is allowable in letters that does not obtain in life, like speaking in iambic pentameters; and on the positive claim that the dramatic arrangement of life in a book is a means of producing pity, terror, catharsis or any other emotion that it is proper to feel in the presence of a work of art. The latter claim rests on the assumption that an artificial arrangement of life in a pattern of event and a curtailment of life in the interests of a pattern of event can be a source of aesthetic satisfaction.

Still the falsification of life remains. We may say that this falsification is tacitly admitted between the writer and the reader, just as a composer of opera tacitly agrees with the audience that people do not communicate by singing at each other; it exists all the same. There is no such falsification of life in *Ulysses*. Of course *Ulysses* is not just a "slice of life", as it was once assumed to be, though even as a slice of life, if that were conceivable, it would still be very great. (Samuel Beckett has said in conversation with the present writer in 1959 that Joyce thought it was perhaps "over-constructed": some of the commentators seem to suggest that it is constructed to the exclusion of everything but the construction and is the "greater" for that.) But the necessary limitations of Joyce's form do not result in a falsification of life as do those of the ordinary novel of self-sustaining event. In *Ulysses*, for the first time in fiction, life could be almost completely itself. Where in the novel of event each picture, each person, each happening, each thought has to be subordinated to the over-all pattern, in *Ulysses* they are allowed their own importance. Nothing is a mere turning point in the narrative, a mere link in a chain of causation, a puppet called upon to give the story a twist or a push. Though there is event – there is a good deal of real drama in the episode of the funeral carriage: the stony silence with which, as Irish Catholics believing in the last sacraments, his companions greet Bloom's assertion that sudden death is the best, and the unfortunate reference to suicide – it has its own right to exist independently. Conversation, anecdote, thought, desultory impression, image and happening are freed at least from their long subordination to plot. They do not have to play a part; or to suffer drastic curtailment because they are counted as irrelevant. Of course they have to have some significance: *Ulysses* would be a terrifying monstrosity if they had not. Each is, in fact, an epiphany, to use Joyce's own terms of greater or lesser importance; but their importance is not that of mere contributing factors to a story. This is the texture of life, not the artificiality of contrived event; and, as a result, *Ulysses* is a prose work much of which one can read as one does a poem, for the epiphanies and the words themselves, not for the sake of a story to which they contribute, though they do, of course, contribute to the total impression the book makes.

Succeeding in this, Joyce has succeeded in eliminating the underlying falsehood of the novel. Though there may be a tacit agreement between the reader and the writer that things do not happen as the novel suggests, that they are not so isolated, nor clear-cut, nor interlocked, nor dramatic; and that most of life is composed of experiences which do not serve the novelist's purposes, there nevertheless remains a residual feeling on the reader's part that things ought to be like this, that fiction is in some way better than fact, a feeling that is bad for fact, for living, and, one might add, bad for fiction too. The various confusions about "naturalism" and "realism" do not help matters. Zola, the great prophet of naturalism, is full of the most preposterous melodrama. Nor, for all that we hear about the influence or non-influence of *Ulysses*, has the novel, even the so-called serious novel, altered very much, if at all, in this respect: event is still preponderant at the expense of texture.

But along with this liberation of ordinary living from the shackles of plot, goes an enormous extension of the range of life included. If one of the simplest but most important functions of the writer is to extend the recorded area of human experience, Joyce has flung the frontiers further out than any writer of this century – and it is to the particular honour of this century that whole new tracts of human experience, never before explored, have been brought under the amending and meliorating rule of the artist's compassion. Whatever his secondary purposes may have been, whatever intertwining strands of meaning and experience *Ulysses* contains, whatever the point of the story, if there is a point, all his statements go to show that Joyce considered it a major, indeed *the* major part of his vocation as a writer to speak the truths that had never before been spoken.

As his brother points out, he was a realist and an extremist who had had the advantage over most writers of having to conduct his after-dinner discussions about life in a country in which the dinner itself was often lacking. From the time when he told Stanislaus that "he had no doubt that most artists, even the greatest, belied the life they knew", so that "literature . . . was a parody of life" and came to believe, according to Stanislaus, that "the poetry of noble sentiments, the romantic music, and the dramatic passions, with a dominant love theme, which culture offered him as a true poetic insight into the universal problems of human life, did not fit in with life as he knew it" – his primary purpose as an artist was clear. He ended his first adolescent manifesto with a quotation from Ibsen: " 'What will you do in our society, Miss Hessel?' asked Rorlund – 'I will let in fresh air, pastor,' answered Lona." And in *Ulysses* itself he writes of the "secrets, silent, stony" which "sit in the dark palaces of both our hearts: secrets weary of their tyranny: tyrants willing to be dethroned".

Part of this process was technical: ordinary living had to be freed from the distortions of plot, from the skimping and twisting essential in the novel of event, of men and women in dramatic conflict, so that it could achieve its own entelechy. But along with this liberation from the tyranny of narrative went a tremendous extension of the amount of life included. Joyce includes so much that had never been included in art before, of man not only in his basic sexuality but in his basic sordidity as well, that he must stand as one of the great liberators of the human spirit from the tyranny of its own secrets. And not only did he bring such things within the scope of expression; he brought them, which is more important, within the scope of art.

IV

A man's message is his way of seeing. Instead of asking whether Bloom will or will not get his breakfast in bed in the morning, and what, if anything, is the significance of the meeting between Bloom and Stephen, it is perhaps better to ask what spirit pervades and informs *Ulysses*. The mood of a book should operate on the reader more surely and a great deal more subtly than anything that could be described as its message.

"The theme of *Ulysses* is simple", says Richard Ellmann in his book, *James Joyce*, "casual kindness overcomes unconscionable power." Harry Levin, in *James Joyce*, however, will have nothing to do with such calendar mottoes. He thinks that the book offers no hope and no comfort, that there is only the author's creative intensity, beating down "like an aroused volcano upon an ancient city, overtaking its doomed inhabitants in forum or temple, at home or at brothel, and petrifying them in the insensate agonies of paralysis." (Incidentally it is difficult to make out from Levin's celebrated study whether he enjoyed reading the book or not.) In an early work, about which I understand he now has his reservations, Hugh Kenner thought that the book was a gargantuan, ironic machine, and he favoured the dilemma of Modern Industrial Man, the dead remains of classical and Christian civilisation being incapsulated in the speech of the characters, whose language is the language of eighteenth-century Dublin, in order to show how the mighty are fallen. That the language of the nameless narrator of the Cyclops episode is the language of eighteenth-century Dublin one is inclined to doubt. It is sufficiently obvious that neither he nor the Citizen are Industrial Men, or industrious men either, for the matter of that. Many people have found the book terrible. George Orwell believed that it was "the product of a special vision of life, the vision of a Catholic who has lost his faith. What Joyce is saying is 'Here is life without God. Just look at it!' " (Apart altogether from whether we really feel that Joyce is saying anything like this when we read the book, it is perhaps worth remarking here that though all the evidence goes to show that he was a cheerful sort of unbeliever it is rather to be doubted whether, as Eliot has pointed out to the present author, anybody brought up as an Irish Catholic could ever, deep in his being, envisage the world as "Godless".) William Empson thinks that Bloom's isolation and Stephen's megalomania are so monstrous that, if the book is to be bearable, it must have a happy ending. He thinks Joyce meant to indicate that Stephen went to bed with Molly, the first woman not a whore he had ever been to bed with, and that this not only produced an enormous improvement in his character, but was the means of restoring conjugal relations between the Blooms.

All this disagreement would seem to suggest that there is a deep inherent difficulty in deciding what are the values of the book, even, let us say, to put it perfectly simply, in deciding whether it is a cheerful book or a very gloomy one.

The values with which we are surrounded in life are, so to speak, concentric: near at hand are those of the parental, or, later, the human circle in which we move, outside them the values of society and beyond that again what are alleged to be the values of God or of the grave. Before discussing his larger vision it would be as well to see whether Joyce accepts, rejects, endorses or modifies the ordinary close-at-hand values of society and it is perhaps instructive to compare him with a famous, and in many ways remarkable, novelist who is said to have attacked them. Thackeray's *Vanity Fair* is an instructive contrast in several respects. *Vanity Fair* is ostensibly an attack on society, on high society for its unwarrantable scorn for all beneath it, on a universally uncharitable attitude towards poverty and misfortune, on the hypocrisy that abounds on all levels of the social ladder and the cheating, dishonesty, calculation and toadying that it masks, in particular on the Victorian marriage-mart as a form of respectable prostitution. Yet the book itself is deeply involved with society also. Thackeray assumes that his readers are normal middle-class people with normal middle-class values, though they are evidently supposed to be better-hearted than he thinks the world is in general. If he is hard on society he is even harder on Becky. Her father, the Soho painter, is treated just as we would expect such an arty, "dissolute" character to be treated for the benefit of such an audience. The counterweights in the book, feminine virtue as exemplified by Amelia and masculine decency, honesty and kindliness as represented by Dobbin are, frankly, in an adult world, ridiculous. Much play is made of Amelia's innocence, gentleness and charitableness as an example to us all, but as a moral yardstick this is nursery nonsense, for if she had been born in a slum these virtues would have had to undergo considerable modification, probably for the better: as she is in the book, Amelia and her virtues, so-called, are simply the product of upbringing, education and good middle-class shelter. Again the contrast between Dobbin and the others is altogether jejune as a matter of serious morality, for Dobbin's virtues depend on his money: indeed the exercise of his vaunted virtues is generally simply an exercise of his money. An even more fundamental flaw in the book is Thackeray's complete acceptance of the struggle for money, for success, for rank and position as important and interesting in itself. It is not simply that the world finds it so and therefore he must write about it: but that he finds it so himself and expects us to do so as well. Generally speaking he is hopelessly, and to a large extent unconsciously, involved with the majority of the values of society. When we ask ourselves who his ideal reader would be, we are forced to conclude that it would be somebody like Amelia herself, a gently brought up girl who accepted the so-called values of innocence and decency as alternatives to those of the world.

Thackeray quite obviously expects the reader to share his beliefs, his prejudices and his values: his book is written in the assurance that there is a common ground and that it is quite easily reached by people of good-will. Joyce does not seem to have any prejudices, whatever about values or beliefs. As far as can be seen, initially at least, what he expects from the reader is only a level of literacy and a freedom from atavistic reaction to sexual abnormality, dirt, drink, dishonesty, failure (how failure sets Thackeray off, one way or the other!) and all societal obstacles to admiration or compassion, or at least a cool regard. The people of *Ulysses* are a pretty battered lot. Debt, drink, idleness afflict practically all of them, Stephen included. Bloom is not idle, but he is not very industrious either, and his record of false starts and lost jobs in Cuffe's, Wisdom Hely's, Thom's and elsewhere certainly amounts to failure, a failure from which only the nine hundred pounds and the insurance policy inherited from his father protect him. Part of his past, the making up to Mrs Riordan, for example, or the suggestion to Molly that she should pose in the nude for the rich dilettantes in Merrion Square, are not very creditable in terms of the sort of values we imbibe from Thackeray or indeed any of the writing of the past. Nor would the rest of the people in the book appear, by these standards, very prepossessing. The three old men who foregather in the Ormonde would not have much to say for themselves in most courts of judgment of life. Ben Dollard of the bass baritone has squandered his substance and reduced himself to penury; Bob Cowley is in the hands of the bailiffs, Simon Dedalus's daughters are near starving while he drinks. Yet there seems to be nothing much on their consciences that a ball of malt and a bar of a song will not amend. Is Joyce's attitude towards them condemnatory, compassionate or indifferent? Are we supposed to admire them as they evidently to some extent admire themselves?

The first thing one is forced to conclude is that if *Ulysses* is an examination of hell, or futility, or an unredeemed decay, or anything else of that nature – which it is frequently alleged to be – it presents some very curious characteristics. Here is a passage from *Stephen Hero* which is an illuminating contrast to the tone of *Ulysses*. Stephen has gone to the Adelphi Hotel to look for Cranly. He finds him in the billiard-room and sits down beside him to watch the game:

> It was a three-handed game. An elderly clerk, evidently in a patronising mood, was playing two of his junior colleagues. The elderly clerk was a tall stout man who wore gilt spectacles on a face like a red shrivelled apple. He was in his shirt-sleeves and he played and spoke so briskly as to suggest that he was drilling rather than playing. The young clerks were both clean-shaven. One of them was a

thickset young man who played doggedly without speaking, the other was an effervescent young man with white eyebrows and a nervous manner. Cranly and Stephen watched the game progress, creep from point to point. The heavy young man put his ball on the floor three times in succession and the scoring was so slow that the marker came and stood by the table as a reminder that the twenty minutes had passed. The players chalked their cues oftener than before and, seeing that they were in earnest about finishing the game, the marker did not say anything about the time. But his presence acted upon them. The elderly clerk jerked his cue at his ball, making a bad stroke, and stood back from the table blinking his eyes and saying "Missed that time". The effervescent young clerk hurried to his ball, made a bad stroke and, looking along his cue, said "Ah!". The dogged young man shot his ball straight into the top pocket, a fact which the marker registered at once on the broken marking-board. The elderly clerk peered for a few critical seconds over the rim of his glasses, made another bad stroke and, at once proceeding to chalk his cue, said briefly and sharply to the effervescent young man "Come on now, White. Hurry up now." The hopeless pretence of those three lives before him, their unredeemable servility, made the back of Stephen's eyes feel burning hot. He laid his hand on Cranly's shoulder and said impetuously: "We must go at once. I can't stand it any longer."

If this is hell, and it is, we are out of it in *Ulysses*. There is no one in *Ulysses* whose life is a hopeless pretence or who presents an aspect of unredeemable servility. Indeed there is scarcely anyone who does not bear himself with panache, with gaiety, with scurrility or with pride. Bloom, though insulted, certainly feels no inferiority. And it is instructive to compare the mood of the portraiture in *Ulysses* with Joyce's treatment of the same people in *Dubliners*. It comes as something of a shock to realise that the Ignatius Gallagher whose scoop we hear about in the *Freeman's Journal* office is the vulgarian who appeared from London in 'A Little Cloud'. The Lenehan of *Ulysses* is a great deal less insufferable (and more cheerful) than the Lenehan who hangs about while Corley extracts money from the slavey in 'Two Gallants'. Martin Cunningham, Jack Power, McCoy, Tom Kernan are all treated harshly and satirically in the earlier book but with what almost amounts to gentleness in the later. But the strangest blossoming concerns someone who had appeared only in the *Portrait* and *Stephen Hero*. Simon Dedalus now at last attains those legendary dimensions that the *Portrait* had grudgingly hinted at. He is given size, humour, style and pathos; it is made quite clear that he retains his daughter's amused affection even though he refuses her the money he proceeds to spend in the Ormonde; and his song in that place is given its full worth of beauty. We see him well away now on his downward path, in the glory of his scandalous autumn, and we leave him in full voice.

Joyce openly enjoys his material in *Ulysses* and grants it a worth which, for any but satirical purposes, is denied to it in *Dubliners*. I have no wish to suggest that the book is Pickwickian or that Simon Dedalus is a first cousin of the Cheeryble brothers; nor that the book presents a happier view of experience simply because it is funnier than *Dubliners* or the *Portrait*. But the humour of *Ulysses* can scarcely be other than sympathetic, for the simple reason that most of it is made by the characters themselves. It is their tongues and imaginations, the vitality of their language, the grotesquery of their wit which, as much as anything else, draw us back to the book and make it, whatever else it may be, one of the funniest in the language.

And there can hardly be any question but that Joyce enjoys them just as they enjoy themselves. The Citizen is well aware that he is giving a performance, albeit straightfaced, and he is certainly enjoying himself. In *Dubliners* the comedy is of a kind that gives Joyce and the reader bitter and mordant amusement – the asinine conversation about the doctrine of infallibility in the story, 'Grace', for example – but which the characters themselves can hardly be said to share. *Dubliners* may be comic; it is anything but humorous. If the man who wrote *Dubliners* has looked upon the Gorgon's head, the man who wrote *Ulysses* has certainly not been turned to stone.

And it is often forgotten how much of *Ulysses* explores the lives of people other than simply Bloom and Stephen: when Joyce's narrowness of scope as a novelist is complained of, it should be remembered how skilfully and often how movingly he touched in the whole background of a minor character's life: Martin Cunningham's wife, J.J. O'Molloy's attempts to borrow money, the Dignam household, Mrs Breen's marriage, Father Conmee's complacency, Zoe's patter. Hundreds of such details, flitting across Bloom's mind or emerging from some conversation, evoke, seldom without compassion, the lives of a dozen others.

The people of *Ulysses* are not a cross-section of the bourgeois world: they are Joyce's father's world, that narrow world of drink and song, of debt and redemption, of vulgarity, wit and seedy gentility that his father inhabited. It is through singing that they are, for the most part, acquainted; and Joyce himself loved song. "The humour of *Ulysses* is his; its people are his friends. The book is his spittin' image", he said to Louis Gillet after his father's death. And, apart from their feeling for song, the people of *Ulysses* are by no means without their virtues: their ready understanding of misfortune, their willingness to help each other beat the rap, their refusal to judge each other by the standards of mere respectability are apparent. *Ulysses*, says Harry Levin, is an epic "entirely lacking in the epic virtues of love, friendship and magnanimity", but he seems to be forgetting or ignoring something deeply important in the characters' attitude to each other:

> For a few days tell him, Father Cowley said anxiously.
>
> Ben Dollard halted and stared, his loud orifice open, a dangling button of his coat wagging brightbacked from its thread as he wiped away the heavy shraums that clogged his eyes to hear aright.
>
> What few days? he boomed. Hasn't your landlord distrained for rent?
>
> He has, Father Cowley said.
>
> Then our friend's writ is not worth the paper it's printed on, Ben Dollard said. The landlord has the prior claim. I gave him all the particulars. 29 Windsor Avenue. Love is the name?
>
> That's right, Father Cowley said . . . But are you sure of that?
>
> You can tell Barabbas from me, Ben Dollard said, that he can put that writ where Jacko puts the nuts.
>
> He led Father Cowley forward linked to his bulk.
>
> Filberts I believe they were, Mr. Dedalus said, as he dropped his glasses on his coatfront, following them.

And along with their readiness to help, however desultory, idle or unreliable it may be, they have a gaiety and courage in face of their own usually well-deserved misfortunes, which is part of an attitude to life that may at bottom be weak and self-deceiving, but which also augurs a certain generosity and recklessness of spirit not markedly characteristic of the bourgeois world. Apart from Stephen's student friends and the librarians these people are all, or nearly all, failures of one kind or another. Even the editor of the *Freeman* is, according to Ned Lambert, a "sad case" of "incipient jigs". That Joyce should have thought an exposure of their limitations and weaknesses worth the full weight of so much of the book is inconceivable. Many judgments on the people of *Ulysses* seem to proceed from a sort of upset liberalism or shocked Protestantism which finds them and their humour an outrage, but these judgments are certainly not shared by Joyce himself. Yeats was nearer the mark when he agreed that *Ulysses* was "cruel" but added that it was "our Irish cruelty, and also our kind of strength". A great deal of the humour of these people is admittedly cruel, but then it is *Galgen-humor*, the product of misfortune, and those who find it too cruel would probably find most Irish humour so, from Lever's to Samuel Beckett's, and might profitably even take a closer look at some of the humour of Somerville and Ross.

The confusion of morality with mere respectability which is almost endemic in the English mind is entirely absent in Joyce, and the vulgarity of judgment by mere status is entirely absent from his book. The people of *Ulysses*, though they belong, very roughly speaking, to a certain social class, form an almost completely classless community. Though the realities of money and survival are known to them, the irrelevancies of the social structure are not important to Joyce. Nor does *Ulysses* contain any lingering traces of a morality – sexual, social, monetary or hygienic – unconsciously adopted from respectable society and silently assumed to be held in common with the respectable reader. Joyce has shifted the process of judgment of human behaviour altogether away from that governed merely by social reflex. And this is one of the ways in which he is a specifically modern writer, reflecting the real consciousness of our time; for whatever else may be said about it, and with all its vulgarities, its violences, its half-baked caricatures of serious creative purposes on its head, ours is a time of liberation from merely societal values. That his book is in large part governed by this spirit of tolerance and liberation is all the more remarkable in that it is populated not by artists or anarchists or beats or professional rebels of one kind or another, but by some of the outwardly ordinary people of Dublin in 1904. It is as if the lid had been pulled off ordinary society to reveal the falsity of the lie that people are divided into the respectable and the criminal: to reveal in all its outrageousness the unbiddable eccentricity, weakness, humour and unreliability of man.

V

But if, as is suggested, the dominant humour, the spirit that pervades and informs the book, is sympathetic, it would seem an odd sort of book about Dublin for the young man we know as Stephen Dedalus to have written in after-life. And we are surely meant to understand that Stephen did write the book we are reading. Indeed, as we shall see later, his forthcoming authorship is referred to in it. If the book is tolerant, if it is more than tolerant, and is, in some sort, a celebration of its material, it is admittedly hard to imagine Stephen Dedalus maturing to write it, for we know from the *Portrait* what Stephen Dedalus thought of the Dublin of his youth. But it is possible that we are meant to be surprised; that part of Joyce's point is that we should be surprised.

We can easily imagine Stephen going on to write books of other kinds: something rather Paterish perhaps, or like those passionate novels of dedication by D'Annunzio which the young Joyce admired even more than he admired Flaubert's. Something in the neo-Baudelairean fashion of the *fin de siècle* is not altogether unlikely or, to be more generous, something as original and as terrible as a new *saison en enfer*. It would certainly have been difficult to predict that after he had described his revolt in the *Portrait*, and the world from which he revolted in *Dubliners*, and gone on to the justification and triumph of revolt and severance, it would take the form of a humorous, but by no means caustic celebration of the goings on in the world he had left: Miss Douce snapping her garter for the benefit of Blazes Boylan, the Citizen's monologue, the meditations of Father John Conmee, the singing in the Ormonde, Gerty Mc Dowell exposing her drawers for the delectation of Leopold Bloom, Lenehan's story about "what star is that, Paddy?" – the whole conception of the saintly Leopold himself. In other words, a celebration of everything from which he had revolted. The creation of Leopold Bloom certainly seems an odd final triumph and climax after all that aesthetic flag-waving, more especially if the attitude of his creator to him and to his fellow Dubliners is neither ironic, vengeful nor despairing. And it will perhaps seem even odder if we compare the draft *Stephen Hero* with the finished *Portrait* of the same young man, for Stephen Dedalus is made certainly, and it seems deliberately, less likely than his prototype Stephen Hero to be the eventual author of *Ulysses*. The differences in this respect between the draft and the finished book are at first sight puzzling; but they are also instructive and they cast light on *Ulysses*.

The *Portrait* is, of course, technically far more sophisticated than its predecessor. The two signs of technical mastery – the absence of overt description and formal explanation – have been achieved, while *Stephen Hero* is full of explanation, description and emphasis. The pacing of the finished book is admirable while the judgment of pace in the fragment is atrocious.

Yet, and this is the odd thing, the eye behind *Stephen Hero* often seems colder, more ironic and more sophisticated than the eye that drew the *Portrait*. Whereas the *Portrait* is a huge advance in sophistication of technique and the handling of material, the youthfulness and romanticism of its subject are heightened, rather than the reverse. All Stephen's crises and relationships are handled much more coolly, not to say cynically in *Stephen Hero*, than they are to be later on in the *Portrait*. His attitude to his parents is much more fully and humorously conveyed; his feelings about Emma are much more cynically and perceptively elaborated than in the later book, where they are reduced to a cipher of romantic love. And there are instructive contrasts in the handling of certain episodes. One concerns the girl whom Stephen encounters wading in the stream at Dollymount Strand just after he has decided to reject the claims of the Church and feels for the first time the sensuous, pagan beauty of the world. Though the account of the episode itself is missing from the fragment, there is an unmistakeable reference to it. In the *Portrait* Stephen had seen a girl, her legs bared to the hips, her face "touched with the wonder of mortal beauty . . . and when she felt his presence and the worship of his eyes her eyes turned to him in quiet sufferance of his gaze, without shame or wantonness". At length, Stephen turned away from her and suddenly set off across the strand . . . "singing wildly to the sea, crying to greet the advent of the life that had cried to him". The reference to the episode in *Stephen Hero* strikes a different note. Here Stephen is described as going to exactly the same spot to stare at the children and the nurses (presumably the "gay light-clad figures of children and girls" of the *Portrait*).

> He used to stand to stare at them sometimes until the ash off his cigarette fell onto his coat but, though he saw all that was intended, he met no other Lucy: and he usually returned to the Liffey side, somewhat amused at his dejection and thinking that if he had made his proposal to Lucy instead of to Emma he might have met with better luck.

This is rather different from, "Her image had passed into his soul for ever and no word had broken the holy silence of his ecstasy" of the *Portrait*: at least he found out her name.

We are on a lower, more mundane plane of reality in *Stephen Hero* than we are to be later on in the finished book. In fact the *Portrait*, with its exalted Stephen, its impressionist background, its shadowy cast behind the brilliantly lit central figure and its successions of dramatic monologues, is written in a mood of dramatic zeal and enraptured fervour which seems odd in a man who was recasting a much more casual, homely and cynical work of his adolescence, and which is much further from the principles of detached classicism he had already formulated.

Another illuminating instance concerns Stephen's apostasy. The famous conversation with Cranly at the close of the *Portrait* is duplicated in *Stephen Hero*, but the tone of it is altogether different. Where in the *Portrait* the suggestion is not so much disbelief as satanism, "I will not serve", in *Stephen Hero* Stephen states quite plainly that he no longer believes; and his attitude in general is more human, more forthright and lacking in the Jesuitical subtleties which add a perverted prestige to the attitude of Stephen Dedalus.

> . . . Look here, I cannot talk on this subject. I am not a scholar and I receive no pay as a minister of God. I want to live, do you understand . . . I don't care whether I am right or wrong. There is always the risk in human affairs, I suppose . . . the whole affair is too damn idiotic. Give it up. I am very young. When I have a beard to my middle I will study Hebrew and then write to you about it . . . . You urge me to postpone life – till when? Life is now – this is life: if I postpone it I may never live.

For some reason then, between the abandonment of the draft shortly after he left Ireland and the beginning of serious work on the *Portrait* in 1909, Stephen became a much more sombre, single-minded and heroic figure with a faint suggestion of incense and sulphur about him, and his relations with the world became less haphazard, human, and comic. The world itself became a grimmer adversary while the world of beauty to which the soul aspired became more sensuous and more ecstatic. The reason, I suggest, becomes clearer if we put out of our heads the common, if curious notion that Joyce wrote only about what happened to him up to the age of twenty-two. Suppose he intends to show us that it is surprising that the youthful Joyce matured to write *Ulysses*, that he is congratulating himself on the danger he has passed, and commenting on what has happened to him in the interval. In order to do this most clearly it would be necessary to exaggerate the youthful romanticism and aestheticism of Stephen; and this, between *Stephen Hero* and the *Portrait*, is what he did. It would be necessary for us also to assume that he had, while writing *A Portrait of the Artist as a Young Man*, some more or less definite glimmerings of the temper, form and dominant attitudes of the later book – that it would be, by contrast to the work of revolt, a work of acceptance. All the evidence shows that the idea of *Ulysses* was conceived in Joyce's mind at the same time as *A Portrait of the Artist* was begun; that it grew as the *Portait* progressed and that he was ready to begin it immediately the *Portrait* was finished: *that the two are, to all intents and purposes, one book*. So that whatever shifts of emphasis in the final version of the *Portrait* are to be accounted for, the reason most probably lies in the design of the two books as a whole. At a certain point in *Ulysses*, Buck Mulligan makes an interesting reference to the book itself.

> Buck Mulligan bent across the table gravely.
> They drove his wits astray, he said, by visions of hell. He will never capture the Attic note. The note of Swinburne, of all poets, the white death and the ruddy birth. That is his tragedy. He can never be a poet. The joy of creation . . . .
> Eternal punishment, Haines said, nodding curtly. I see. I tackled him this morning on belief. There was something on his mind, I saw. It's rather interesting because Professor Pokorny of Vienna makes an interesting point out of that.
> Buck Mulligan's watchful eyes saw the waitress come. He helped her to unload the tray.
> He can find no trace of hell in ancient Irish myth, Haines said . . . . The moral idea seems lacking, the sense of destiny, of retribution. Rather strange he should have just that fixed idea. Does he write anything for your movement?
> He sank two lumps of sugar deftly longwise through the whipped cream. Buck Mulligan slit a steaming scone in two and plastered butter over its smoking pith. He bit off a soft piece hungrily.
> Ten years, he said chewing and laughing. He is going to write something in ten years.
> Seems a long way off, Haines said, thoughtfully lifting his spoon. Still, I shouldn't wonder if he did after all.

Ten years, almost to the month, after that conversation, *Ulysses* was begun in Trieste. They had not in fact driven his wits astray, by visions of hell or otherwise, but I think we are meant to realise that it had been a pretty near thing. Mulligan's "Attic note" here is far too close to Stephen Hero's "classic temper" to be mere coincidence. Joyce was writing among other things his own epic, and with him everything had, like justice, not only to be done, but to be seen to be done. The point in elevating Stephen Dedalus, in making him more limited and more satanic, is evidently to show the dangers that he ran and to make his ultimate triumph in achieving the "classic temper" more plain. Joyce is congratulating himself on having attained it, "a temper of security and satisfaction and patience" which acknowledges that "as long as this place in nature is given us it is right that art should do no violence to the gift." And he is pointing out the dangers Stephen Dedalus ran of succumbing to "the romantic temper . . . an insecure, unsatisfied, impatient temper which sees no fit abode here for its ideals." Empson is right. The book has a happy ending. Stephen not only wrote it, but he wrote it in a particular way, looking back in a particular way from the stand-point of what then he was. It is significant that Stephen Hero's praise of the classic temper is omitted from the *Portrait*, as is his curious reference to the romantic, idealistic side of his nature as "the monster in him". And his clear-cut realisation that the failure to reconcile the world as it is, with the ideal world of the imagination, is, "however disguised or expressed, the most utter of pessimisms", is not allowed to jar on Stephen's self-communings in the completed book:

> The spectacle of the world which his intelligence presented to him with every sordid and deceptive detail set side by side with the spectacle of the world which the monster in him, now grown to a reasonably heroic stage, presented also had often filled him with such sudden despair as could be assuaged only by melancholy versing. He had all but decided to consider the two worlds as aliens one to another – however disguised or expressed the most utter of pessimisms – when he encountered through the medium of hardly procured translations the spirit of Henrik Ibsen.

VI

It is striking how clearly Joyce, in his own career, sums up the *fin de siècle* and its immediate aftermath, the advent of modern literature. There is an aesthetic revolt. A brave, proud satanic but "languid" young man scorns the world as it is and rejects its paths in favour of his own right to follow and create an ideal beauty. The *fin de siècle* artist turns his back on the meanness, squalor and ignobility of the world. Then suddenly in the aftermath we find modern art as never before concerned with that world and attempting to bring all that very squalor within its compass: within, that is to say, in some way or other, the compass of "beauty".

Stephen is right to revolt against and abandon the Dublin he knew, and the parental environment into which he had been born. While remaining personally within it he was unlikely to accomplish much. "When the soul of man is born in this country there are nets flung at it to hold it back from flight. You talk to me of nationality, language, religion. I shall try to fly by those nets." Physically and spiritually of course he did. *Ulysses* is in no sense a double apostasy. Its author is not finding sustenance or illumination in the spiritual values of its characters. But he is in their human value, and in their human reality. In the Proteus episode, while Stephen is communing with himself on the strand, contemplating a visit to his uncle, he reflects on his family. We hear, in this reflection, his real, "consubstantial father's voice" for the first time, commenting on his in-laws:

> O weeping God, the things I married into. The drunken little costdrawer and his brother, the cornet player. Highly respectable gondoliers. And skeweyed Walter sirring his father, no less. Sir. Yes, sir. No, sir. Jesus wept: and no wonder by Christ.

And Stephen imagines also his uncle's greeting:

> Sit down or by the law Harry I'll knock you down.
>
> Walter squints vainly for a chair.
>
> He has nothing to sit down on, sir.
>
> He has nowhere to put it, you mug. Bring in our Chippendale chair. Would you like a bite of something? . . . the rich of a rasher fried with a herring? Sure? So much the better. We have nothing in the house but backache pills.

And he reflects:

> Houses of decay, mine his and all. You told the Clongowes gentry you had an uncle a judge and an uncle a general in the army. Come out of them, Stephen. Beauty is not there.

Yet, if the purpose of Stephen's revolt, and, in whatever sense, the purpose of the artist, was the creation or extraction of some form of beauty, and if *Ulysses* was the justification of that revolt and the fulfilment of that purpose, then beauty must lie there, even in those "houses of decay" which are its subject.

If, to put it simply, the book was his father's "spitting image", it is in the contemplation of that image that beauty must lie.

Ulysses executes a complex movement of reconciliation and acceptance: towards the world of its author's father, towards the "sordid and deceptive" world of ordinary living; and, because the self, having abandoned the heroic lie, is not seen to be part of that world, towards the self as well. For Stephen and, ultimately, because art achieves the general through the particular instance, for us, they are one and the same. He had been tempted to reject the world of mundane, sordid and deceptive detail, as well as his father's houses of decay, in favour of an ideal beauty. That to reject the mundanities and sordidities of this world is also to reject a great deal of the self, every human being knows, in whom "the monster" who favours the ideal has not grown to dominatingly "heroic proportions". It was through the concept and the creation of Leopold Bloom that Joyce, with many characteristic ironies and subtleties, but also with immense simplicity, achieved the multiple apotheosis he desired. "There is", says Lenehan, "a touch of the artist about old Bloom. He's a cultured allroundman, Bloom is . . . . He's not one of your common or garden . . . you know . . . There's a touch of the artist about old Bloom."

There is indeed, for "As we . . . weave and unweave our bodies, Stephen said, from day to day, their molecules shuttled to and fro, so does the artist weave and unweave his image." And a few pages later we are reminded of another Jewish character in the same young man's assertion that Shakespeare "drew Shylock out of his own long pocket".

There are many parallels between Bloom and Stephen just as there are many resemblances between Bloom and the mature Joyce. Boylan stands in relation to Bloom as Mulligan does to Stephen: accenting his isolation, making a mockery of his attitudinisings, representing a worldly glitter and a sexual flamboyance which neither Bloom nor Stephen possesses.

> Wit. You should give your five wits for youth's proud livery he pranks in. Lineaments of gratified desire.

To a large extent, though not nearly to the same extent as Stephen, Bloom rejects the values of the society within which he moves. Both are humiliated; both are excluded, partly by choice and partly by force. Both are infidels, though both are concerned with and coloured by the ancient faiths within which they were nurtured. Both of them have deep and complex feelings about the histories of their races and their ancestral religions; but, nevertheless, to both of them history is a nightmare from which one must struggle to awake. Both have reason to feel remorse about the dead.

But their contrasts in resemblance are no less interesting than the resemblances themselves. Whereas Stephen is almost overwhelmed by his remorse, Bloom recovers his balance comparatively easily. In the brothel Bloom finds the thought of his ancestral background a source of strength; Stephen finds the thought of his merely another source of remorse. Parallel to Stephen's dramatic defiance of convention and society runs Bloom's comic, often shaken, often degraded, seldom dignified, never wholly triumphant, but still stubborn, courageous and, in the main, successful attempt to achieve the same end: to be oneself. But Bloom has merely to remain himself, whereas Stephen has to become. Confronted like Stephen by mockery, assault, the temptations of the flesh, Messianic ambition and remorse, Bloom, unlike Stephen, has attained to a certain magnanimity.

In general, where we find a resemblance, in circumstance or personality, between the two, and when we see its end, we can say that the difference is that Bloom is more mature than Stephen and seems to body forth – with some irony of course and some caricature, but nonetheless fairly faithfully – the differences between Stephen and the mature Joyce.

But Bloom had to be made inclusive not only of the circumstantial Joyce, but of the human nature that Joyce and all men shared. If the pretences to heroism were to be stripped away and *Ulysses* was to be the first great masterpiece of unheroic literature; if Bloom was to survive as the first great anti-hero, standing in for all unheroic men, including the self, if the "silent secrets" sitting in the dark palaces of all men's hearts which were "weary of their tyranny" were to be dethroned, the avatar had to be subjected to, and his power of survival tested against, the most open and the most cruel tests.

This frequently ridiculous, often humiliated man is seen in every possible intimacy and exposed to every possible nuance of contempt. He is put to flight by physical threats; he is cuckolded; he masturbates before our eyes; most of the atavisms born of fear and shame by which we are accustomed to react to others and judge ourselves are flouted. Nor does Joyce spare him his humour. From the episode of John Henry Menton's hat to the silly questions about Gibraltar in the coffee stall, he is exposed to it. Even such ambiguous qualities as his wariness at fence sometimes desert him in favour of a boyish and ridiculous vanity for the truth. And the cruellest cut of all is reserved till last. Molly may or may not be Gea Tellus or the Great Earth Mother; she is certainly Bloom's wife. She knows him through and through and she spares him nothing. If she remembers his romantic insistence on Howth Head, she also remembers his peculiar request in Harold's Cross Road. Joyce's purpose in ending the book with Molly's monologue has been much debated; yet it seems fairly obvious that if his purpose was the total exposure of Bloom, and the exposure of him in the most candid light, no tribunal could equal in intimate knowledge and ultimate frankness the thoughts of his woman.

Yet the remarkable thing is that in some way Bloom survives all this, even Molly's inquisition, though shakily as usual. "Let them go and get a husband first that's fit to be looked at", Molly says of the Miss Kearneys; and she recognises that he is in some sense or other superior to his mockers:

> . . . theyre a nice lot all of them well theyre not going to get my husband again into their clutches if I can help it making fun of him then behind his back I know well when he goes on with his idiotics because he has sense enough not to squander every penny piece he earns down their gullets and looks after his wife and family goodfornothings . . .

Her final "yes" may or may not have the allegorical implications her admirers have read into it; it may or may not be a "yes" to life; it is certainly a repetition of her original acceptance of Bloom.

Nor does the reader withhold his assent, as the long book draws to a close and we get to know Bloom through intimacies of body and soul to which no other character in literature had ever previously been subjected. Joyce set out to show man in a light he had never been seen in before; to expose him to a gaze more omnipresent and more exacting than any to which he had ever previously been exposed. He weighted the circumstances against his man; he put him in situations which normally arouse only our contempt; he exposed him to the jibes of the cruellest wits in Europe; he brought the elaborations of his own irony gleefully to bear upon him. Yet it is the measure of his success in his ultimate purpose that the man not only survives but survives triumphantly, as the first great hero of unheroic literature; that he arouses not only our compassion and sympathy, our affection and humorous understanding, but, before his long chapter of humiliations is over, our profoundest respect.

That Bloom's own qualities, often overlooked by criticism,

and always derided by the other characters, had something to do with this miracle we must admit; though they are certainly not the whole story. He is at least averagely kind. He performs, for example, most of what are known in Catholic theology as "the corporal works of mercy" during the day: he visits the sick, comforts the afflicted, buries the dead, shelters the homeless, etc. Though no combatant, he can bring himself to assert vital truths in the teeth of the opposition.

> But it's no use, says he. Force, hatred, history, all that. That's not life for men and women, insult and hatred. And everybody knows that it's the very opposite of that that is really life.
> What? says Alf.
> Love, says Bloom. I mean the opposite of hatred.

And he pays for this, and for similar pronouncements, in more ways than one. It is typical of Joyce's method that it is the enunciation of this simple and terrible truth that brings down upon him Hynes's cruel and brilliant sneer about his own abilities as a lover – "I wonder did he ever put it out of sight" – just as it is his display of learning in Lenehan's story of coming home beside Molly in the sidecar which exposes him to the jibe, so amusing to the teller that he momentarily collapses with laughter, about "that's only a pinprick".

His own humour, his irony, his subtlety and his intelligence are, in general, easy to underestimate. His mind only works in clichés in the coffee stall scene when he is tired, and it does not seem to have been noticed that he is here making a mistaken attempt to impress Stephen as a sort of literary man and thinker. What he utters are the clichés of editorial journalism, particularly provincial journalism of a sort that is written in Ireland to this day, though it was probably more widespread everywhere in 1904. It is just the sort of language we might expect Bloom to use in order to impress Stephen intellectually at the beginning of their acquaintance. (The general unpopularity of this extremely funny and engaging section of the book with critics who are not particularly well acquainted with Ireland, may stem from their lack of recognition of the precise kind of language he is talking.) Before that, as S.L. Goldberg has pointed out (he is very good on Bloom's process of thought, suggesting that his stream of consciousness, far from being "jelly-fish", is actually composed of illuminating and rewarding epiphanies), Bloom's quiet ability to think for himself, his equanimity without insensitivity, above all, perhaps, his combination of moral seriousness with a generally humourous, caustic, but tolerant cast of mind are remarkable enough. Joyce's purpose would not have been well-served either if Bloom had been merely the sort of stupid, acquiescent, bumbling mediocrity which earlier criticism often made him out to be. It was necessary that he should be deprived of certain dignities and exposed in certain lights, that he should be the opposite of Napoleonic and often the apotheosis of the foolish, but it would not have done, either, to make him out merely a dull cretin. In his kindness and his gropings after better things he is surely as human as in his *niaiseries*. Joyce had to be fair twice over.

Nor is he dull in any other sense. The fact that he is not a scurrilous wit like most of the others, that he is grave and quiet in demeanour and talks seriously when he believes the issues are serious, should not disguise the fact that his mind has a constant and perhaps predominantly humorous cast:

> All kinds of places are good for ads. That quack doctor for the clap used to be stuck up in all the greenhouses. Never see it now. Strictly confidential. Dr Hy Franks. Didn't cost him a red like Maginni the dancing master self advertisement. Got fellows to stick them up or stick them up himself for that matter on the q.t. running in to loosen a button. Fly by night. Just the place too. POST NO BILLS. POST NO PILLS. Some chap with a dose burning him.

But it must be repeated that it is in no way primarily because of his intellectual or moral qualities that Bloom so arouses our interest and so commands our affection. (It should not, really, except to critics, be necessary to prove that he does the latter: no character in contemporary fiction has such a widely variegated personal following.) I mean my Ulysses to be a good man, said Joyce to Frank Budgen right enough; and we can see that he is, however strange the definition of goodness might seem by orthodox standards, but it is not this in the end. When we ask what it is, we are forced ultimately I think to recognise that here is the familiar: the worn, familiar, comical, shabby, eroded but not collapsed face of humanity. In his vulnerability, his weakness, his secrecies, his continuous but uncertain ability to remain upright, his clinging to a few props, his constantly threatened dignity, Bloom commands that affection in the midst of comedy which we give to our own image, stained and worn as it is. Joyce has given him an almost infinite complexity as well; because the book is technically, for all its faults, a *tour de force*, we learn about Bloom as we learn about nobody else in fiction while we go along. And his creator has also breathed life into him and surrounded him, on this one day, with a world masterfully rich in the comic and in living detail. But his ultimate triumph was to extract this ordinary poetry of humanity from him; and it is a strange one, for his creator was Stephen Dedalus, that well-known aesthete.

VII

Joyce's movement, as he was subsequently to demonstrate at length, was circular. By "the commodious vicus of recirculation" one came back to where one started, to the father and the race. He had in particular (as, it is alleged, has all humanity in general) a fallen father, "foosterfather". The fall began in the dark wet winter of Parnell's downfall and death, when John Joyce began that long downward progress in which the instincts of a dandy and a gentleman, a Corkman and a boaster, a whiskey-drinking "praiser of his own past" were to consort oddly with, and to succeed only in accelerating, that decline into "squalor and insincerity" of which Stephen Hero speaks. The two falls, Parnell's and his Parnellite father's, were for ever after symbolically one in Joyce's mind. He was to harmonise them humorously and to entwine them with all other falls and fathers in *Finnegans Wake*. In *Ulysses* he has achieved out of the resentments and limitations of adolescence, even out of the justified attitudes of revolt and the judgments he was entitled to make about his spiritual and carnal inheritance, an attitude of compassion, tolerance and delight, which returns to that inheritance what it gave him: pride, humour, a love of song, a sense of style and a knowledge of the obverse of these coins, the degradations, the inescapable Irishness of life. The contrast between Stanislaus's attitude to his father, as expressed in *My Brother's Keeper*, and Joyce's is almost a parable of the difference between the viewpoint of the good man and the artist. The one is a judgment, harsh, clear and unforgiving. The other is an acceptance.

Yet, important though this movement was for Joyce – this achievement, like Shakespeare (according to Stephen), of the spiritual paternity of his own father – it is not the whole story. Like "the greyedauburn Shakespeare", walking in Fetter Lane Joyce was "weaving and unweaving his own image" and seeing himself as he then was "by reflection from that which then I shall be"; and he was also attempting to incorporate and to redeem aspects of our common humanity which had never been incorporated victoriously into literature before. It is here that Leopold Bloom enters, contrasted in his humility yet his continuing, if comic, integrity, with Stephen Dedalus; the self-image transmuted into an Irish Jew with ancestry somewhere in central Europe, with "a touch of the artist" and yet without the artist's redemption from the conditions of ordinary living. For Bloom does represent ordinary living, though isolated and set apart. He is pragmatic, yet a visionary; mean and careful, yet often in trouble out of generosity or fineness of spirit; betrayed and betraying, yet loyal after his fashion in the primary instances of love; ridiculous, yet dignified; spat upon, yet victorious; sensitive yet complacent, with the complacency which turns out in the end to be one of humanity's great defences, a clinging to the moment and the necessities of the moment, a form of continuing courage. All this adds up to the inescapable Jewishness of life. Bloom is not heroic, in the old sense. Nor is he abysmal, in the old sense, as any character in literature with certain of his characteristics would have had to be before him. In him, for the first time, our unpromising, unpoetic, unheroic image is found to have surprising possibilities for pride and for poetry.

The greatness of *Ulysses* is partly technical. A new prose form has been achieved, free from the distortions of dramatic narrative, and not dependent for its intensity on dramatic confrontations and resolutions. Yet it has intensity: a matter of language, of density of life, of immediacy of texture, in a word, of poetry. That the texture is yet "ordinary" proves that intensity, poetry, resides here too, its extraction being a matter of language and of the pitch of interest with which the ordinary is contemplated and then evoked.

In this sense it can hardly be otherwise than "on the side of life", ordinary, continuing life, as against dogmatisms of one kind or another. Such poetry cannot avoid possessing, in Coleridge's word, geniality; and if this were all that were to be said it would still be enough. Poetry is enough. The book does not have to be "about" anything, except, of course, Leopold Bloom.

Yet over such a large area, an uncoloured contemplation and evocation of life is tantamount to impossible. There remains the question of the author's vision. One cannot prove syllogistically that the temper of the book is what Joyce called "the classic temper", that it is an act of acceptance and an act of *pietas*. One can only appeal to the reader's response to its abounding humour, its creative zest, its ability to anneal the spirit (all of which are inseparably bound up with its poetry and its "geniality"); and one can only try, as I have tried, to show that

Joyce meant it to be received in this way and that, in part, he wrote a saga about a young man who achieved this classic temper. It is not necessary to seek profundities of meaning in *Ulysses*. Criticism has performed no service for Joyce by the suggestion that we must unravel the book before we can understand it; and that patience, skill and drudgery in unravelment are the primary qualities required of its ideal reader. They are not the sort of qualities commonly found in those most remarkable for receptivity and generosity of response to art or anything else. The suggestion that they are essential is part of the academic claim to indispensability – let alone usefulness – which has followed in our time as a result of the vesting of academic interests in literature. Yet it is also the duty of the critic to seek to interpret a book in the spirit in which it is written. Whether the facts that *Ulysses* is partly a strange act of *pietas* on Joyce's part; that Bloom, as well as being plain Leopold Bloom of Eccles Street, is a mediator between the artist and mankind; or that the book is a work of abounding comedy, full of "profane joy", make it greater than if it were a work of hatred and disgust, is a question difficult to answer. We can only fruitfully say that all great works are full of intensity, and that there is not therefore so much difference between opposing visions as criticism may be tempted to suggest.

It is certain, however, that if we can describe *Ulysses* in this way we claim it to be more important than it would be if the whole enormous structure had been raised in support of some theory about metempsychosis, some illumination of comparative myth, or some conviction about the decline of Western man. It is in the redemption of our common and ordinary humanity from its own "deceits and sordidities", and the totality as well as the poetic intensity of its statement of the conditions of ordinary living, that its originality and its importance for us lie. More than any other book *Ulysses* marks the end of heroic literature, and with the advent of Bloom man takes on a new poetic interest for his complex mundanity rather than as an actor of greater or lesser strength and tragic resonance. The resonance is there, and the tragedy as well as the triumph, but they are otherwise revealed. In no previous work, to take but one of his characteristics, had a "good" man been shown who was not altogether "normal" sexually.

We have become suspicious of the notion of progress, but there is a sense in which there is progress in the arts. We cover more ground, we say what has not been said; partial and limited like the visions of other artists of other eras though ours may be, we extend both the ordinary recorded area of human experience and the reclaimed area of poetic compassion; and we in our time have been honest. *Ulysses* has faults, of eccentricity, of mere display, of mechanical thoroughness. Yet in the way it encompasses ordinary living and the way it gives to much that had been denied it the intensity and texture of poetry, *Ulysses* is a landmark, perhaps the most important single event in the great breakthrough that has been achieved in this century.

JAMES JOYCE:
Footnote for a Poet

Joyce's poetry has been a mystery to friends and enemies alike. It has seemed to need accounting for; and both parties have done their share, what has bothered most being an apparent dichotomy between the prevailing tone of the poems and the outlook revealed in the rest of the work. One, labelled "romantic" and even "mawkish" has been contrasted with the other, labelled "realistic", even, in earlier days, "cynical" and "brutal".

To some people, like Rebecca West, the poems have been evidence of a hidden sentimentalist, a man who permitted himself a sort of private dishonesty and indulgence behind the facade of the complex and sometimes impenetrable prose. But admirers, like Professor William York Tindall, have been anxious to account for them also, and have done so in the usual academic way by insisting that they do not mean what they appear to mean.

According to Professor Tindall the poems in *Chamber Music* are all concerned with a simple bodily function, various scatological references and meanings being hidden inside these apparently so-innocuous verses. This is an attempt to toughen them up, so that it would appear more likely that the author of *Ulysses* should have written them, Professor Tindall being one of the first and most prominent representatives of the hidden meanings school.

Joyce had begun to write poems towards the end of his time in Belvedere, that is to say when he was about fifteen or sixteen, or at least to collect the poems he was writing into an exercise book which he labelled, probably most appropriately, 'Moods'.

When he was at University College this collection was supplemented by another, called 'Shine and Dark', the new verses, following Gogarty's example, being inscribed in the centre of large sheets of paper. In 1901, in his third year at University College, he burnt all that he had written except for a small handful, one of which, 'The Villanelle of the Temptress' is in *A*

Portrait of the Artist, postdated, and a few new ones which he decided to retain and which went into *Chamber Music*. The story that George Clancy was in possession of two early collections at the time he was shot by the Black and Tans is probably not true.

And so the poems in *Chamber Music* are not quite juvenilia, at least not unless we count *Dubliners* juvenilia, for he was still adding poems to the collection after he had written 'The Sisters', 'Eveline' and 'After the Race'. To say that they reveal a totally contrasting sensibility would be an understatement. These poems are cloudy, vague and burdened – in so far as they are burdened with anything – only with an inchoate romantic yearning. They are as different from the mood of *Dubliners* as rose water is from schnapps. When George Russell said that they were "as delicate and dainty as Watteau pictures" he was wrong, for they have nothing of Watteau's exactitude, Joyce himself was nearer the mark when he spoke to Colum of a lyric being "a simple liberation of rhythm": of rhythm that is at the expense of everything else, including meaning, exactness of imagery, even syntax.

By the time the book appeared, however, Joyce had lost interest in it. This was in 1907, when Elkin Matthews brought it out in light green boards at one and sixpence and with what various learned authorities have variously called a harp, a lute and a spinet on the title page.

Joyce himself called it a "pianner" and though the book's publication was the occasion of a lengthy and very favourable review by Arthur Symons in the *Nation* – the first extended notice of any kind he had received from a major literary figure – his pleasure in the event was dulled by the fact that negotiations about *Dubliners* had reached a most dispiriting impasse and that he had had most of the verses on his hands for five years. Life, as usual, had bestowed its gift too late and among too many confusions. He thought the poems "pretentious" but claimed that they had "a certain grace". Two years later he told a correspondent: "There is no likelihood of my writing any more verse unless something unforeseen happens to my brain."

In fact the abandonment was not to be as total as that, for in Trieste in the three years beginning in 1912 he wrote eight poems; in Zurich in the last years of the Great War three more; while in Paris he wrote two poems, including the beautiful *'Ecce Puer'*, which came to him as late as 1932. But an abandonment nevertheless it was, and for a reason which Stanislaus Joyce had put his finger on somewhat earlier: "What I was beginning to notice was that not all Jim's personality, nor even the most distinctive part of it, found expression in verse, but only the emotive side, which in one respect was fictitious. It is not so with true poets."

In other words, Joyce's poetry was not inclusive enough. A great humorist, with a humorous view of life, he had not succeeded in including this view in his verses. A great pioneer in the exploration of the sordid and unspoken aspects of existence, he had not succeeded in exploring them in poetry either. And he never would.

Yet Pound's comment, when he handed back the poems collected as *Pomes Penyeach* – "They belong in the Bible or in the family album with the portraits" – is woefully unjust. There is a streak of honesty, an admission of complexity and a recognition of the ironies of existence in them, "ninetyish" though some of them still are, which is missing from the earlier book, and at least three of them are successful and moving poems by anybody's standards. Still, if we knew nothing else about their author we should never guess that he was the cool appraiser, the compassionate and ironic explorer of the less lyrical side of life who, when he assembled the little collection, had just achieved a sort of fame as the author of *Ulysses*.

Nor, indeed, aside from the two satirical pieces about Dublin which he wrote as footnotes to his own odyssey and did not, in the ordinary way, publish ('Gas From A Burner' and 'The Holy Office') did it ever apparently occur to Joyce that humour and sordidity could be constituent elements in poems. He was born three years before Pound and six before Eliot. He grew up during one of the recurrent nadirs of English poetry, a period almost as bad as that following the death of Goldsmith. Linguist though he was, he knew nothing about Laforgue and Corbière – who, through Eliot and Pound, were to bring modern poetry into existence; and he probably saw Baudelaire through the same sort of eyes as did Dowson and Arthur Symons. (The "swoons of shame" and "sin-dark naves" of *Pomes Penyeach* have just that tone); 'The Love Song of J. Alfred Prufrock', the first fully inclusive, ironic and anti-lyrical poem in the modern canon, was not published in England until 1917; and Joyce had decided that prose was his métier long before that.

Looking back on his earlier poetic efforts, Stanislaus declared that they were "evidence of the struggle to keep the spirit within him alive in the midst of the all pervading squalor and disintegration" which he saw everywhere in Dublin; an attempt to "seize the elusive eucharistic moments in life and express them in songs for his own relief and comfort". In other words, poetry was an escape, or an expression of the desire to escape. On the one side was "life" with all its "squalor and insincerity"; on the other was "beauty" and some sort of romantic fulfilment; or the hope of beauty and some sort of romantic fulfilment, which hope you kept alive through poetry.

Of course this was a mistake; and in very large part the wonderful intertwined epic of Joyce's life and work was an acknowledgement of this mistake. There was not a separable beauty. There was not a redemption or something to be escaped from. There was not something outside the ordinary conditions of living for which it was in any way admirable or poetic to yearn. As Stephen Hero says, to believe so is "the starkest of pessimisms". There was only life. Interwined with life there was courage, humour, compassion, tenacity, will, even love and honour. Inseparable from the rest of life, were visions and wonders enough, but they were surrounded and coloured, if never finally discredited, by the "squalor and insincerity" which he would not only explore but prove to have, like Rembrandt's flayed ox, its own sort of beauty.

To embody all this he needed an inclusive art; and so he took to prose. A poet is tempted to say, he fell back on prose; but this would not be true either. For another great thing about Joyce is that if he did not know or did not care whether the "squalor and insincerity" could be included in poetry, he certainly believed and was amply to prove that the poetry could be included in prose.

When Stanislaus said that "a poet, whether major or minor, it is impossible to say" was lost to the world in Dublin in 1902, he was wrong. *Ulysses*, more than any other prose work in the English language, has the texture, the intensity, the visual and aural qualities of poetry and could only have been written by a poet.

JAMES STEPHENS:
The Gift of the Gab

That James Stephens was typically Irish, both as man and writer, was something that his contemporaries never tired of insisting; and, as time wore on, and the typically Irish thing began to lose some of the glamour it had once had by contrast with English Edwardian stodginess, it is possible that this did him no good. As Augustine Martin says in *James Stephens: A Critical Study*, he cultivated an image of himself as a sort of other-worldly, unpredictable Celtic phenomenon – in part resembling one of his own leprechauns and in part one of his own loquacious philosophers – so successfully that he became in the end its victim.

The impression of a word-spinner, full of charm and fanciful invention, but with really very little to say, prevailed. And it was helped by the fact that Stephens really did write little or nothing substantial for the last twenty years or more of his life. During these last years his basic mood was one of depression, but his early reputation as a magical talker was extended by his justly celebrated use of the radio, a medium through which – though not, as Augustine Martin says, "week after week" – he continued to project the personality of a beguiling, humorous lightweight, fanciful and poetic enough, but somehow non-serious.

It is of course one of the stereotypes of the Irish writer: someone who has plenty of words and images at his command, but who prefers the ethereal to the actual, and is somehow contemptuous of ordinary human experience. In total this was grossly unjust to Stephens: but then to some extent he may be said to have brought it on himself: and insofar as he was guiltless his friends were ready to weigh in on his behalf. His words, said Padraic Colum, are those "of a man who has entertained words and can let them crowd the doorway and the sills of his mind. In his talk he could go on to what in any other talker would be a superb invention, and then cap it with something extravagant, profound, or poetical, and this with a promptitude that one would remember as a feat."

And Stephen McKenna said that his characteristics were "a seeing power like that of a savage, a song and dance as of a child, the loving tolerance of a mystic discerning in all things, noble or trifling or ugly, always some trace of some god." All of which may have been true up to a point, but is certainly the sort of thing that is hard to live down.

Of course, in any case, critical misapprehension was likely because Stephens was a comic writer and people are always inclined to equate the comic with the non-serious. Also, his chosen prose métier after *The Charwoman's Daughter* was the tale in which other-worldly beings – leprechauns, faeries, demi-gods or whatnot – move in and out of the actual world and play a part in human events; and as the harsh light of an Irish dawn succeeded the Celtic twilight this may have become a little embarrassing to serious criticism. Though modern critics are not notorious for having a sense of the ridiculous, nor markedly averse to breaking butterflies on wheels, they may have felt that to be analytic in Stephens's case would be to invite derision; while those who genuinely enjoyed his work may have decided that there was little to say about it and perhaps the less said the better.

So he became one of those authors who are enjoyed in secret, without being subject to critical analysis. This is not a bad fate, but it tends to mean nowadays, when people read classics or semi-classics mostly for academic reasons, that the author in question goes unread. Some of Stephens's best books are no longer in print.

An attempt to resuscitate his literary reputation is probably long overdue; but it is to be hoped that the academics will tread more warily than is their wont. References to Stephens's "fictive morphology" do him no service. If I interpret the word morphology correctly it has to do with form and structure; and the earlier attitude to Stephens is the more correct: he had a sort of story-teller's gift and a sort of story-teller's flow; but he had no structural capacity and hardly any powers of invention. The facts that he had to fall back on existing material, the Irish folk-tale and saga stuff, and that he eventually dried up completely go far to prove that.

Where the earlier attitude was wrong was that it missed out on a sort of realism, concentrating instead on the fantasy and the charm. He rather fancied himself as a poet: in 1913 we find him saying that his poems have been unjustly neglected in favour of *The Charwoman's Daughter* and *The Crock of Gold*; and that in ten years time the balance will be reversed. He also rather fancied himself as a realist, one who brought poetry down to the circumstances of ordinary life. There had been a good deal of "realism" about since the urban poets of the 'nineties, Henley, Davidson and Symons amongst them. And there was a good deal of "realism" among the Georgians. Rupert Brooke tries hard to be bang up to the minute sophisticated; and of course there were the efforts to be urban, even proletarian made by Masefield, W.W. Gibson, Gordon Bottomley, W.H. Davies and others.

What lets most of them down is their rhythm and their diction. They were pre-Ezra Pound in precept and pre-T.S. Eliot in practice. Stephens's poem about the Four Courts cab driver, for example, goes thumpety-ump in a way that is entirely inappropriate to the urban, anti-poetic subject:

> The driver rubbed at his nettly chin
> With a huge, loose forefinger, crooked and black.
> And his wobbly violet lips sucked in,
> And puffed out again and hung down slack . . .

What is wrong with Stephens as a poet is not that he is an Irish twilighter but that he is an English Georgian, sometimes school of W.H. Davies (when he is trying to be visionary) and sometimes school of W.W. Gibson (when he is trying to be urban).

In fact he may well stand as a perfect example of the "poetic" Irishman whose real genius is for prose. And in *The Charwoman's Daughter* he does achieve something of the sort of urban realism that he fails to find or invent a poetic diction for.

As an account of the extreme poverty of the tenement slums of the Dublin which Stephens knew, the book has its share of indignation; and one of the marks of the true realist, technical interest and accuracy, is certainly not lacking. When Mary goes charring her mother gives her elaborate instructions:

> All through breakfast her mother advised her on the doing of her work. She cautioned her daughter when scrubbing woodwork always to scrub against the grain, for this gave a greater purchase to the brush, and removed the dirt twice as quickly as the seemingly easy opposite movement. She told her never to save soap. Little soap meant much rubbing, and advised that she should scrub two minutes with one hand and then two minutes with the other hand, and she was urgent on the necessity of thoroughness in the wringing out of one's floor cloth, because a dry floor cloth takes up twice as much water as a wet one, and thus lightens labour; also she advised Mary to change her positions as frequently as possible to avoid cramp when scrubbing, and to kneel up or stand up when wringing her cloths, as this would give her a

> rest, and the change of movement would relieve her very greatly, and above all to take her time about the business, because haste seldom resulted in clean work and was never appreciated by one's employer.

It was written seventy years ago; and there may be those now who will believe that the whole thing is, in spite of its truth to slum circumstance, its pity and its indignation, vitiated by the fact that it has a wish-fulfilment outcome instead of some sort of a class-conflict outcome: Mary and her mother get the classical solicitor's letter telling them that they have come into a fortune; and she marries and – presumably – keeps her young poet, who is clearly an autobiographical projection. The great Dublin general strike, which called the attention of Europe to the slum tenements and was a victory if only because in the long run they could no longer be tolerated, was just a year away. O'Casey, who was to write great plays about slum tenements (though only because he left the Citizen Army and was guilty about not turning up in 1916) and his bitterer sort of truth overshadow it. Yet it has its own sort of truth; and that Stephens was the kind of man and the kind of writer who liked happy endings may or may not be unfortunate, but it was a fact. He could not have ended it otherwise, even to ensure himself another sort of approval; and if he had it would have been a fake. There are those who find it schmaltzy. Others may think that for a seventy-year-old book it has a wonderful readability; and that, having survived thus far, it will continue to outlive the various "books of the month" of the years in between. The present writer is of the latter school of thought.

He was, in fact to return to the theme of slum life again in the story 'Hunger' in the collection *Etched in Moonlight*. The title says nearly everything that is to be said about it; for there is scarcely any event, except the departure of the unemployed house painter for Scotland and the discovery of his death there. It is the story of a state; and the state is the state of being hungry, the only other theme in it being the fierce maternal anxiety of the wife for her starving children. Those who believe that Stephens had little or nothing to say, but only a sort of story-telling faculty and a certain amount of charm should read it.

For the truth is that he had a great deal to say, while having even less than the usual amount of inventive faculty, of which the Irish, generally speaking, have very little. The story 'Hunger' is strongly reminiscent of the story of the clerk-prisoner in *The Crock of Gold.* In each case there is a basic situation: the bread winner can just about support his family while he has a job and his health. If he loses either he and they are doomed, as in the pre-social insurance world, which Stephens presents in starker terms than any other writer of his time, English or Irish, such people indeed were. But the presentation of the material in the account of his life which the clerk-prisoner gives is more in the nature of tract than story: there is little narrative substance, little description or re-creation, only a stark and terrible human situation with an inevitable end.

Nor, in his masterpiece, *The Crock of Gold*, are his powers of fictional embodiment – his ability to find, in Eliot's well-worn phrase, "an objective correlative", for whatever it is he wants to say – very evident. More often than not, he just decides to say it. His friends may or may not have been right about his conversational inventiveness. They were surely accurate about his conversational flow. Few books, even Irish books – and the Irish novel of this century has seen an extraordinary flowering of talk of one kind or another – have so much discourse in them.

Broadly speaking it is of three kinds. There is, first of all, the comic discourse in which facts and ideas are to some extent mocked; while the language employed achieves a pitch of absurd precision which is, alas, rare in the presentation of either fact or idea through normal methods of communication. There is no record of Stephens ever having read Thomas Love Peacock, but there is something of Peacock in this:

> The Philosopher drew his chair closer to the visitor until their knees were jammed together. He laid both his hands on Meehawl MacMurrachu's knees –
>
> "Washing is an extra-ordinary custom", said he. "We are washed both on coming in to the world and on going out of it, and we take no pleasure from the first washing nor any profit from the last."
>
> "True for you, sir" said Meehawl MacMurrachu.
>
> "Many people consider that scourings supplementary to these are only due to habit. Now, habit is continuity of action, it is a most detestable thing and is very difficult to get away from. A proverb will run where a writ will not, and the follies of our forefathers are of greater importance to us than is the well-being of our posterity."
>
> "I wouldn't say a word against that, sir", said Meehawl MacMurrachu.
>
> "Cats are a philosophic and thoughtful race, but they do not admit the efficacy of either water or soap, and yet it is usually conceded that they are cleanly folk. There are

> exceptions to every rule, and I once knew a cat who lusted after water and bathed daily: he was an unnatural brute and died ultimately of the head staggers. Children are nearly as wise as cats. It is true that they will utilise water in a variety of ways . . ."

And so on and so forth. Whether or no Stephens ever read Peacock, it is certain that Flann O'Brien read Stephens; and we get the same delight in each case. The impression is of an instrument being kept in tune; and doubtless the instrument of prose discourse is improved by such exercises.

The same can hardly be said of some of Stephens's expressions of his own philosophy:

> First, like a laughing child, love came to labour minutely in the rocks and sands of the heart, opening the first of those roads which lead inwards for ever, and then, the labour of his day being done, love fled away and was forgotten. Following came the fierce winds of hate to work like giants and gnomes among the prodigious debris, quarrying the rocks and levelling the roads which soar inwards; but when that work is completed love will come radiantly again to live for ever in the human heart, which is Eternity.

Whether or no he was ever an actual subscribing member of the Dublin Society, there seems to be a good deal of the fashionable Theosophical blather of his time about this; but it is as well to distinguish these philosophical maunderings from the third sort of discourse in Stephens's books, a humbler sort of thing which may be called the expression of a personal point of view, often indubitably wise. Mostly this is about the relationship of the sexes, which he sees as a sort of immemorial conflict, beneficial to both parties, in which only victory or defeat constitute disaster: so long as the conflict continues, and the balance is kept, all is well. Male preponderance or female preponderance are equally wrong. To that extent he is a liberationist. To the extent that he saw male and female as opposite polarities whose eternality is well established he would offend the sort of female liberationist who believes that the object of the female part should be to become more like the male; but not those who delight in intermingling:

> Extremes must meet, it is their urgent necessity; the reason for their distance, and the greater the distance between them, the swifter will be their return and the warmer their impact: they may shatter each other to fragments or they

> may fuse and become indissoluble and new and wonderful, but there is no other fertility. Between the sexes there is a really extraordinary freedom of intercourse. They meet each other something more than half way. A man and a woman may become quite intimate in half an hour. Almost certainly they will endeavour to explain themselves to each other before many minutes have elapsed; but a man and a man will not do this, and even less so will a woman and a woman, for these are the parallel lines which never meet.

Because so much of his books consist of this sort of discourse and because it is necessary to rescue him from the charge of being the sort of writer to whom "words alone are certain good", it is as well to pay attention to Stephens's view of things. And he really has a great deal to say about a number of related topics; much of it, in one sense or another "true", though about the topics concerned it would be perhaps enough to be merely illuminating: the conflict and union of opposites, the nearness of love and hate, the importance of desire and the disappointments of satiety. He knew a great deal about hard times, having been born in the utmost poverty and deposited in the care of a foundling institution. It would seem nowadays to invite the most obvious of retorts to say that he knew a great deal about the riches of poverty also; but he does – it is part of his system of opposites – he knows the dreams of beggary and the intoxications of its occasional windfalls. If he has a message it may be that struggle and effort are the conditions of human life. "His ally and stay was hunger", he says of the young man in *The Charwoman's Daughter*, "and there is no better ally for any man: that satisfied and the game is up; for hunger is life, ambition, goodwill and understanding, while fullness is all those negatives which culminate in greediness, stupidity and decay." And towards the conclusion of the book Stephens declares that "Next to good the most valuable factor in life is evil. By the interaction of these all things are possible." Like Yeats, he believes in the dialectic.

But of course it would be as wrong to treat Stephens as a thinker who must be judged by the validity of his views as it would be to treat him as a feather-brain with some sort of fluency and some sort of charm. He was a literary artist: at least as much entitled to those views as are the essayists of the world; indeed his books often do seem to be a series of short, loosely-linked essays in a sort of contrived narrative setting. It is perhaps the case that he never found his métier. It may even be that he had no métier to find. *The Crock of Gold* differs from *At Swim-Two-Birds* in that it is to a large extent a mere hold-all, and not a construction. The signs are plain in it that it was written serially. *The Charwoman's Daughter* offends some people because the author is too present and too voluble; but *The Demi-Gods* is certainly an underrated book, probably because this world, or at least the literate, English-speaking part of it, had enough of other-worldly, Celtic beings at a certain point of its existence. It has a delightful heroine, one of Stephens's most memorable girl-women; the intrusions of comment are pointed, humorous and successful; and the more overtly philosophical, or theosophical flights are not too frequent. But all of Stephens's books, including also *In The Land of Youth* and *Irish Fairy Tales* can be recommended to a certain kind of reader. He or she will be one who is to some extent, at least, responsive to charm, and to literary expression as a vehicle for personality, as it is in the case of most essayists. But charm can soon pall and turn into a liability rather than an asset, unless, so to speak, it is otherwise backed up. A reader responsive to prose will therefore find more to enjoy in Stephens's discourse than one who is merely looking for whimsical beguilement; and so will one who is responsive to a mind which plays freely, humorously and often quite wisely on certain subjects, particularly perhaps the differences between men and women, which today are not dealt with freely and humorously so frequently as we might sometimes think. One wishes, since he would have wished it, that there was more to be said in praise of his poetry than there is. His translation of O'Bruadair's lament and a late poem, 'Strict Care, Strict Joy' are so far above the rest as to entitle him to the name of poet but one should be chary about employing it, for there is a lingering belief that Stephens's prose is an expression of the poetic sensibility as it was once popular to define it in Ireland – whimsical, fanciful and non-serious – and if anything could be calculated to do his reputation as a prose writer further damage, it would be the perpetuation of that sort of notion.

THOMAS MacGREEVY: Modernism not Triumphant

Thomas MacGreevy occupies a place of peculiar importance in the history of Irish letters in that he was the first specifically and consciously modern Irish poet. To put this fact in some sort of perspective it perhaps helps to know that he was born (in Tarbert, county Kerry) in 1893, or only five years after T.S. Eliot; that he lived in London and Paris during most of the nineteen-twenties and -thirties; that the one and only book of verse he published during his lifetime appeared in London in 1934; and that he did not return to live in Ireland until 1939, when those who had composed the nucleus of a specifically modern movement a little earlier had been well scattered or silenced. (There were to be other such movements and poets.)

One should also perhaps recall or become aware of the facts that apparently only once during MacGreevy's lifetime did anybody acknowledge that he was an innovator (Samuel Beckett in *The Bookman*, 1934); and that from the time the present writer became aware of MacGreevy's work around about 1943 or 1944 until he died in 1967 he does not recall anybody adverting in any serious way to the fact that he was a poet at all, and this though from 1950 onwards he was frequently mentioned in the newspapers as Director of the National Gallery.

It is true that John Lyle Donaghy, Denis Devlin, Brian Coffey and Samuel Beckett had published poems or even one or more small collections before MacGreevy's book appeared in 1934 and that Devlin, Coffey and Beckett were also in one way or another innovators, while Donaghy at least wrote free verse; but MacGreevy had been publishing poems before any of them had and, as far as the employment of certain techniques discovered elsewhere was concerned (to go no further for the moment), he was the forerunner.

When Beckett praised Coffey and Devlin in the same article in *The Bookman*, he did so because they had, he said, submitted themselves to the influences of "Corbière, Rimbaud, Laforgue, the *surréalistes* and Mr. Eliot, perhaps also to those of Mr. Pound." In doing this he placed them in what was then the central line of development for modern poetry – leaving out Rimbaud and the *surréalistes*, the Eliot line. It is here that MacGreevy is to be placed also. Beckett said that his book was "probably the most important contribution" that had been made "to postwar Irish poetry". In 1934, it was. Since there is in informed circles now a fairly general agreement that we have to go back a bit to find the true line, it may still be more important than some people might think.

MacGreevy was in the First World War. It is not clear whether his one and only war poem ('*De Civitate Hominum*', one of the finest and least known poetic products of the holocaust, worthy of comparison with the work of any of his more celebrated fellow-soldiers, except that it cannot be compared, being in diction and imagery a truly modern poem, which Owen's or even Rosenberg's are not) was written at the time; but assuming he began to write poetry in his early twenties what is remarkable is that he made no false starts. Let it be said to his credit that there are no Celtic crepuscularities in his work and that instead he came immediately under the influence of Ezra Pound, T.S. Eliot and the French; from the point of view of critical doctrine really the one nexus of influence: Pound's.

It has, of course, been impossible for anybody in this century to write good poetry in English without taking to heart the discoveries, the prohibitions, the injunctions and the principles of Ezra Pound; and even Yeats only became a great poet when he began to listen and learn in about 1909 and swept out the inversions, the poeticisms and the rubbish. The kernel of principle was in the desperately needed negatives and prohibitions ('A Few Dont's for Imagists' says most of it) but it is not to be expected that a young man still, in spite of the war, in his twenties would escape positive influences altogether, or that he would completely avoid getting the message of experience through somebody else's apparatus. Neither the Dean nor the Dublin setting can conceal the fact that this is too obviously a Poundian poem:

Vanessa is of today
And intelligently interested
In everything that goes on.
But she is also a very little
Of the English eighteen-nineties.
Her parents knew young Oscar . . .

While this is too close to early Eliot:

I might have tittered
But my teeth chattered
And I saw that the words, as they fell,
Lay, wriggling, on the ground.

Still only good poets are capable of learning anything other than how to imitate and what MacGreevy learned (in practice, most rewardingly I think from Eliot) demanded an attribute of a very rare order: he had an ear which enabled him to distinguish between *vers libre à la* Eliot and *vers libre* as the lazy man's hold-all.

Eliot's sort of free verse did not, as we know, catch on in the nineteen-twenties or -thirties. The reason is probably simple. Most people's hearing equipment was just not sensitive enough. To make the claim for MacGreevy that he was one of the very few who were able to write free verse deriving from, but not necessarily imitative of, Eliot is therefore to award an Irish poet of the era a not inconsiderable place in the international scheme of things. But I go further: MacGreevy wrote, after Eliot himself, the most perfectly modulated free verse written in the period in England, Ireland, or America.

Juan de Juni the priest said,
Each J becoming H;

Berruguete, he said,
And the G was aspirate;

Ximenez, he said then
An aspirated first and last.

But he never said
And – it seemed odd – he
Never had heard
The aspirated name
Of the centuries-dead
Bright-haired young man
Whose grave I sought.

Whether from Eliot or otherwise, he had learned also that the liberation from rhyme had in fact created new possibilities for the employment of rhyme.

Eliot had said in 1917: "Freed from its exacting task of supporting lame verse, it could be applied with greater effect where it is most needed. There are often passages in an unrhymed poem where rhyme is wanted for some special effect." MacGreevy's best poems frequently have unexpected rhymes irregularly placed to superb effect. And there was one further thing he learned, whether from Eliot, the *surréalistes* or otherwise: the image is autonomous and is not an algebraic symbol for something else. Neither is it raw material for the metaphor industry.

These things are broadly, one supposes, in the realm of technic, though it is difficult to see, in the case of the last at least, how technic can be separated from the capacity for experience, in this case the capacity to relate visual experience to all other, to feel visually. In the matter of the experience in the poems, of "what he had to say" that was his own, MacGreevy may be described as being primarily concerned with the bright moment or the illumination which is almost but not quite overwhelmed by the indifferent and frequently awful surround.

> My rose of Tralee turned gray in its life,
> A tombstone gray,
> Unimpearled.
> But a moment, now, I suppose,
> For a moment I may suppose,
> Gleaming blue,
> Silver blue,
> Gold,
> Rose,
> And the light of the world.

Samuel Beckett (again in 1934; this time in *The Dublin Magazine* and the only decent review MacGreevy apparently ever got) declared his concentration on such moments to be a form of prayer. Certainly to the extent that he was concerned with them he was a lyric poet. Because of the sardonicisms of context of which he insisted also on being aware, he was a modern lyricist, like, say, Hart Crane. Because the experience and its context were frequently Irish he is, apart from his nativity, an Irish poet, but further than this, MacGreevy was, in fact, an intensely patriotic man who drew a good deal of sustenance from some central Irish reality which he (convincingly) glimpsed. This does not make him any less universal; other poets from other lands have had these feelings about their natal place and the experience carries (one might even instance Hart Crane again, though I wouldn't want to push the comparison any further). MacGreevy anyway is not a dealer in local colour, mere accidental properties or the picturesque. It is simply that his special illuminations about what he saw as God's creation relate often to the part of it called Ireland, though they may be related to Continental Europe too, as in the 'Nocturn of the Self-Evident Presence'.

> I see no immaculate feet on those pavements,
> No winged forms
> Foreshortened,
> As by Rubens or Domenichino,
> Plashing the silvery air,
> Hear no cars,
>
> Elijah's or Apollo's
> Dashing about
> Up there.
> I see alps, ice, stars and white starlight
> In a dry, high silence.

Well, in 1934, the little blue book appeared from Chatto and Windus. According to Thomas Dillon Redshaw, who edited his posthumous *Collected Poems*, it "received remarkably little attention save for Samuel Beckett's acute review in *The Dublin Magazine*." When those *Collected Poems* were issued in 1971 (by Michael Smith, from the New Writers Press, to whom all honour for the enterprise) the editor had only five poems to add to the little collection of thirty-seven years before.

So once again we are confronted with the Irish flawed achievement and we have to ask what went wrong. To all intents and purposes after 1934 MacGreevy was silent, though he was to live for another thirty years. It is tempting to blame Ireland and indeed I do not think that Ireland is entirely guiltless in the matter. As I remember it, MacGreevy's position in Dublin was the ambiguous one of the returned exile. He was the one who had tried and (the assumption was) failed in literary London, he was also the ex-Parisian who had known Joyce. (In fact there were locals who got more mileage out of one meeting with Joyce than MacGreevy was at all interested in getting out of a fairly intimate acquaintance.) A man of exquisite manners and great dignity, he was, as I recollect it anyway, locally a bit of a joke. What Samuel Beckett called "the antiquarians, delivering with the altitudinous complacency of the true Gael the Ossianic goods" occupied the foreground. One doesn't suppose that the cosmopolitan MacGreevy was asked for many poems.

Add to this that circumstantially he had a hard enough time of it until he got his gallery (there were those who employed him, but the *Father Matthew Record* was perhaps not the ideal ambience for his talents) and it may be concluded that Ireland must bear some portion of the blame, if blame there be. Although a poet's silence is not altogether to be explained in external terms, external reasons have always more to do with it than people like to think. Let us honour him now anyway as best we can. He wrote at least ten poems that will outlive masses of more talked of products, some of them among the best written anywhere in English in this century, which, now one comes to think of it, is not bad at all.

FRANCIS STUART:
Religion Without Revelation

Black List, Section H is the rather enigmatic title of a novel by Francis Stuart which first appeared from the Southern Illinois University Press. Though it was, in fact, its author's twenty-second book and twentieth novel, he had some trouble finding an English publisher for it, Martin Brian and O'Keefe eventually, to their credit, entering on territory where others evidently had feared to tread.

The American edition has both a preface and a postscript by a Professor Harry T. Moore. In the preface Professor Moore says that "it is the story of an Irishman who in early youth marries a famous beauty, is a poet and novelist, breeds racehorses, owns a poultry farm, is imprisoned at the time of the Irish Civil War, travels widely in Europe, and spends the Second World War in besieged Berlin (though not as a Nazi or even as a Nazi sympathiser). Few novels or our time have so wide a range, so great a depth, and few are so magnificently written."

He is here guilty of at least two misdescriptions of fact. In the first place, the hero of the novel does not breed racehorses but buys (in the early 'thirties, for forty guineas) and keeps in training one two-year-old filly; and in the second, the novel can by no means be described as "magnificently" written unless Professor Moore claims entitlement to use that word as a mere amorphous, almost meaningless term of praise.

A lot hinges on this and so it is as well to be clear that the writing is not splendid, formally beautiful, grand, rich or exalted. It is, on the contrary, painstakingly and painfully exact, scrupulous, careful of detail and sparing of effect; and it is all these things to such a degree that Stuart sometimes gives the impression of clumsiness. There are occasional clichés which are evidence of a grip which is perhaps over-tight being suddenly relaxed through exhaustion, but there is no fine writing, no cloudiness or fake. This is important because the story is in essence the story of a spiritual quest and we all know books about spiritual quests in which the ultimate theophanies, described in fine or poetic writing of one kind or another, are fake. In fact even in describing *Black List, Section H* as an account of such a quest one has to be careful, for Stuart is here at least a religious writer who is denying himself a religious terminology and who does not claim either a special truth or a special revelation. He takes us through most of a lifetime and upwards of four hundred pages and he leaves us (almost) nowhere – which is one of the reasons why his book is so disturbing and also why it will endure: its truth is not only independent of dogma or theology, but also independent of the possible revelations sought, the very simple and sufficient fact of the matter being that they are not vouchsafed.

There are other reasons also. There are, for instance (a minor reason), some real people, given their real names, in whom posterity will be interested: Yeats, Maud Gonne, the author's first wife and, among the living, Liam O'Flaherty may be mentioned. The book is in fact autobiographical, which, of course, is a risk to take, for while there are ways of synthesising fact which may be valid and also valid ways of transferring fact to the fictional plane, they are not the same thing and they do not mix. Stuart is, however, concerned with breaking down the barriers between art and life as some other people, Joyce and Borges in their different ways among them, have been also (Yeats is accused by the hero of maintaining those barriers). And it can certainly be said for this essay into the usually dubious sphere of autobiographical fiction that there is none of the usual, however disguised, narcissism. There is no attempt to make the hero in any way whatever larger than life. That he is a highly unusual person must be agreed: but he is not put forward as being himself more adventurous, more decisive, or more sexually successful than is the rest of humanity; while even the sort of self-mockery that is often the obverse of such assertions, the comic mock-modesty that often reinforces the never quite put forward claim, is absent. Stuart sees the comic side all right; smuggling a machine-gun back from Belgium during the Irish Civil War the hero spends the voyage imagining not the direful consequences of being discovered smuggling arms, but the acutely embarrassing ones of being also discovered to be smuggling French letters. And unlike other Irish or Spanish or whatever civil war heroes, he is somewhat less heroic and committed than the merits of the cause would seem to demand, spending a train hold-up, which is the only time he sees action, in a state of partial funk, being re-called to the realities of his situation when a country girl passenger smiles at him sympathetically and whispers "Up de Valera". De

Valera, was of course the leader of the republican cause; but he was also, in H's eyes, one of the most reactionary leaders on either side. In the sexual encounters the very real and convincing unfulfilments are stressed as often as are the fulfilments, where there is fulfilment: the actress whom he meets through a friend of O'Flaherty's in London keeps her breasts heavily bandaged even in bed and a curious "chemical whiff" seems to come from the "muffled up and apparently untouchable part of her". Since the subject is never mentioned between them in the months of their association H never finds out why. And so far from always feeling more lyrically or more intensely than the majority, H is subject to a sort of switching-off feeling, so that his life often seems to him and to us like a record of non-participation, a sort of not-thereness.

That this latter state is more familiar to the complicated, self-conscious being which the artist often is than the more vaunted, and more often claimed emotional states is probably true; but the real point is that the main pitfall of the autobiographical fictional mode, the pretence that the hero has somehow lived "more fully" than the rest of people is avoided. *Black List, Section H* is, by one definition or another, a work of fiction; but its author is a born truth-teller. And if another of the dangers of the life-chronicle mode is sprawl, it too has been avoided; to such an extent that a second reading discloses that the main themes have been laid down straight away and are seldom departed from. On the very first page, for example, we find that the hero writes a letter to a Dublin newspaper "on the subject of Home Rule". He guessed that, "coming from the heart of the Unionist North, the letter would have a good chance of being published", but it was not for the sake of seeing his name in print that he had composed it or because he had any ultimate interest in "Irish or any other kind of nationalism". No. "What was behind it was an instinct, far from conscious, to cut himself off from the world of his cousins once and for all." When the letter is published, though, the only person to comment on it is his Aunt Jenny and so far from resulting in his being put forever beyond some sort of pale, "for years he was to notice it, from time to time, put away, with newspaper clippings about her prize heifers, in the empty half of her silver cigarette case".

The incident is typical, both in its impulse and in its frustration; and after it few of his political adventures or misadventures should come as any surprise. Through his marriage with Maud Gonne's daughter he becomes involved with nationalist circles and drifts, almost by accident, into the Civil War. From the beginning, though, he dislikes the assumption of the "absolute rightness and moral purity of the nationalist cause". "Under either de Valera or Griffith, art, religion and politics would still be run by those who at best used them to give themselves power, prestige and a good living."

His main impulse is in fact a dislike of moral complacency and a hope of unsettling it in some way or another. A book he later writes has for its heroines two girls who are tarred and feathered and tied to the Church railings for associating with the British terrorist-police known as the Auxiliaries, in other words, in a foreshadowing of H's own fate, "collaborating with the enemy":

> He believed that the near-despair of being utterly cast-off from society and its principles could create the inner condition conducive to the new insights it was the task of the poet to reveal.
>
> The girls tied to railings symbolized for H the poet who is exposed and condemned for his refusal to endorse the closed judgements and accept the categorical divisions into right and wrong that prevailed. If he survived the ordeal there would flow from the depths of his isolation fresh imaginative streams to melt the surrounding freeze-up. Yeats, for all his superb craftsmanship and intellectual passion, was not going to cause any real alteration or reorientation in inner attitudes because he had not been forced to this point of extreme loneliness.

He is attracted to a Russian writer, Rozanov, because he was a Tzarist among revolutionaries and anathema to the Tzarists. What he fears most and would most like to disperse is any and every "gathering mass or consensus of thought", whether liberal or authoritarian, because he feels, like some of the characters in his books, "that even a liberal doctrine held in common tends to produce that sort of assured moral attitude that is fatal . . . Such psyches only thrive in periods of mental doubt and upheaval". And out of a sort of amalgam of these attitudes he not only accepts an invitation to give readings and lectures in Nazi Germany just before the war but assents when asked to broadcast for the state radio after war has broken out.

There is, to be sure, some passive acquiescence in the dictates of chance in this. Indeed far more than in most novels the obscure workmanship of drift is acknowledged in Stuart's. As has been said, and as indeed he says himself, H's life is to a large extent "full of omissions and non-participations". Refreshingly in a work of fiction situations are allowed to develop as life-situations do, through nobody's choosing, and to continue after they have lost their reality. Sometimes, as in the hero's marriage, elements of the haphazard and the meaningless co-exist with real pain; or, as in the case of an affair with a London actress in the nineteen-thirties, elements of the grotesque with flickers of real feeling.

But in the case of the German sojourn there is also a very deliberate choosing. To begin with "the mere existence of all those dubbed as monsters by enlightened opinion exerted a certain spell on him as, at least, the antithesis of all the mediocrities in the public eye and home" and he has a hope of sorts of "an imaginative revolution, a sudden jerk forward in consciousness, especially as expressed in poetry and fiction, which . . . . might only take place after a new political or social cataclysm". In other words, his hope is for apocalypse.

It is not long, however, before he comes to realise that "to imagine the postwar world as a place where fundamental changes would be general was an illusion" and in fact from the first he has known that his real object was to divorce himself irrevocably from what he sees as the intolerably complacent and hypocritical world in which most people live – just as he had once wanted to divorce himself irrevocably from his Northern cousins.

That this is part of a larger quest for a sort of reality which the pressures of that world, its conventions, its systems of morality, its conspiracies of agreement on both feeling and conduct are concerned to deny is apparent throughout. Although the main expression of H's desire to put himself beyond the pale and to become himself the outcast or the criminal is the departure for Germany (where he soon begins to dream of going on to Russia) his writings are an attempt to explore what happens in the psyche of those who have put themselves beyond bounds in other ways. He experiments with alcohol, with mysticism, with orthodox religion.

He traces the usual path of the bohemian. If there was in fact going to be any religious homecoming at the end of the book you could put a lot of it in 'Hound of Heaven' terms. He ravens through, and eventually casts aside, mystical authors such as St. John of the Cross and St. Catherine of Siena. Only the humble, non-intellectual Bernadette Soubirous, seems to him to have something of

> the pure, near-manic clarity that accompanies states of possession experienced by poets, mystics, and madmen, and to which he himself responded obsessively. For him it was the song of the hidden psyche, inaudible to well-balanced normally functioning brains, announcing its kin-

ship to angels or demons as in the poem of Emily Brontë:

> He comes with Western winds, with evening's wandering airs
> With that clear dusk of heaven that brings the thickest stars;
> Winds that take a pensive tone and stars a clearer fire,
> And visions rise, and change, and kill me with desire.

There were passages in the Gospels with these peculiar, limpid notes of the psyche's secret song, like the description of the disciples coming from the lake in the evening and slowly recognising the hidden Jesus tending a fire on the shore.

But the vision of Jesus, hidden or otherwise, is not vouchsafed to H as it has been to so many other literary men in our time. There are the tantalising hints. There is the conviction that in the outcast state "at the point of extreme loneliness", something is revealed, but that is all. And the novel, like the search, contradicts itself by virtue of the fact that H is, after all, an artist. Like all artists worth their salt at the table of humanity, whatever his wish for a "beyondness"; whatever indeed his fleeting, tantalising sense of its occasional immanence may be, he still is deeply immersed in "mere" sensations and sense experience. For the most part he avoids overt description; but, as befits a novel which is, after all, in one sense or other historical and political – even if in another sense a-historical or a-political – the European cities of the ninteen-twenties and -thirties, Vienna, Prague, Berlin, London, and, of course, Dublin, are wonderfully evoked, often through bakery smells, the taste of the food, or even of the fog. Nor are his experiences on the green sward of the raccourse neglected: or the complicated emotions and daydreams that the study of the form-book bestir in him.

As far as surface and visual experience is concerned H's "switchings off" do not matter. If, like Beckett and Joyce, though in a very different manner and through a very different mode, the straightforward realistic mode of the autobiographical chronicle novel, he undermines the pretence to emotion that so many lyrical writers have been guilty of, the surfaces of the world continue to trouble and entrance and disturb him. In fact when finally the outcast state is reached, and H, soon to be imprisoned and disgraced, crouches in the bomb-shelter, the only revelation that is vouchsafed him is that all may be physical in the end: "The psyche, as the consciousness thought of itself, imagination's unique locale, its beautiful pattern of roots in the deoxyribonucleic acid, drawing up its 'vast ideas' from deep in the past, could it be annulled, reduced to a spot of slime on a collapsing wall?"

Still, what is remarkable about the novel is the combination of a search for "something other" and "something beyond" with a refusal to admit that more than a hint of it, if that, has ever been found. At any previous time in the world's history such a book would have been couched in religious or philosophical terms, and reached a religious or philosophical conclusion. But, in spite of the hero's brief religious and mystical experiments such terms are, it seems, tacitly denied him; and it is evidence of something in our politically hag-ridden age that so much of such a book should be taken up with a search among political dislocations and destructions for the new reality. One recalls Thomas Mann's famous remark to the effect that in the seventeenth century the destiny of man was discussed in religious terms, in our time in political.

The collapse he witnesses at the end is of course not it. The sharpening of perception and the heightening of humble sensation which H experiences at this point in company with the German girl who is now his lover are beautifully conveyed, but they are more a matter of escape into a blessed ordinariness of experience than a product of the gigantic dislocations and destructions which are to be seen all round.

There may be a message here about the triumph of the artist over the dissatisfied spirit; but it is yet very likely that the dissatisfactions expressed have still a long way to go; that Stuart's book stands at the beginning of an era in which the disinherited religious spirit, seeing no fit abode among the world's complacencies for its ideals, will express itself in contradictory, unavailing and destructive protest.

All the more honour to him then for the refusal to indulge it with fake revelations and resting places even at the end of the line.

SAMUEL BECKETT:
Murphy Becomes Unnamable

Europe has now had a written literature, all shone and polished and fitted for the expression of permanent truths, for more than three thousand years; and it had God knows what in the way of oral epic and heroic tales before that. It is no wonder that we are self-conscious; and that so much of our literature now makes a comment, ironic or sarcastic or whatever, on what went before it. The growth of this process of comment has been a creeping one: you could conceivably say that Shakespeare was a commentator; you could certainly say that his contemporary, Miguel de Cervantes Saavedra, was; but in the nineteenth and twentieth centuries it has, like everything else, speeded up.

The shock to ancient values brought about by the naked triumph of commerce over all other systems of valuation whatever was extreme; and involved an abandonment of notions enshrined in literature and stretching right back through the eras of aristocratic pretence and chivalric pretence to the very dawn itself, which notions were done no good either, of course, by the industrialisation of war.

And while commerce was triumphing over the hitherto themselves profitable pretences of all aristocratic and religious systems, its machines were bringing to an inconclusive end our romantic affair with nature, which affair had naturally reached a pitch of screaming intensity just before the machine age came in.

So modern man's necessity to enquire and to comment, to contrast and to compare became different in kind from that of his predecessors; and a new sort of self-consciousness was born. If the self-consciousness of the romantics, of Rousseau and Byron and a great many others had elements of self-delight in it (indeed was, whatever its agonies, principally composed of such) that of the protagonist of Dostoevsky's *Notes From Underground* had none. It might therefore be seen as one of Joyce's triumphs that he got a little self-delight, at least of a humorous sort, back into the self-consciousness; as well as a measurable assertion of pride in the difference between contemporary man and his predecessors; but however that may be, contrast and compare he did, endlessly posing Bloom, and Bloom's questions, against the real Ulysses, wondering which was which and what was what; and how Homer's man stood up to his own redoubtable fellow and so on.

This contrasting and comparing became the basic technique of modern literature. It is the basic technique of *Ulysses'* great epic counterpart, *The Waste Land*, published in the same year. It is, as suggested in the last chapter, the basic technique of *At Swim-Two-Birds*. And there was indeed a great deal, principally in the matter of emotional intensity or even emotional simplicity, to contrast and compare with.

Most of the literature of the past dealt with the heights of human experience. It took the exalted moments of lyrical emotion – of love, or even perhaps of hate – and it sought to enshrine them in words which matched their intensity. It celebrated those virtues which were proper to heroic struggle or great achievement, courage and loyalty, will-power, ambition and resolution among them. Even when it dealt in crime or villainy or despair it was interested in the extreme rather than the average – and except in some very great examples which are still a wonder to the world, Shakespeare's *Hamlet*, or the same gentleman's *Troilus and Cressida*, it never allowed the new ingredient of *Notes From Underground*, destructive self-consciousness, to enter in. And when it presented its exalted emotions and destinies for contemplation it often put them in the rich context of public event and spectacle – the death of princes, the fall of dynasties, the meetings and separations of star-crossed lovers whose fate was or became a public spectacle.

Indeed much, you might say, to contrast and compare with – more particularly since what all this literature of instinctive struggle and overwhelming passion, of ecstatic communion with nature and kinship with its presumed purposes left out was the major part of human experience. For life, as we all know, does not consist of a series of exalted moments; and many of the exalted moments of which it did consist, or used once occasionally to consist, were dependent on the acceptance of values which commerce has made ridiculous and which the new element of self-consciousness has consequently undermined – not much use Roland blowing his horn in the passages of Spain if kingship and fealty had turned out to be a fraud like all other frauds; and perhaps not much point either in Macbeth feeling all that guilty if you knew, as Balzac knew, what some of the admired figures of the contemporary political and commercial world were up to.

But yet the literature of the past had put us all under an indubitable burden, both of emulation and gratitude, and it had created archetypes about which we all felt uneasy; so, partly in response to these archetypes, but partly, of course, also as independent representatives of mankind, modern literature put forth its anti-heroes and anti-heroines, a long and curious gallery, which includes Dostoevsky's civil servant, Bouvard and Pécuchet, Madame Bovary, Kafka's K, Leopold Bloom, and, perhaps last of all, the individual who subsists in Samuel Beckett's novels.

Three at least of these, *Molloy, Malone Dies* and *The Unnamable* form a sequence, often referred to as "the trilogy", and to describe their principal protagonist as an individual is admittedly to postpone for a moment the question of why he is a man of many names: but even judged as different people, Molloy, the dying Malone and the often re-named Unnamable will be seen to have certain characteristics in common.

Taken together they may be said to compose a sort of archetypal Beckett man, the most extreme of all the anti-heroes and the one from whom all vestiges of the heroic or even the likeable have been most thoroughly eliminated. Thus while Kafka's K is deeply and often painfully involved in the world's affairs, anxious to do right and even to see that justice is done, the Beckett man regards everything that concerns his busy fellows as a snare and a delusion. While Bloom is full of fellow-feelings, the Beckett man is a loner, and his principal emotion when confronted with another human being is fear.

> Morning is the time to hide. They wake up, hale and hearty, their tongues hanging out for order, beauty and justice, baying for their due. Yes, from eight or nine till noon is the dangerous time . . . It may begin again in the early afternoon, after the banquet, the celebrations, the congratulations, the orations, but it's nothing compared to the morning, mere fun. Coming up to four or five of course there is the night-shift, the watchman, beginning to bestir themselves. But already the day is over, the shadows lengthen, the walls multiply, you hug the walls, bowed down like a good boy, oozing with obsequiousness, having nothing to hide, hiding from mere terror, looking neither right nor left, hiding not provocatively, ready to come out, to smile, to listen, to crawl, nauseating but not pestilent, less rat than toad. Then the true night, perilous too but sweet

> to him who knows it, who can open to it like the flower to the sun, who himself is night, day and night.

The Beckett hero does not believe in the brotherhood of man; and questions of equality are disposed of by the eager admission that he is, in all respects, inferior. He lays no claim to any virtue that can be named, except the saintly ones of resignation and humility; or to any talents or skills except those forced on him by the exigencies of a probably ludicrous, arbitrary and undignified circumstance. He has a certain low cunning; and if set a useless problem, such as how to ensure that no one of sixteen sucking stones is sucked more than once in any one cycle, he, like Molloy, will set about solving it.

The attitudes of the Beckett man are in fact almost a complete reversal of those we have all been encouraged, by our educators or our atavisms, to adopt. There is no hitherto esteemed notion, whether of honour, dignity, trustworthiness, courage, energy, ambition or goodwill, which he has not learned – he might even say by bitter experience – to scorn or to disregard. He believes that most of what we call learning, or science or philosophy, is a fraud, to be described as time-wasting except that it was probably invented to pass the time, and so is time-filling rather than otherwise.

> Yes, I once took an interest in astronomy. I don't deny it. Then it was geology that killed a few years for me. The next pain in the balls was anthropology and the other disciplines, such as psychiatry, that are connected with it, disconnected, then connected again, according to the latest discoveries. What I liked in anthropology was its inexhaustible faculty of negation, its relentless definition of man, as though he were no better than God, in terms of what he is not. But my ideas on this subject were always horribly confused, for my knowledge of men was scant and the meaning of being beyond me.

Born into an unending stream of instruction and exhortation, often maddeningly imprecise, very likely inaccurate, seemingly useless, the Beckett man believes that the most shameful moments in his career were those in which he was deluded enough to try to learn; and he holds by his rejections with a fierce tenacity, often catching himself on in the nick of time, when another one than he might have admitted to an emotion or a thought that was, in one way or another, worth the having. In this, as in other respects, he is the most anti of anti-heroes;

and he raises in its most extreme form the question of the point we have arrived at.

It is not, of course, the boring old question of why go on living which the early critics of the plays discussed, often under the impression that it was something called the existentialist dilemma. It is rather more, in fact, the question of why go on writing – why, at least, go on creating fictions – and it is raised not only in general terms because literature seems to be seen as the enemy which has positively fed our delusions, but in particular ones because Beckett's work seems to have its own underlying heroism and to be, in some way or other, a positive assertion, if not of the importance, then, more peculiarly still, of the inescapability of literary utterance.

Murphy, the first and most orthodox of these novels, was originally published in 1938, and at that time, it seems, was readily ignored and rapidly forgotten. Superficially it might seem to bear only a remote relationship to the later work. *Murphy* is set in the recognisable world (Dublin and London) with a background that is scrupulously evoked and a geography that is painstakingly exact. This outer world, in accordance with Beckett's presumed purposes, tends to vanish as the serial scheme of his novels unfolds. Those who know Dublin may fairly easily identify the opening scene of *Watt* as the tram stop by Portobello Bridge over the Grand Canal, and the train journey as from the old Harcourt Street station to Foxrock, in whose vicinity Mr. Knott lives; and there may be lingering traces of the county of Dublin landscape in *Molloy*, but it would be presumptuous to set the jar in which the Unnamable in the book of that name is incarcerated, in Paris, if indeed it is meant to exist at all, since he himself is dubious:

> That the jar is really standing where they say, all right, I wouldn't dream of denying it, after all it's none of my business, though its presence at such a place, about the reality of which I do not propose to quibble either, does not strike me as very credible. No, I merely doubt that I am in it. It is easier to raise a shrine than bring the deity down to haunt it.

Though the book in which he appears is not part of the trilogy which is generally bound up in one volume and regarded as a self-contained work, Murphy is acknowledged by the Unnamable, the culminating figure of the trilogy, as being among his predecessors. This first novel therefore remains an acknowledged part of Beckett's grand prose design and, since it is comparatively so straightforward, it provides a sort of first course in Beckett, a clue to that "meaning" which has been so much debated. Here in its pristine sparkle is his sardonic disgust with the whole "colossal fiasco", the world of hope, movement and action. Wylie, who, like Murphy, has been a pupil of the Cork philosopher Neary, believes that:

> The syndrome known as life is too diffuse to admit of palliation. For every symptom that is eased, another is made worse. The horse-leech's daughter is a closed system. Her quantum of wantum cannot vary.

Neary, though intellectually he agrees, is still driven to seek some sort of palliation in the "anthropoid" Miss Counihan, in the friendship of Murphy, later in Celia. Murphy himself has gone far beyond mere palliatives. From fret, seeking, mere contingency, from the tender ambitions on his behalf of Celia the whore who loves him, he desires to retreat into the privacy and inviolability of his own mind, whose delights are, in ascending order, reversal of the direction of the kick, contemplation and darkness, the sensation of being "a mote in the dark of absolute freedom . . . caught up in a tumult of non-Newtonian motion". These states of bliss he can satisfactorily achieve only in his rocking chair, and though he declares to Celia "I need you, you only want me, you have the whip, you win" and goes out each day obediently to trudge around looking, or not looking, for a job, he would agree with the opinion expressed (by the author himself, no less!) in Beckett's first published work, a monograph on Proust, to the effect that "wisdom consists not in the satisfaction but in the ablation of desire".

So when he eventually finds a job, as a male nurse in a lunatic asylum, far from being horrified by the psychotics around him,

> The most easily identifiable of his immediate feelings were respect and unworthiness . . . the impression he received was of that self-immersed indifference to the contingencies of the contingent world which he had chosen for himself as the only felicity and achieved so seldom . . . The issue therefore, as lovingly simplified and perverted by Murphy, lay between nothing less fundamental than the big world and the little world, decided by the patients in favour of the latter, revived by the psychiatrists on behalf of the former, in his own case unresolved. In fact, it was unresolved, only in fact. His vote was cast. 'I am not of the big world, I am of the little world' was an old refrain with

> Murphy, and a conviction, two convictions, the negative first. How should he tolerate, let alone cultivate, the occasions of fiasco, having once beheld the beatific idols of his cave? In the beautiful Belgo-Latin of Arnold Gelinceux: *Ubi nihil vales, ibi nihil velis.*

Murphy is a fairly straightforward narrative, and it is worth noting that Murphy makes an outstandingly good male nurse and his death is not suicide but accident – no Beckett character commits suicide. This book gives expression to an attitude which is at the core of all Beckett's work: not of renunciation, for there is nothing but filth to renounce, but rather of desire, of yearning for selfhood, true selfhood at last.

Watt has no exterior logic in its narrative and is therefore more likely to tempt readers into interpretation of meaning, as allegory, parable or symbol. Though funny enough in parts, it is less so than *Murphy*, which is very funny indeed. In language, in evocation of the physical world, shades of light and dark, twilight and day, it is the most poetic of Beckett's prose works. Its core seems to be, oddly enough, Watt's own haunted pursuit of "meaning" in the events and images surrounding him from the moment he enters Mr. Knott's house, a pursuit that has a very bad effect on him and eventually drives him into a lunatic asylum – he who previously

> had not seen a symbol, nor executed an interpretation, since the age of fourteen, or fifteen, and who had lived, miserably it is true, among face values all his adult life, face values at least for him. Some see the flesh before the bones, and some see the bones before the flesh and some never see the bones at all, and some never see the flesh at all, never never see the flesh at all.

As in the incident of the blind piano tuner it was the "fragility of the outer meaning" which "had a bad effect on Watt, for it caused him to seek for another, for some meaning of what had passed, in the image of how it had passed". It is only towards the end of his stay in the house that Watt learns "to accept that nothing had happened, that a nothing had happened, learned to bear it and even, in a shy way, to like it. But then it was too late."

This wavering between an actual, apparent incident and an elusive something beyond it, the fact that a pot, for example, has somehow ceased to be a pot for Watt and yet he can find no other name for it, his constant failure to find satisfying correlations between such things as the hour of Mr. Knott's rising and the hour of his retiring, or to fix Mr. Knott himself in any constant physical appearance, this reduction and at the same time dreamlike extension of experience and image gives the book a strangely disturbing, ghostly, unsettling, but nonetheless also indemnifying power, which is not least among the kinds of poetry at Beckett's command.

But it is in the trilogy composed of *Molloy, Malone Dies* and *The Unnamable* that Beckett's originality is most evident and his general purpose becomes more clear. Whatever about being in a conceptual sense "understood", the trilogy can be received and apprehended with excitement on almost every page. The beauty and exactness of Beckett's prose needs no demonstration. He has invented a new instrument, whose beauty is an ironic beauty, not only in the sense that the statements made are ironic, but also in that the syntactical structure of the prose is, in keeping with the author's purpose, an ironic comment on all syntax and all expression, while even in the "translations into English" – if that indeed is what they are – which Beckett has made, or for which he acknowledges responsibility, its rhythms are as individual and as haunting as any in the language.

The asceticism of this prose is one of its most notable features, an austerity in keeping with the macerations of false experience which are intended. It is a prose which denies itself all spurious ornament and adjectival embellishment, even, for the most part, the alluring joys of metaphor. And the boredom of description which, at least nowadays, is almost always and almost necessarily a concoction and a falsification, is rigorously avoided. Thus Molloy breaks off a description with a refusal to "relapse again into a wealth of filthy circumstance"; and Moran interrupts an account of the birds he heard singing in the night, with the ironic declaration: "If I had heard of other birds that cry and sing at night, I should have listened to them too." Beckett is intensely aware of the possibilities of corruption inherent in all attempts to embellish one's language, the harm that can be done by the little words that continue to fester and corrupt the rest of the statement long after they have been indulged in.

Many of the stylistic devices that he mocks may once have been viable, but they are so no longer; and in this, as in the vision of life he is concerned to express, Beckett is struggling against the backwash of false feeling which three thousand years of literature have left in their wake.

Of course all comic artists, as well as some serious ones, exaggerate. If you are going to reject the picture of a humanity always on the *qui vive* to prove itself honourable, brave, capable and subject to fits of significant emotion – which picture literature has been concerned for three thousand years to present as the truth – you will be inclined to do it either with fury or with levity for, after all, the deception has been enormous. Beckett prefers the latter, so that to say he exaggerates is to say no more or no less than that he is a comic artist. He overstates the falsehood of what literature has offered us; of the lessons humanity thinks it has learned. He exaggerates the futility of action. He labours the emptiness, the barrenness, the loneliness, not so much as an expressionist painter exaggerates the agony of the features, but as Chaplin caricatures the grotesqueness of mishap while the audience rocks with laughter.

Exaggerate though he does, however, there is no mistaking the fact that Beckett is, like most comic artists, in deadly earnest.

At one point in the trilogy the sum of what all delusions of action amount to is given brilliantly comic expression by the creation of an opposite figure, if not exactly a hero then, at least, a sort of comic obverse of the anti-hero, and very definitely a man of action, besotted, like so many we know, with the thought of his own capacity; and asinine in the conviction that capacity and application somehow amount to a morality in themselves. This is Moran, to whom the second part of Molloy's book is given over. He begins as a scrupulous, correct, punctual, affirmative and obtuse bore, gladly undertaking the task assigned to him by his mysterious employers, which is to track down Molloy and make a report on his whereabouts and condition; and he ends as a partially paralysed wreck, like Molloy himself, his idiotic and ultimately fragile illusions shattered, his dream of action vanished.

Is Beckett's work, then, a final farewell to all quest, enquiry and endeavour? Does this ultimately quietist gospel reject the validity of all forms of heroism, struggle and effort? Not quite. Moran's last words are:

> I have spoke of a voice telling me things. I was getting to know it better now, to understand what it wanted. It did not use the words that Moran had been taught when he was little and that he in his turn had taught to his little one. So that at first I did not know what it wanted, I understood it, all wrong perhaps. That is not what matters. It told me to write the report. Does this mean that I am freer now than I was? I do not know. I shall learn. Then I went back into the house and wrote. It is midnight. The

> rain is beating on the windows. It was not midnight. It was not raining.

We have here, in one simple passage, all the elements that are to become so familiar to readers of the trilogy as a whole: the categorical imperative; the difference between this imperative and all the others which have been directed at us; the possibility of liberation through obedience to it; the necessity to lie in order to obey; the departure from the truth; and the compulsion to return to it again. The compulsion to utter, to make a report on things, is of course the artist's; and so there remains one privileged victim who is not exempted from the necessity to sustain, in one way or another, the role of hero; who is indeed not exempted, in a very specific sense, from the necessity to at least pretend.

The trilogy may be seen as a series of subsidences. Moran comes inevitably to resemble Molloy – paralysed, crawling, almost resigned. Malone's efforts to amuse himself with the story of Macmann are unsuccessful; and Macmann becomes, all too obviously, Malone:

> What tedium. And I call that playing. I wonder if I am not talking yet again about myself. Shall I be incapable, to the end, of lying on any other subject? I feel the old dark gathering, the solitude preparing, by which I know myself, and the call of that ignorance which might be noble and is mere poltroonery.

It is in the last book, with its successive collapses of pretence, its peelings away, monologue within monologue, of falsification, that these subsidences are explained. Murphy in the lunatic asylum, Molloy crawling through the forest, Malone lying on his bed, Mahood in his jar under the tarpaulin, Worm, the reduction of them all whom no threat or torment can bring to life, are all, we now learn, fictional creations of the Unnamable. They are, it appears, attempts on his part to create and sustain fictional identities, surrogates for himself if he has any self, made at the bidding of those obscure masters who rule him. They are part of the double and contradictory burden that afflicts him, forced on the one hand to be and to create something other than himself in order to placate one set of powers, while knowing at the same time that behind them remains that other, who, as he says, "will not give me quittance until they have abandoned me as inutilisable and restored me to myself".

It is these contradictions which compose a "labyrinthine

torment that can't be grasped, or limited, or felt, or suffered, no, not even suffered". There is, on the one hand, the command continually to utter something, and on the other, the command to utter that which is, for some obscure reason, because of some terrible necessity to expiate, important:

> It is difficult to speak [he declares] even any old rubbish, and at the same time focus one's attention on another point, where one's true interest lies, as fitfully defined by a feeble murmur seeming to apologise for not being dead. And what it seemed to me I heard then concerning what I should do and say, in order to have nothing further to do, nothing further to say, it seemed to me I only barely heard it, because of the noise I was engaged in making elsewhere, in obedience to the unintelligible terms of an incomprehensible damnation.

"It all boils down to a question of words" says the Unnamable, for he has no hands, and hence cannot be required to keep up a continuous clapping noise, as if calling the waiter; nor legs, and therefore can scarcely be expected to dance the Carmagnole. He speculates as to what the expiation that is required of him might have been like if it had not been a question of words – a simple job perhaps, sorting and arranging things, or carrying water in a thimble from one set of containers to another, tanks perhaps secretly connected by underground pipes, so that his work could be undone as rapidly as he did it, while yet he could be deluded from time to time by attacks of carefully arranged hope.

It will be obvious, however, since for him it is a matter of words, that his position is that of the artist. The trilogy is an epic written in the only terms in which it may be possible to construct an epic today. Behind the flagellations and macerations of literary experience lies something incomprehensible: the necessity to create more literature. No reality is presupposed outside the artist's own need, which would make his struggle comprehensible. Though the Unnamable sometimes believes (if that is the word) that behind the voices with their command to utter and to be at all costs, there may exist another who requires true utterance and true being; and that if he succeeeds in pleasing them they may leave him

> in peace at last, and free to do what I have to do, namely try and please the other, if that is what I have to do, so that he may be pleased with me, and leave me in peace at last,

> and give me quittance, and the right to rest, and silence, if that is in his gift.

yet in this labyrinth this other, too, may be a delusion and the voice may be his own.

And in the Unnamable's curious compulsion to "say words, as long as there are any, until they find me, strange pain, strange sin", there lies one final contradiction. The artist who is concerned only with the truth can arrive at it only by means of a fiction. The creations of the Unnamable – Molloy, Malone, Macmann and the rest – stand in Beckett's scheme, not only as surrogates of the Unnamable's non-existent personality, but as an illustration of this tortuous irony in the artist's search for himself. For there is a sense in which the voices are right, or at least appear to be right. It does seem that it is only by the adoption of a fictitious mechanism and the entry into a labyrinth that may never lead back to the self, that the self can be revealed. It does seem that it is only by the saying of words on other subjects, "even any old thing", that the words will be found which will discover the self and release it from its torment. This is the dilemma that Melville hinted at when he said how he would have preferred the "utterance of a great soul in repose" to the plays of Shakespeare. And it is the explanation of the dialogue of Yeats's 'Vacillation':

> *The Soul.* Seek out reality, leave things that seem.
> *The Heart.* What, be a singer born and lack a theme?
> *The Soul.* Isaiah's coal, what more can man desire?
> *The Heart.* Struck dumb in the simplicity of fire!

For there is no doubt that the attempt to speak directly of the truth, without a fiction or a mechanism or a construction of any kind, does lead to barrenness and silence. It is the liars who are creative; it is lies which are germinal, even of the truth. And yet, should it not be otherwise? Hence the Unnamable's guilt and agony, whichever course he adopts.

The commandment is to create as well as to utter: indeed it is only through creation that utterances of any significant sort can be achieved; yet even after all suspicion of a plot has been dispensed with, all creations are fictions and all fictions are lies. "We are getting on", says Malone after he has succeeded in creating Saposcat. "Nothing is less like me than this patient, reasonable child, struggling all alone for years to shed a little light upon himself, avid of the last gleam, a stranger to the joys of darkness. Here truly is the air that I need, a lively tenuous air, far from the nourishing murk that is killing me". But almost immediately the knowledge returns that in this form of externalisation of the true self (the bringing to light of which is the whole object of the exercise) may be danger: "If this continues it is myself I shall lose and the thousand ways that lead there. And I shall resemble the wretches famed in fable, crushed beneath the weight of their wish come true."

But if, as the reader of the trilogy gradually discovers, all Beckett heroes are one hero; if, behind them all, looms the figure of the artist who created them, may it be that the views on action and endeavour, honour and probity expressed so often are peculiar to the artist?

Many years ago, in an essay on Proust already quoted, Beckett spoke of Proust, driving to the Guermantes Hotel

> to receive the oracle that had invariably been denied to the most exalted tension of his spirit, which his intelligence had failed to extract from the sismic enigma of tree and flower and gesture and art, and suffer a religious experience in the only intelligible sense of that epithet, at once an assumption and an annunciation, so that at last he will understand . . . the dolorous and necessary course of his own life and the infinite futility – for the artist – of all that is not art.

The key phrase – "for the artist" – must give us pause. Is it only for the artist that all things other than art are futile, "an expense of spirit in a waste of shame"? To answer this question we must step outside the trilogy, or outside those prose narratives which have been declaredly subsumed into the general scheme of the Unnamable.

And here, surely, in the plays and elsewhere, the finding is the same. Molloy communicates with his mother by knocking on her forehead, one for "yes", two for "no", three for "money". In the play *Endgame*, the hero's parents live in two dustbins on the stage, mumbling, resigned, pathetic, grotesquely and unfittingly sentimental. "It's suicide to be abroad," says Mrs. Rooney, in the beautiful radio play *All That Fall*, "but what is it at home? The gradual dissolution." "Be again on Croghan on a Sunday morning, in the haze, with the bitch, stop and listen to the bells . . . Be again. Be again," says Krapp, most romantically-minded and most lyrical of Beckett's central figures; but adds after a pause, "All that old misery. Once wasn't enough for you".

Though the figures in the novels are fictional projections of the Unnamable, or of the author himself, made in response to the incomprehensible demand to utter and create, they have enough substantive reality to embody what used to be called, twenty-odd years ago, and particularly in the land where Beckett lives, the human condition, at least as their creator sees it.

We are not all octogenarians, living on soup, paralysed on a bed. But by reducing his characters to the extreme simplicities of need and satisfaction, Beckett does succeed in laying bare both the realities of our need and the grossness of our illusions. All is caricature and yet all is real. This is our world and not just the worst of it, as it would be if these were literal accounts of the existence of *clochards* or crippled old men; but like an X-ray or the face of one sleeping off guard, it is the reality behind the distractions, the rain, the umbrellas and the taxis. The substantive conviction that lies behind Beckett's work is not to be judged by whether his characters' voices echo realistically among the stage-settings: nor is its richness to be measured by what Molloy calls its "wealth of filthy circumstance". The author, through the Unnamable, may disown these creations, but he has created them nonetheless. Some part of Beckett's strength is realism, about the body as about the soul; and a great part of his destructive power. Molloy enjoying the hospitality of the kind lady called Lousse; Malone waiting for the skinny old hand to push in his food and remove his chamber pot, scribbling away meanwhile in his exercise book with the stub of a pencil (a French pencil, he is careful to assure us); Mahood in his jar on the pavement outside the cafe near the slaughterhouse – they are all real enough. And while it may not be exactly the realism of Balzac, Zola or C.P. Snow, or even of Beckett's old mentor James Joyce, it suffices for the sort of conviction as well as for the sort of shock Beckett wishes to produce.

When Molloy proceeds to wonder whether he has ever known what is called true love, and recounts the experience which he thinks may have amounted to a knowledge of that famous state; when Malone counts his possessions and the Saposcats agonise about their son's progress in examinations, these reductions and enlargements of common experience can be seen to have their own awful validity. And when his people and/or their creator denounce the values of the world, and express their ironic astonishment before the delusions of the world, they mean it too. These delusions, induced and encouraged by literature, have, of course, done damage; so though the denunciations and disillusionments are expressed with a certain amount of ironic zest, this should not blind us to the fact that the conviction which lies behind them is a truly quietist one. Whether it could also be expressed in the terms of any established quietist religion or formulated quietist philosophy, is, of course, another matter. The nearest Beckett has ever come to any extra-fictional statement of belief along these lines is in the statement already quoted from the essay on Proust: "Wisdom consists not in the satisfaction but in the ablation of desire".

In any case the only call to action now admitted is the command to create; and one cannot call it moral because it is described, specifically, as incomprehensible. Nevertheless it must be obeyed and though the Unnamable's difficulties are specifically those of the imaginative creator of embellished fictions which must have some degree of substantive reality in order to suffice, in one form or another the imperative has been known to every artist who ever lived. What is different is the knowledge that it is incomprehensible and therefore merely (and terrifyingly) categorical. In this form it has been the peculiar (and dubious) privilege of the artist only since the divorce between art and society took place at the beginning of the bourgeois era. As such, it is familiar to the small proportion of the population which has shared the artist's agonies since the day of Charles Baudelaire; and that it is not recognised as the shockingly simple preoccupation (the strength as well as the simplicity of which being themselves sufficient proofs of genius) which lies at the root of Beckett's work is a tribute to the ability his critics, like Joyce's, show in ignoring the obvious.

But if all action is ridiculous save the creation of works of art, what becomes of the exemplars, the heroes of action, even the "good", if confused, men, the Pierre Bezuhovs of the world, whom it used to be, in part at least, the purpose of poets and novelists to present to us? "There are no great men", said Baudelaire, "save the poet, the priest and the soldier. The man who sings, the man who offers up sacrifice and the man who sacrifices himself. The rest are born for the whip. Let us beware of the rabble, of common sense, good nature, inspiration and evidence." But somewhere about the mid-part of this century, after the second war to save democracy, after Churchill and Eisenhower and Stalin and the bomb, soldiers and priests went the way of all others; even the creation of Leopold Bloom became impossible; and the poets found that there was no-one to admire but a *confrère*, usually dead, no-one to respect save another artist who had rejected all forms of activisim and divorced himself from the values of commerce and the market-place. Yeats, who was born forty years before Beckett, had had artists enough in his pantheon but yet believed in soldiers and men of action as more humble people believe in footballers. Baudelaire's admirer, T.S. Eliot, presented a priest for the positive admiration of mankind. While if Kafka, like Eliot, was a quietist, his hero was nonetheless tortured by a call to duty; and could stand in for all who were still so tortured, even if they knew that most activity was either harmful, idiotic or destructive. Beckett belonged to a different era.

The attractions of an art of despair in a century of frenetic activity do not need explaining; nor perhaps does the paradox that the effect of an art of despair, as of all art, is one of elation. Yeats believed in the contemplation of heroes, he-men and swordsmen as an example to us all, though he liked them to come, as often they did come, to a sticky end. In other words he believed, probably correctly, that it is by the contemplation of its own bravery, resourcefulness and ingenuity, its limitless and boundless courage and tenacity, that humanity pulls itself up by its own bootstraps; though the liking for a tragic outcome was certainly the expression of a preference for non-societal heroes, even non-societal soldiers, freebooters if not revolutionaries. But by the time we come to Beckett non-societal heroes have gone the way of all others. Man is, by definition, non-societal and there is no news in that. The mythmakers, the artists, have no myth but that of their own persistence: ". . . I don't know, I'll never know, in silence you don't know, you must go on, I can't go on, I'll go on." Will it suffice? It has sufficed up to now at least, for art at least. Beckett has gone on, and the honour as well as much else must be his. It would be surprising, though, if the society which permits the artist no myth but himself could itself go on much longer. It would also be surprising if in the transition other heroes and heroism were not discoverable and discovered.

If that comes about, though, it will not come out of a conviction that the bootstraps are necessary, or that the pulling up process is desirable. The commissar or the critic who believes either of these things may produce something, but it will not be art of any importance. It will come out of another "shift in sensibility", a new mode of experiencing the world among the artists themselves, probably consequent on a change in the world to be experienced. There are signs that this has already happened. The great masters of the first stage of the modern movement, of whom Beckett is the ultimate, have receded a little. The despair – religious in the case of Eliot, less specifically so in that of Beckett – produced great art; but now that we have been a little further through the mill we can perhaps see it for the luxury it was.

PATRICK KAVANAGH:
Alive and Well in Dublin

That Patrick Kavanagh was a "natural" all are agreed; and the agreement seems to have inhibited criticism to a serious extent. Since his death there has been surprisingly general local agreement about his "greatness" – or is it his "stature"? – but seldom can such agreement have been less backed up by people prepared to say why they feel as they do. The itinerant foreigner, stumbling upon a national conviction of which perhaps he was previously quite unaware and looking for a critical *raison d'être*, will be disappointed. Nobody is prepared or able to advance one; and it would seem therefore as if instinctive, spontaneous poetry – primitive poetry as one might say – can call forth only instinctive, unexplainable reactions.

Of course whether he was a primitive in any real sense or not, there is a sense in which Kavanagh may be said to defy criticism, or at any rate the sort of criticism we are getting used to. You can look in vain in his poems for elaborate metaphors, correspondences, symbols and symbolic extensions of meaning, the sort of thing that academia feeds on. Kavanagh was, up to a point anyway, a direct poet. His subtleties are the subtleties of perception, not of elaboration; and academic criticism – which in any case is often obtuse about perceptions, or even baffled by them – would therefore, even if it was prepared to turn its microscopic attentions in his direction, probably find it had little enough to say. That this is a good enough reason for not saying anything seems to be proved by the few rather ludicrous efforts there have been to make Kavanagh the subject of currently fashionable critical method.

But if semeiology is at a discount in his case, neither is there in his poems really anything that turns out to be a coherent life-view in the philosophical sense, a *weltanschauung* to which a critic with a mild talent for paraphrase and popularisation might conceivably turn his hand. You could, it is true, perhaps go on about contemporary Ireland and his relationship to it; and this is what the odd, brave American critic, caught with Kavanagh for one of those dreadful monographs, has usually done, making emergent Ireland and its consensus views into a *weltanschauung* which Kavanagh, their hero, was against.

Of course Ireland, in this respect, usually turns out to be a disappointment. It is not as coherent an either/or in Kavanagh's case as it might be. And there is an indubitable difficulty, experienced particularly by Americans, in accounting for or even understanding Ireland's preposterous complications and contradictions.

But if this is the case – that Ireland is, for critical purposes, something of a disappointment as a life-view – Kavanagh's response to it, from the standpoint of the explicatory critic at least, must be regarded as disappointing too, for in the end there does not seem to be anything opposed to Ireland except the poet's individual existence. And while it may or may not be a drawback (it may or may not *have been* a drawback – and I have said elsewhere that in a somewhat overlooked sense I hold that it was) in Kavanagh's case that he had no ideology to oppose to recent Irish history, the fact certainly throws the critic. If it narrowed and constricted, even in terms of sheer bulk, of what he would have called "mileage", the work itself, what the poet had to say, it equally narrows and constricts what the critic can say about it.

There remains, of course, the relationship with nature, about which, at first sight anyway, there might seem to be much to say, even if only by dint of reference to Wordsworth and by dragging in pantheism and the religious sense. But in the case of the relationship with nature the critic soon enough comes to another easily discernible full stop, for over and over again the poet says about nature and the visible world that to name it and advert to it and declare one's consciousness of it with love and passion is enough, and not infrequently declares further, which must be even more disquieting, that this is all you can do. So that on the subject of man's relationship with nature nobody could ever say of Kavanagh, as Arnold said Leslie Stephen did of Wordsworth, that his poetry "is precious because his philosophy is sound"; that it "is informed by ideas which fall spontaneously into a scientific system of thought"; or that "his ethical system is as distinctive and capable of exposition as Bishop Butler's".

And so we come again to the primitive, over whose achievement the critic can do little but exclaim. What is odd about the primitive categorisation, though, is that, although Kavanagh's work does over-all give the impression of a fierce originality both of statement and technique, this originality is less apparent in his early work, whatever its merits, than in his later.

At the precise time when he was being regarded in Dublin as an untutored *naif*, late come from the fields with poems springing directly from his experience of nature and blessedly free from literary influences, he is at his most derivative. Several of the lyrics in *Ploughman and Other Poems* have direct literary references. The impression they give is one of a fully learned and absorbed accomplishment rather than otherwise. Georgian may not be the precise word, but the verse-turns and line endings suggest a man whose acquaintance with fairly recent poetic literature had been (however he came by it) profitable and is being put to good literary use:

> Splendours of Greek,
> Egypt's cloud-woven glory
> Speak not more, speak
> Speak no more
> A thread-worn story.

may be better than Humbert Wolfe, but it is Humbert Wolfe all the same; just as Byron's lyrics may be better than Tom Moore, but are Tom Moore all the same.

Though some of Kavanagh's life-long themes are already being enunciated: the recall to innocence, the distrust of experience, learning and acquired wisdom, the relationship of asceticism to truth, the eternality of nature and its readiness to respond only to the pure in heart; and though there are poems of great beauty and charm here, some of them springing directly out of his own life and circumstance; in scarcely any instance, if we had come across the poem without knowing anything about its author, could we have identified the voice or, even, been inclined to regard it as a highly original one. Even ploughmen, after all, were not rare in the literature of these islands before Kavanagh – there is an explicit reference to John Clare in the second poem – and however beautiful the title poem, there is nothing said in it that Robert Burns, Clare himself, or even James Hogg or Robert Bloomfield might not have said.

In only one poem, 'Inniskeen Road: July Evening', a statement of the psycho-sexual loneliness of the sensitive adolescent, is there something absolutely unparalleled and irreplaceable. The circumstance is economically and sardonically evoked, and yet with a sort of tenderness:

The bicycles go by in twos and threes –
There's a dance in Billy Brennan's barn to-night,
And there's the half-talk code of mysteries
And the wink-and-elbow language of delight.
Half-past eight and there is not a spot
Upon a mile of road, no shadow thrown
That might turn out a man or woman, not
A footfall tapping secrecies of stone.

And then, with complete honesty, the poet's own isolation, the unsurmountable barrier that separates him from the life of the others, is counterpointed to the picture of common happiness:

I have what every poet hates in spite
Of all the solemn talk of contemplation.
Oh, Alexander Selkirk knew the plight
Of being king and government and nation.
A road, a mile of kingdom, I am king
Of banks and stones and every blooming thing.

Of course the psycho-sexual loneliness of adolescence had been the subject of ten thousand poems before; but the young poets concerned had for the most part – Leopardi is perhaps an exception – presented the emotion as something other than it was, something as vague as a general condition of mankind. Kavanagh universalises too, on behalf of all awkward, shy and suffering people, poets or not; but the difference between their productions and Kavanagh's is the lack of explicitness; and as time went by explicitness was more and more to become one of his virtues, perhaps even, it might be claimed, the characteristic which above all marks him out. It was an explicitness quite different in kind from literary "outspokenness", which is, more or less, what people found in *The Great Hunger*; and though courage, frankness and an end to concealment were necessary to it, its difficulties did not lie in the simple human ones of being courageous and being frank.

The difficulty was rather the perennial one of a tone of voice, a way of presenting the real self in its relationship to the external world, to the writing self and to the reader. To that extent it was, besides being a "life-difficulty" – the necessity to be frank, to call things by their names – a literary difficulty. Its solution was necessary to Kavanagh's ultimate purpose and ultimate achievement; though for quite some time after the publication of *Ploughman and Other Poems* his efforts to solve it are neither too apparent nor too successful. His own subsequent opinion of *The Great Hunger* is well-known; and it may be that what he afterwards apprehended was a change, or at least an uncertainty, temporary but putatively disastrous, of direction.

The Kavanagh themes revealed in *Ploughman and Other Poems* would not have made him either a very original poet or (probably) a very convincing one if they had been all there was to his work. All of them are more or less open invitations to sentimentality or – what is perhaps worse – unfounded assertion with moral overtones; and he certainly does not avoid either of these things altogether or consistently.

At the same time, considered simply as a poet of nature (which is partly what he was), he may be thought to have failed in what is often considered to be a nature poet's primary undertaking: nowhere does he seek to delineate or describe nature in such a way that the reader shares his experience of it; nowhere in fact does he present.

The most he does (or, to put that in a less pejorative way, what he does instead) is advert to his own experience of nature – or sometimes, man-made objects which have strong, probably childhood associations – and to declare that the experience is in some way both significant and consolatory. The stance is that of the poet looking, experiencing and remembering: not, as in so much English nature poetry, that of the observer in whom the physical embodiments of nature have created certain emotions and who seeks to recreate those emotions for the reader by describing or delineating the physical fact. This calling attention to the feeling engendered as much as to the thing itself is a characteristic of the very first poem in his *Collected Poems*:

> I turn the lea-green down
> Gaily now,
> And paint the meadow brown
> With my plough,
>
> * * *
>
> I find a star-lovely art
> In a dark sod.
> Joy that is timeless! O heart
> That knows God!

It was to become his common practice, as time went on; and it was held against him in a review of the *Collected Poems* by Patrick Fallon which remains one of the best pieces of Kavanagh criticism yet written. The objection would have had more damning effect, though, except for something the critic missed;

but that something is all-important and once recognised it gives his work, amongst other things, coherence. Whether he knew it or not, whether he put it to himself in that way or not, Kavanagh was writing a personal epic.

It was an epic unusual in certain respects. It was related to his life, but not, as epics usually are, to extra literary achievement. It was not a matter of belief or conversion to belief, yet it had a good deal to do with faith. There is no question of philosophic certainty or the spread of conviction; and yet philosophical acceptance as it was once understood – the maintenance of a philosophical balance – was as important to it as anything else.

In Kavanagh's sense, to survive as a poet means to go on having the same experiences – very largely those of intimate communion with the ordinary visible world of everyday – whose intensity marked them out as specifically poetic in the first place. This survival is related to spiritual integrity because it can only be experienced when certain forms of ambition, fretfulness and regret have been cast out. It is related to literary integrity also because the statement of the experience "without clap-trap" is all that is permitted; and to go beyond that into the world of speculation, argument, belief, "profundities" of one kind or another is to be, in one way or another, a fraud.

> Mention water again,
> Always virginal,
> Always original...
> Name for the future
> The everydays of nature
> And without being analytic
> Create a great epic...

Openness and faithfulness to the importance of the humble is essential; and so are the ancillary things such as humour, balance, "uncaringness" and even cynicism – the avoidance of the ever-present danger of being taken in by anything that is not, by the touchstone of the ordinary, known-to-be-valid poetic experience, genuine. It has to be made clear that the ultimate self is incorruptible; and, however aberrant, has maintained its integrity and refusal to compromise. To demonstrate these things, and the narrowness of the escape, a strong element of confessionalism is needed. We have heard a good deal about "confessional poetry" since: indeed Kavanagh, most confessional of poets, lived into the era of its most extreme fashionability without ever being mentioned in those particular dispatches. But the confessional element in him has to be strong, and the right tone of voice has to be achieved for it because, without the admissions he makes, the claim to have maintained philosophical balance, to have preserved his integrity, to be still able to commune, in the fullest sense, with nature, with the man-made weir over which the water streams by the canal, with the corner of a gravelled yard in the hospital, with

> The length of Gibson Square
> Caught in November's stare

would be invalid. And unlike most of the "confessional" poets, Berryman, Lowell and others, that he lived to see hold the centre of the stage, he confesses still, as he did in 'Inniskeen Road: July Evening', to things that have certainly no legend-making qualities in themselves. In an increasingly permissive and star-struck era, the things that most confessional poets admitted to – mistresses, casual affairs, marriages, conversations with T. S. Eliot – were certainly not thought of as being to their discredit. What Kavanagh admits to is shabbier and less glamorous: sexual frustration, sexual and literary envy, literary inactivity, mere poverty, time-consuming drunkenness. Yet without this sort of confession, the claim to have maintained his values, his integrity, above all the "innocence" through which the eye can see the canal weir or the yard of the hospital for what it is, would be mere lyricism of a different sort. It would be mere W. H. Davies. So too, of course, with physical survival; and with the accompanying refusal to be soured by experiences of poverty and humiliation. Both have been endangered; both have been achieved. But against that survival and that refusal the enemies listed in the satirical poems he began to write in the nineteen-forties are variously leagued.

Many of them are tempters. They will allow survival – indeed they will ensure it, if he will consent to become the pre-conceived idea of the poet, particularly the Hiberno-Celtic poet. They stand nearly always for the fraudulent, both in art and life, preferring a more ebullient or allegedly profounder kind of poetry, demeaning the humble experience which is to him, specifically, the poetic; advancing the claims of others to have had and expressed experiences more passionate and more rewarding. That this means usually grosser and more riotous is in keeping with the Hiberno-Celtic idea of things.

In thus defining the enemies of his vision through satire Kavanagh added a dimension to his personal epic; but it is not too much to say also that in these crude-seeming, casual pieces, with their apparently careless rhythms and far-fetched but often brilliant rhymes, he has written also, to use Joyce's phrase, a chapter in the moral history of his country. It is the chapter relating specifically to a new phenomenon, the "art-loving", liberal middle-classes of independent Ireland; and they are all here: the theatre-lovers, the patrons, the bohemians, the "card-sharpers of the arts committees". Though their place in the over-all scheme of Kavanagh's work is to make the triumph of "innocence" more apparent, from the point of view of the value of the satire it matters not. The motive of satire never matters. These still significantly unpopular poems, unpopular with readers and with critics who have their own versions of the "poetic", alike, are as accurate a picture of a side of Irish life which has universal extension as one could wish. If to be that is unimportant, they are unimportant; but it ought to be clear that in dismissing them as such, those critics who are in general sympathetic to Kavanagh's work, Michael Schmidt and Seamus Heaney among them, are deploring the subject not the poems; indeed in Heaney's case they are specifically dismissed as part of "the Dublin thing". Joyce is allowed the possibility of universalism where Kavanagh is not.

But one way or the other, there is no doubt that the poet himself sees them as part of the personal epic which he is writing; and once this aspect of his work is understood, much else falls into place also, including, incidentally, his own later dislike of *The Great Hunger*. In that poem, for the first and last time in his life, he who could not do so even in prose attempted an act of social and imaginative projection, adopting as the hero, or anti-hero, of a life-story which has in its beginnings at least much in common with his own, a created "character" from whom his own most important characteristic has been removed. The presence of personal themes like sexual frustration, land attachment, land inertia, probably only aggravated in his own eyes the offence, for if in epic fact the poet has escaped or transcended these things, the nearness of the Maguire figure to his creator only falsified the record.

And the sub-theme of "coming to Dublin", so beloved of sentimental critics and myth-makers, themselves perhaps peasants who had made the trek to the big city; and who though promoted to the radio, to newspaper criticism or even university lectureships were still suffering from one of the simpler varieties of nostalgia, also becomes rather a different kettle of fish when the existence, the total shape and purpose of the epic is kept in mind. Though some of the worst and weakest poems – mostly in *A Soul For Sale* – seem to trade in the merely nostalgic and regretful aspects of the move and a good deal has been made by simplistic legend out of the disillusion-with-literary-Dublin side of things, to concentrate on these matters is to do less than justice to

Kavanagh's sophistication and sense of proportion. The confrontation with the aspects of Irish society, literary and para-literary, which he encountered in Dublin, was integral to his epic right enough, but mere nostalgia or regret for a more natural order of things – which he never believed rural society represented anyway – played very little part in it. The theme of escape in fact predominated over that of regret. More important than either is the theme of the second escape: that which was accomplished after the escape from the country and was from the wiles, snares and traps set for him by the bourgeois "art-lovers" of the city.

But this listing and cataloguing of the objects of satire, and giving them as a good satirist should, plenty of rope to hang themselves with – allowing them to condemn themselves with their own voices – is the nearest he came to utilising any sustenance from outside, whether in the way of social reality, belief or myth. In the writing of the satires he expressed what is indeed a social passion, but beyond that he propagates nothing and presupposes nothing except perhaps a God who is manifest in the humblest objects of creation:

> No System, No Plan,
> Yeatsian invention
> No all-over
> Organisational prover.

In the end this has a narrowing effect, as he comes to realise:

> O Kavanagh repent
> And start to invent
> An amenable myth...
> To meet every condition
> Outside genuine passion.

And with the final conclusion, in the last poem in the *Collected Poems*, that

> Nature is not enough, I've used up lanes
> Waters than run in rivers or are stagnant
> But I have no message and the sins
> Of no red idea can make me pregnant.

the epic comes to an end. Elsewhere I have remarked on the poignancy of this conclusion.

Now, I am not sure that it is not fitting, for, if this is an epic, it must be in some sort seen as a reductive one – not quite as reductive as Beckett's perhaps, but reductive all the same; and the admission at the end that nature and the natural object would only carry you so far is part of it.

True, Professor Denis Donoghue is not satisfied. He says Kavanagh made no synthesis; that the – I think it was – "encompassing and controlling mind of the great poet such as Wordsworth" is absent. In talking like this he is, of course, echoing Leslie Stephen, though perhaps without knowing it; and is committing the common error of the critic, particularly the academic critic, that of having an ideal poet in mind rather than a real one.

"Encompassing and controlling minds" belong to the world of politics, or, at the least, philosophy; not to that of poetry. Certainly Wordsworth did not have such a mind; and it may be doubted whether, amid all their torments, jealousies, ecstasies and uncertainties, Shakespeare or Dante had one.

Yeats, who pinned his faith to the carrying power of belief and myth, may seem an unlikely source to look to for confirmation of Kavanagh's achievement; yet one recalls his resolution at the beginning to prove that the ordinary day to day feelings of a lifetime were sufficient for poetry; and towards the end his sad enough remark about the smallness of the part of the total personality that can ever be brought to birth in verse. Kavanagh brought quite a lot of the total personality to birth in his verse and it is an achievement the more remarkable because humour and irony were as much a part of his being as the poetic affirmation.

The achievement would not have been possible if he had not found a language which fitted his purpose; but somehow the humour, the uncaringness, the humility and the philosophical balance all became reflected eventually in the diction he used. It is doubtful if his particular version of epic would have been plausible otherwise today.

Out of weakness more than muscle
Relentlessly men continue to tussle
With the human-eternal puzzle.

There were gulls on the pond in St. Stephen's Park
And many things worth a remark.
I sat on a deck-chair and started to work

On a morning's walk not quite effectual,
A little too unselectual
But what does it count in the great perpetual?

If he is anything, in the philosophic sense, he is an Emersonian transcendentalist: "And herein is the legitimation of criticism, in the mind's faith that the poems are a corrupt version of some text in nature with which they ought to be made to tally... The path of things is silent. Will they suffer a speaker to go with them? A spy they will not suffer; a lover, a poet, is the transcendency of their own nature, – him they will suffer. The condition of true naming, on the poet's part, is his resigning himself to the divine *aura* which breathes through forms, and accompanying that." But he does not have to be an Emersonian transcendentalist, or a subscriber to, or inventor of any other system – supposing Emersonian transcendentalism to amount to a system – to be a great poet, for what Leslie Stephen said about Wordsworth was, as Matthew Arnold knew, rubbish. Wordsworth's poetry was not informed by "ideas which fall spontaneously into a scientific system of thought". Nor was his ethical system as distinctive and capable of exposition as Bishop Butler's, supposing Bishop Butler's to have been anything whatever of the sort.

Of course Wordsworth, like Kavanagh, frequently adopts a moral tone: he suggests – in 'The Prelude' he even says – that his way of looking at, or absorbing the beauty of nature, is morally elevating; though Kavanagh is, in a way, easier to take about this if only because he has more sense of humour. Like Kavanagh, too, he got a good deal of "the life of his time" into his poetry, sometimes under the heading of distractions from, if not positive dangers to, the ideal state of receptivity. (In Kavanagh's case the life of Dublin also comes in as ancillary circumstance, sometimes happy circumstance.) As did Kavanagh, Wordsworth believed in a certain innocence or openness, being able to look through the eyes of the boy that once was, as essential to the re-assurance, the at-oneness-with that he desires above all else. Unlike Wordsworth's nature (which includes more people) Kavanagh's nature often includes a man-made thing, or a combination of natural and man-made things, the man-made often mouldering back into nature. One is reminded of the work of certain modern painters: Vlaminck's painting of a shed, for example, or Utrillo's Paris walls, where some sort of emotional *rapport* between the painter and what he is looking at exists. Neither poet is really very specific about the God who may or may not be manifest in creation, whether natural or man-made, though sometimes, because he is inclined to slip into Catholic terminology, Kavanagh certainly sounds more specific. On the other hand Wordsworth's insistence on the mighty or majestic spectacle, the awe-inspiring moment, makes his at-oneness-with altogether different from Kavanagh's; and the present writer is old-fashioned enough to call Wordsworth's attitude pantheistic, whatever people say nowadays, though of course this does not mean that he had a "system" or is worthy of being spoken of in the same breath as Bishop Butler. But nevertheless Wordsworth certainly allows himself "isms" – liberalism in the old English sense, conservatism, patriotism, rural virtueism, which Kavanagh sedulously forbids himself, and in one great poem Wordsworth certainly expresses a belief in some form of metempsychosis.

Unlike Wordsworth, of course, Kavanagh lived in a time of philosophical breakdown, when, paradoxically, certain poets were congratulating themselves on the "mileage" they could extract from isms and systems and beliefs which they acknowledged had no more than the status of myth: in other words on the use they could make of large-scale lies. One recalls the remark which I have recorded elsewhere about "all that junk that Auden has in his mind" and about how he "knows it's lies, but when he throws it on it does to make a blaze". He was envious, but he knew that this envy was one of the temptations which integrity had to struggle against.

> We have no game no more
> Someone stole our game
> And left us high and dry
> On a beliefless shore
> But it ain't no shame
> Plainly the only thing is not to be a bore

If this is existentialism, that is a bonus of which Kavanagh was unconscious. As the poems themselves, his personal epic, insist, he maintained his uncaringness as well as his humour and humility in face of the mystery, disclaimed profundity and all philosophy except in the old sense in which the word implies balance and a preparedness to accept whatever the day brings. Thus he maintained the open, wondering and delighting eye which made the at-oneness-with possible. In affirming his own ability to do this in the face of much adverse circumstance, much temptation and many enemies, he declaredly re-assures other people of the possibility. Because of this; and because his sensibility is, specifically, a grateful one, his poetry is a poetry of affirmation, both individual and universal. That is perhaps the most difficult kind of poetry to write to-day; and his ability to write it, up to the designated end, was a good trick to turn on those who claimed that their "myths", in other words their lies and artificial systems, were "life-giving".

LOUIS MacNEICE:
London and Lost Irishness

If there is an identity, things can go wrong with it; just as if there is a tooth, there can be toothache. There is an ailment called "a crisis of identity" from which many of us, North and South, are said to be suffering; indeed it is a sort of new addition to the long Irish list. Its symptoms are too well-known now to need re-hashing here, but among them is a concern about one's "roots" combined with an inability to decide just exactly which they are, or even whether they are to be found in this island at all.

If anybody could be said to have been specially singled out for such a disability, it might be thought to have been the late Louis MacNeice. He was born in Belfast, which made him a Northerner of sorts, but he was the son of a Church of Ireland bishop, and was therefore, in a sense, cut off, or at least separated from, many of the Irish creeds and their attendant traditions at once: from peasant Catholicism, North and South; urban Presby-terianism; and, even, Church of Ireland though his ancestry was, from the remaining strands of that Church's traditions in the South.

He was therefore deprived, if that is indeed how we should look on it, of all sorts of things which have given the rest of us sustenance: the holy water font in the hallway and the touching faith in the Blessed Virgin, the banging of drums and the re-assurances to be derived from the emotion of multitude, even the cosiness of the Southern, small-town vicarage tennis party or the lost splendours of the hunt ball. He would also, presumably, have been deprived in his cradle of the particular neuroses, obsessions, inhibitions and melancholias which go with any or all of these things and which the one-time Catholic novelists amongst us at least find so fruitful.

Whether he was or not, his separation from Ireland was rendered physical and geographical by the fact that he went to an English public school, to Marlborough to be exact, and sub-sequently to Merton College, Oxford, where he was more or less the contemporary of W.H. Auden, Stephen Spender and Cecil Day Lewis. These three poets, as all the world now knows, awoke one morning to find themselves famous and became the fashionable younger poets of a brief decade.

In so far as it matters now, he was with them but never quite of them. He was never a Communist, for example, and in his early verses he appears to look sufficiently askance on the fashionable Marxism of the day to be called by Yeats, in the preface to the infamous *Oxford Book of English Verse*, "anti-Communist". He was not in *New Signatures* or in the more overtly political *New Country*, the two famous collections in which the poet-impresario Michael Roberts brilliantly succeeded in setting the tone of subsequent proceedings and in presenting his contributors as a homogeneous group to which it was a pity not to belong.

However, he collaborated with Auden in *Letters from Iceland* and, again in so far as it matters, he became one of the big four who were discussed almost to the exclusion of everybody else (a fact which has adversely affected their reputations in varying degree ever since). What mattered in this respect (and does matter still) is that MacNeice was unmistakeably contemporary, bang up to the minute almost, the poet of an urban world of jazz and taxis and neon signs, and even, to a greater extent than some of those overtly committed to political beliefs, of

> Conferences, adjournments, ultimatums,
> Flights in the air, castles in the air,
> The autopsy of treaties, dynamite under the bridges,
> The end of *laissez faire*.

It is possible for a poet, as it is for an artist of any kind, to relish his material even if he disapproves of it on various grounds. In that sense at least MacNeice liked the urban world with which he dealt and he is much more the laureate of the nineteen-thirties even than Auden, certainly more than Spender or Day Lewis. He liked surface. He even liked what used to be called glamour; and his poems have a sort of nimbus of sophistication about them just as the neon signs themselves had. Of course there is cynicism and disillusion but they are lightly enough borne, and there is even a suggestion of "the show must go on" about the attitude. Personal unhappiness when it showed in his verse was presented as an inevitable part of the life of the big city, its doubts suggested only by the wry phrase, the mental shrug, the deliberately insufficient irony which are the traditional defences of the big-city dweller and the stock-in-trade of the sort of comedians and cabaret artists he is supposed to approve. Judging from the poems at least, it seems that MacNeice had found his country. It was called Cosmopolis.

This part of his work wears, I think, extraordinarily well. MacNeice had far more expertise and more technical resources to draw on than any other member of the group except Auden. There were other poets of the city but they did not quite capture, as he captured, its glitter and excitement. Much of what he wrote at the time is poetic journalism, but unlike some of what was to come later, it has the energy, vitality and immediate excitement of good journalism, and that this kind of thing can quite easily last we know from Byron. 'Autumn Journal', a long poem in a loose but sustaining form, susceptible of many variations in which the poet waits in London for the war that did not quite come in September 1938, listening to the news on the wireless, reflecting on a broken marriage, thinking, amongst other things, of Spain, remains one of the most readable really long poems of our time. And whatever about his differences from the then "Marxists", it contains the most poetically successful statement of the wish for democratic socialism that anybody of the decade made.

Then the war that wouldn't quite come came. MacNeice fire-watched. He went abroad on British Council business. He joined the BBC. And for one reason or another, after the war at least, something undoubtedly happened to his talent. The concentration on surface that had been so attractive now seemed superficial. The poems were frequently travelogues, character sketches or, worse still, anecdotes, the sort of thing that accomplished poets tend to write when they are stuck. Had Cosmopolis let him down as a source of poetic excitement? The question is complicated by the fact that something had undoubtedly also happened to Cosmopolis itself which could not have been foreseen. MacNeice had always been a zestful prophet of its doom: in numerous poems, indeed, doom (rather than, say, Marxism or religion) had supplied the answer to many of the questions which the mere existence of Cosmopolis raised. But the war had turned out not to be Apocalypse after all and no-one had banked on the incertitudes and sordidities of the seemingly endless post-war.

When the present writer first went to London around this time, he was surprised when somebody talked of MacNeice as an Irish poet. The fact was so, of course, at least in the literal sense of birth and ancestry, and there were the references to Ireland and the Irish passages in the poems, but to him MacNeice had always seemed at least as cosmopolitan as Auden. And where Ireland was indeed the theme of MacNeice's work it was in much the same way as the Hebrides had been, or Iceland, or Spain. There might be references to being Irish and turning one's back on it, but the view was an outsider's all the same, touristy and with an emphasis on what seemed at the time to be the picturesque elements, violence included. It was even more surprising, therefore, on meeting him to find that his Irishness seemed to bulk rather larger in MacNeice's own consciousness than one would have expected.

There was at the time, however, a sort of fashionable Hibernophilism in the circles in which he moved and when one saw him in the George in Great Portland Street, or in the Stag's Head, his back to the counter, a drink in his hand, a little cohort of BBC employees round him, it was frequently in a sort of little Ireland or would-be Ireland that he stood. The general feeling was rather one of romantic exile or London refugee-dom than of anything more fruitful and positive, whether in the way of return or departure. To an eye other than that of one of his immediate circle he seemed indeed something of a beached figure, one who belonged to an era that had ended in hiatus, without a country other than a part of literary London and a particular corner of Cosmopolis that was really no man's land.

Does Cosmopolis always then turn out for the poet to be merely a state of exile and despair, however modified, in the end? Unfortunately MacNeice's work does not really prove anything either way. Whatever developments there may have been in it towards the close of his life (and it is now almost *de rigueur* to see some) they were not the produce of his renewed Irishness. The Irish poems of the latter years at least are no advance on those of the 'thirties and the posthumously published 'Prologue' to the projected MacNeice-Rodgers anthology is in fact inferior to 'Valediction' or the Irish parts of 'Autumn Journal' and 'Eclogue from Iceland.'

Partly because of his joy in surface there was always a sense in which MacNeice, even at his best, seemed to be looking for the instant poetry in what he was observing or contemplating. He was always, in other words, a bit of a travel writer. To an Irishman, however, this seems less of a weakness in his poems about other places, even Cosmopolis itself, than it seems in his Irish poems. Granted that these latter are often an analysis of his country's persistent neurosis leading to continuing violence which has now been rendered relevant again: more relevant, indeed than it perhaps was in the "lull" periods in which it was written, but now that it has been rendered relevant again, one can see for one thing that it is not an analysis at all, or at least it is not analytical enough. The feeling that Ireland might be doomed to this kind of thing forever may even have poetic possibilities, just as the accompanying shrug and turning away have a poetic effect when performed by such a master of the shrug and the wry phrase; but (to be rational about it, and MacNeice was never afraid of rationality) it leaves a lot out of account, including the fact that Ireland might be freed from some if not all of these neurotic predispositions by the achievement of a political unity from which nobody could turn back, that is by the achievement of its lost or missed nationhood – or however you like to describe a stage of development probably as essential in the growth of healthy countries as other states are in the lives of individuals.

Taking what is undoubtedly an easier poetic option, MacNeice in other words decided that violence was endemic in the Irish character, not in the Irish situation. It is a comment of sorts on that situation, as well as on the belief that poetry is a vehicle for feeling or impression rather than thought, for acquiescence in tragedy rather than rational hope – a belief that, if challenged, MacNeice might not have agreed with – that some more recent Northern poets have done the same and set themselves up as celebrants of tribalism rather than analysts of politics. However that may be, though, there was, not too long ago a MacNeice evening in the Peacock Theatre, masterminded with his usual skill by Mr. Liam Miller. The poems read were mostly the Irish ones and through emphasis on them there seemed to be an attempt to demonstrate that MacNeice was truly an Irish poet.

Now, in the sense that he was born here, he undoubtedly was. Yet, in a very natural way dictated by his upbringing and background, he decamped to London; and no-one surely can deny that he wrote most of his best poetry while in that place and about that place. And so, at first blush, he might seem to uphold the sort of tradition, the Anglo-Irish tradition, that Shaw and Wilde upheld. The difference, I suggest, is in two things: first, MacNeice's Irishness is, in a way, to be seen in the sort of glamour that the sights and sounds of London, or at least Cosmopolis, had for him. And second, in his case, as never in theirs, there is an admission of the fact that London, or at least Cosmopolis, had let him down. There was, as he said, "the head-shrinking war",

> From which reborn into anticlimax
> We endured much litter and apathy hoping
> The Phoenix would rise, for so they had promised.
>   Nevertheless let the petals fall
>   Fast from the flower of cities all.

And nobody rose, only some meaningless
Buildings and the people once more were strangers
At home with no one, sibling or friend.
  Which is why now the petals fall
  Fast from the flower of cities all.

One thing is certain anyway. The big city, during certain years, brought out the best in him: and the best is very good. It would be ludicrous to wish that the chances either of class predilection or of personal predilection had been otherwise; for there is such a thing as poetic predilection too; and if it had not been operative in MacNeice's case we would all, Irish or otherwise, be that much the poorer.

FLANN O'BRIEN
The Flawed Achievement

The works which Brian O'Nolan wrote as Flann O'Brien are four in number; and the brief list is headed by an indubitable masterpiece, *At Swim-Two-Birds*, the mere mention of which, in later years, appeared to cause him pain. This was perhaps simply and solely because it had had an early and enormous word-of-mouth *succès d'estime* in the city of Dublin, where he worked in the civil service and was, at the time of its publication, though still only twenty-eight, known to a considerable number of people. It is, however, also possible that the reputation it acquired so early inhibited him afterwards creatively in various ways, making it difficult for him to write a fitting successor; that he knew this, sub-consciously at least, and hated his first, great book accordingly; and if this is the case there is a savage irony in the fact that it was not, to begin with, in the ordinary sense indicated by extensive reviews in important journals and sales of any magnitude, much of a success at all. Although Anne Clissmann declares somewhat effusively in *Flann O'Brien: A Critical Introduction To His Writings* that "for one glorious week in April (1939) *At Swim* replaced *Gone With The Wind* as top of the best-selling list in Dublin", when one collates this information with the fact that it sold in all, everywhere, two hundred and forty-four copies in the first six months after publication, it is evident that one has here a perfect example of Irish gigantism, a national tendency to magnify indigenous things beyond the bounds of reality, which caused Flann O'Brien's alter ego, Myles na Gopaleen, constant and sometimes ferocious amusement.

More to the point, although Flann O'Brien's first novel achieved a quite genuine place in the affections of a considerable number of people, there were confusions and misconceptions attending its partial and localised reception which, in the absence of any very perceptive criticism, tended to attract attention to certain superficial aspects of it as well as to conceal (perhaps even from its author) the true nature of what had been achieved.

It is discouraging to be under-estimated and even more so to receive no praise at all; but to have the accidental and secondary characteristics of what has in fact been done elevated above the important ones makes continuance in the true vein difficult, as Flann O'Brien (who was oddly suggestible and anxious for reassurance about anything he wrote) was to find. Criticism where *At Swim-Two-Birds* was concerned tended to lag woefully behind mere enjoyment; and while that situation has its charms, it cannot (to the extent that criticism is ever of any help to an author) have been of much assistance to him. More important for us now perhaps is the fact that seventeen years after his death much of the nature of his achievement and much of its greatness remain unrecognised.

Foremost among the confusions surrounding *At Swim-Two-Birds* have been the related ideas of the prodigiously clever literary jape and the brilliantly opportunistic commentary on or pastiche of the works of James Joyce by a member of a younger literary generation. That *At Swim-Two-Birds* is in part a sort of comic coda to all the previous utterances of the twentieth century is indeed true; but then so is most of the great literature of the twentieth century. That it is in any subservient sense a commentary on, or, in any sense at all, a mere parody of Joyce's works is a woeful misconception.

But the Joycean idea quickly took root, in Dublin and elsewhere. It was known that the book had been praised by James Joyce. Perhaps by a sort of corollary, it was assumed to be Joycean. Through a curious set of chances there were more copies of *At Swim-Two-Birds* available in Dublin in the nineteen-forties and early -fifties than there were of *Ulysses*, and since what could be taken as the Joycean characteristics in Flann O'Brien's book were indeed evident, some quite intelligent people were prepared to take the Joycean domination of it for granted, without any very close examination of the differences between, or even of the properly complementary aspects of the two.

There was, for one thing, the syncretic and eclectic method, known to be Joyce's, whereby a great deal of earlier literature and heroic myth had been included and exploited for some reason pertaining to the contemporary characters and their situation. The purposes of this procedure even in Joyce's case were not yet clear; but in each instance the effect was, whatever else it might be, comic; and so the intention was presumed to be identical. And although both are mentioned in Flann O'Brien's text it was overlooked that the American poets T.S. Eliot and Ezra Pound had been up to precisely the same game.

Allied to this there was in the case of both Joyce and Flann O'Brien the devouring, almost all-consuming interest in the way words exposed their users and frequently mocked them, revealed the false and ridiculous aspects of a culture and an era and allowed individuals and civilisations generally to make fools out of themselves. It is more than possible, though of course Dublin wasn't to know it, that Flann O'Brien, who knew German and was interested in contemporary German literature, got this, if he got it anywhere, from Karl Kraus rather than from James Joyce.

There was, as well, the substitution of an apparent inconsequentiality for the machinery of a dramatic causation. This too had been a feature of *Ulysses*. It was overlooked that *The Waste Land* and the *Cantos* also had abandoned narrative or dramatic causality and continuity, perhaps because, on the whole, it was truly more remarkable that it should be done in prose.

And, finally, there was the exploitation of the merely banal and the undeniably sordid in place of what had been regarded hitherto as the dramatically interesting or the poetically significant. That in this as in the other respects Flann O'Brien was in the central stream not only of Irish post-Joycean literature (of which he was then thought to be the sole representative, for however flat *At Swim-Two-Birds* had fallen in the matter of getting English reviews, it had not fallen as flat as Beckett's *Murphy*) but of the modern movement in general was the more easily overlooked because to add to the other Joycean resemblances there was the identity of subject matter. Irish Catholic students and members of the Dublin lower-middle classes were the principal characters in both Joyce and Flann O'Brien, while in each also the main protagonist was a Catholic student would-be writer with an interest in the fundamentals of literary aesthetics.

This was an accident. There was no way out of it unless to write a fiction of an entirely different sort and in fact Flann O'Brien made the more sensible decision and occasionally adverted to it obliquely in his text. In doing this he was in part, of course, properly calling attention to the fact that he and Joyce were both sharers in and would ultimately be seen as early founders of a tradition. Modern Irish literature in English was in its infancy. He doubtless intended to make his position clear; and in any case a degree of incestuousness is certainly no harm in the case of a threatened and ambiguously positioned literature such as our own.

But he can scarcely have been in any doubt that what he was doing was of significance not only for Irish, but for modern literature in general. It was not only James Joyce, but modern European literature and poetry which had been concerned since Baudelaire with what appeared to be the sordid, unfruitful, desultory and boring aspects of modern life. To these it had juxtaposed fragments of mythology or of archaic splendour which suggested that the dimensions of that life were narrower and its conditions meaner than those of any previous era. *The Waste Land, Ulysses,* the *Cantos* and even 'Hugh Selwyn Mauberly' had continually shocked and surprised by opening up vistas beyond the contemporary in humanity's store of mythology or exhibiting evidence of other values than the contemporary in fragments of its heroic past. Although their purpose in doing this was, as has been said, debated, it was generally agreed that the net effect on the contemporary was diminishment. Leopold Bloom was seen as a comic, sordid and unworthy Odysseus. The seduction by the Thames in *The Waste Land* was in the poem deliberately contrasted for dignity and significance with the love of Elizabeth and Leicester; the abandonment seen as shabby and degrading when the story of Dido and Aeneas was hinted at.

So far as the present writer is aware, until he said so in the nineteen-sixties there had been no-one to suggest that the use of myth in *Ulysses* "cuts both ways"; and that if it cast a peculiar light on Bloom and his contemporaries it also shed an odd one on the pretences of epic and heroic poetry. Joyce had, it was recognised, indulged himself in some rather heavy humour at the expense of the gigantism of Irish saga; but he was not seen as having implied that all the heroes in all the myths were in fact probably no more heroic in essence than Leopold Bloom; and, if the reductionist process that he was in truth applying to all myth, was not apparent to his critical betters, it is not likely to have been apparent to Brian O'Nolan, who was no great critic at all; so little of a critic, in fact, that in the course of a prolonged acquaintance you were exceedingly unlikely to hear him utter a critical judgment – or even a literary remark – of any consequence.

But critic or not, like all artists he must have had a strong sense of his position in time and his relationship to the work of his predecessors; and so it is not at all unlikely that he may have felt, in the nineteen-thirties, in the way artists do feel such things, that a humanisation of myth, a reduction of it to humanity's scale and an exploration of the revivifying as well as the comic possibilities of myth-juxtaposition were long overdue. There was, after all, no such reduction in *The Waste Land*, or in the then unburgeoning *Cantos*; and the reductionist process in *Ulysses* was unrecognised: even Eliot thought that Joyce was up to the same game as himself; and was putting the heroic in simply in order to show up the shabbiness, the formlessness, the disorder and the meannesses of modern life. In any case, a humanisation and a reduction of myth is attempted and brilliantly achieved in *At Swim-Two-Birds*.

The devices used are very numerous and cunning; and they include comic realignments and subsumations of many different sorts. But intricately planned and structured as the book is; and although these devices are all the time comic ones, the triumph is, as it should be, more a matter of feeling than of thought; and in the end it is the extraordinary extension of feeling that counts: to Finn, an old bore who yet has dignity, sharing the fireside in their shabby digs with Shanahan and Lamont; to Sweeny as a representative of all bare, forked humanity in its ultimate distress.

And along with this tender diminishment and humanisation of myth goes a positive elevation of the banal and the inconsequential. Joyce had managed this, of course; indeed it had from *Dubliners* onward been one of his principal concerns and ambitions to do so. But most criticism had, again up to the nineteen-sixties, discerned, from the story called 'Grace' to the scene in Holles Street, a strong degree of impatience and of near Swiftian disgust in Joyce's dealings with the banal. It had failed to distinguish the remarkable difference in the tone of these dealings that is described in an earlier chapter in this book as having occurred between *Dubliners* and *Ulysses*. Certainly in 1938, when Flann O'Brien was writing, the common critical assumption about Joyce was that he was a satirist in the Swiftian vein, possessed of a Swiftian loathing of common humanity, including his own hero, Leopold Bloom. And, though this can now be seen as a misconception, and the celebratory aspects of Joyce's work are acknowledged on all hands, it is certain that Flann O'Brien went even further than Joyce in freeing the banal and the ordinary from its place not only in the plot but in structure. Nothing in *Ulysses* is as free from the shackles of Joyce's own kind of consequentiality and structural significance as the story of the jumping Irishman or the discussion of the fiddle as an instrument in *At Swim-Two-Birds*.

But the younger author went further in one more revolutionary direction than Joyce ever had; and it was a step that was to have dubious and irreparable consequences for him. In abandoning dramatic interest and significance Joyce had done almost everything to abolish the novel as a form except finally to expose the merely wilful and autocratic relationship between the creator and his fictions. Whatever the relationship between the book and Stephen Dedalus, the final step had not been taken. That somewhat ambiguous young man was not openly acknowledged to be the creator of the fiction in which he appeared. The novel as a form was spared the ultimate indignity of being exhibited as the product of one of its characters. And whether or not Joyce's loyalty to the artificer and his conception of him as godlike had remained that of the young Dedalus, the fact was that Flann O'Brien went one better. Prodigiously talented though the author of all the inner books in *At Swim-Two-Birds* may be showing himself to be, he is simultaneously revealing himself as a dependent stripling whose literary activities are merely part-time. "Great man" and rival of Joyce's "god of creation" though Trellis may be, he is yet at the mercy of his own creations and exposed as a frequent victim of the haphazard and the accidental in a way that contrasts strangely and refreshingly with the claim to be the unerring master of extraordinarily deep-laid strategies which had been central to the method and the pretensions of James Joyce (or Stephen Dedalus or whatever god-like creature lurked behind *Ulysses*). It was a brilliantly conceived step; but unfortunately for the taker it was also a brilliantly and deliberately nihilistic one; and partly because of his peculiar relationship with his audience it put him in a position which he found difficult to consolidate or develop and from which he found it also almost impossible to withdraw. For there were special circumstances pertaining to his relationship with his audience which made the process of development – or indeed, if necessary, withdrawal – more difficult than it might have been.

Like all books, *At Swim-Two-Birds* posed the problem of what its author should do next. This was a problem which both the inclusive and the nihilistic strains in the archetypal masterpieces of modern literature had already created for their authors. Joyce's complete change of direction after *Ulysses* is notorious; Eliot's difficulty about finding one after *The Waste Land* almost equally apparent: in the eight years that followed he wrote only one short poem. And in Flann O'Brien's book the nihilistic elements – those which tended to break down if not to abolish altogether the form in which he wrote – had been particularly strong.

At Swim-Two-Birds had been a genuine anti-novel and its author's delight in flouting the restraints and mocking the conventions of the genre had been extreme. What he had done would in any case have rendered either advance or retreat within the boundaries of prose fiction exceptionally difficult but there were special factors obtaining in his case which must have made it more so.

In University College, Dublin he had acquired a reputation for extraordinary cleverness and virtuosity. However and wherever acquired such reputations tend to turn men of true originality and capacity into mere wits and measurers of effect, dinner-table virtuosos and creatures of unfulfilled promise; and in Dublin, although there are no dinner-tables to speak of, such a reputation can be especially deleterious because the conditions and atmosphere of U.C.D. are reproduced almost exactly among the more or less literate in the town at large.

In any other society an artist such as Brian O'Nolan had now (as Flann O'Brien) shown himself to be would have had a better chance of escaping the initial disadvantage of having great things expected of him before he had properly begun. Even here a man of his resources might have dismayed his admirers in unexpected ways, but much now conspired against him.

At Swim-Two-Birds had attracted no worthwhile published criticism to speak of. It had sold a miserable number of copies before Longmans' stocks were destroyed by bombing. When its immediate successor, *The Third Policeman*, was rejected by one or more London publishers in the following year the attractions of other modes of expression for an energetic and ambitious young man whose attitude to literary form was, to say the least, provisional and experimental must have been increased. Within a short space of time after the publication of *At Swim-Two-Birds* and while, presumably, *The Third Policeman* was being monotonously rejected, Brian O'Nolan, had, as Myles na Gopaleen, committed himself to a newspaper column which was, while providing him with an undoubted mode for his talents, to absorb a considerable part of his energies for most of the rest of his life the example of Karl Kraus being, here again perhaps, a sustaining and indemnifying influence.

But even *The Third Policeman*, highly praised though it was on its posthumous appearance twenty-seven years later, shows what a trap his masterpiece and his U.C.D. reputation may have conspired to create for him. Flann O'Brien's first novel had been, on the surface at least, a brilliantly resourceful and quick-witted book. To some (even among its author's admirers) it may have seemed little more. Alternatively however, it was the sort of work which could be interpreted as having a "meaning", which is something that criticism is always inclined to search for: indeed in the case of *Ulysses* academic criticism has kept up the search for thirty years or so and shows little sign of abandoning it even yet. If a book as intricately constructed but apparently as pointless as *At Swim-Two-Birds* is to be more than clever, the argument runs, it must be profound. And whether indeed he was influenced by the desire to show that he had a great deal more to offer than the presumed virtuosity of *At Swim-Two-Birds* or not, *The Third Policeman* seems to betray at the very least an anxiety on its author's part to show that he could write a work which contained an important inner meaning, which was in fact "profound". The usual device of those who wish to do that is allegory. *The Third Policeman* is allegorical.

It suffers, therefore, from the usual fault of allegory in that the world of its author's imagining lacks substance, texture and, even, detail. The book is full of oddly generalised and amorphous description, that of landscape, which occupies such a large part of it, being composed in the most laborious way out of mere landscape elements, like a child's picture; while the people seem to be constructed in the manner of photo-fit pictures with feature added to feature in a painstaking way until the whole is complete. And if the mere anxiety to describe is disquieting enough, apart from its visual aspects the prose in which it is done would have seemed to somebody who had an ear for such matters and was given an opportunity of reading the book in sequence after *At Swim-Two-Birds* to be something of a giveaway. Now that the covers were off was the manipulator of so many modes to be seen to have none of his own?

Nor does the allegory appear, to this reader at least, to be consistent with itself, which all allegory must be or else fail utterly. There is a Faustian theme, within which is included admittedly one brilliant joke: the ambition of Faust in the modern world being to write the definitive book about somebody else, in this case the ineffably tiresome de Selby; but if the narrator is Faust there is too much left hanging and too much contradiction; while if it is all an allegory about man and the machine it is a highly simplistic one. If on the other hand the book is an exploration of guilt and retribution, the variations of mood within such a short compass would seem to vitiate it, for guilt is the most pervasive and unremitting of emotions. Though its pressures may vary, it remains a constant, a fact that Kafka's *The Trial* wonderfully exemplifies; but in *The Third Policeman* it is as if the author's natural bent and zest are pulling him all the time towards the comically inconsequential and the banal but he is refusing to give way, so that in the net result he has substituted an equally false consequentiality for the consequentialities of plot which he had already learned to do without.

Not long after the first rejection of *The Third Policeman* Brian O'Nolan began, as Myles na Gopaleen, to write a column for *The Irish Times*, and he continued to do so on and off for the next twenty-six years. About the merits of this column there can be no dispute, for apart from anything else the prose in which it was written would have made it remarkable, while as an exercise in what he called the "compartmentalisation of personality for the purposes of literary utterance" it was even more so; and in the best years of the column the ingenuity, humour and intelligence as well as the selected compartments of his total personality thus displayed were a constant joy. Such were its merits in fact that "Cruiskeen Lawn" may well have been the best piece of sustained journalism that the last forty years or so have produced in any language, but one thing which many of its admirers have claimed it to be it was not. As satire the column (which in any case never struck this reader at least as having a true satirical intent) was too closely in tune with its audience, too fanciful and too quirky to be more than occasionally worthy of note; and when in its later years it became sometimes querulous and bad-tempered the purposes of satire were not served either.

About the other productions of Myles na Gopaleen opinions may differ. *An Béal Bocht* is true satire, right enough, and although much of the joke may be lost on those whose Irish is not sufficient to grasp it even in the bare bones of translation it reveals itself to be a considerable work, about the human condition as well as the Irish, while the first act at least of *Faustus Kelly* is true satire and is hilarious.

After these works, though, for a very long time, nearly twenty years in fact, there was to all intents and purposes only the column. One sort of promise remained unfulfilled, while another, perhaps that which some of his contemporaries had in their heart of hearts forecast for him, became in its fulfilment a feature of the Dublin scene. For if the man of promise anywhere holds out to his admirers the possibility of brilliant failure, in Ireland's and Dublin's mode of response up to recently the man of genius is always a man of flawed achievement, the prisoner rather than the triumphant possessor of his own talent, the victim of his gift. Besides the difficulty of choosing between expedients with which he was now confronted, and apart altogether from his own temperament and the choices it imposed, Brian O'Nolan had now like others a part to play out which was the result of a curious collaboration between himself and the country to which he belonged.

In considering this it is essential to remember that he was one of the first writers to deploy his gifts in the context and, to some extent, in the service of contemporary, independent and – so far as his audience went – mostly urban and middle-class Ireland.

Because he was that much younger than them and, for many years, hardly known outside Ireland's shores, he was much more its product and its writer than such as O'Connor, O'Faolain and O'Flaherty were. Like Patrick Kavanagh, he wrote directly for it to a far greater extent than they did; and his intimacy with and direct dependence on his milieu were aggravated by the coming of the war as well as by his own not inconsiderable pride in his country and deliberate choice. He was accustomed, in conversation anyway, to speak slightingly of England and America. Unlike most members of the generation which preceded, and some of that which came after him, he never lived in either, whether as lecturer, literary hack or literary exile. For years he had no publisher in either country – no publisher at all, indeed, except the publisher of *An Béal Bocht*. His career, in so far as it is a tragic and incomplete one, was in part at least so for reasons to do with Ireland which are worth more examination and analysis than that country has up to now accorded them, however difficult they may be to separate from other matters, such as his chauvinism, his pugnacious Catholicism, his fierce asceticism and his addiction to drink. These latter were, of course, partly matters of individual character; and to the extent that they were and that they affected his work for the worse rather than the better (and they all, even the addiction to drink, did both) his failure was a personal one. So it was too, perhaps, in the vital matter of the deployment of time and talents. More than once and for long periods he appears to have made the wrong choices among those that were open to him, opting for hand-to-mouth work when even his short-term interests would have been better served by another sort, writing for money even when he had a job as well, and so on.

But social reasons, particularly the expectations of his audience, played a part in these choices too, and to that extent Flann O'Brien's failure was, as well as being personal, a failure on the part of that audience and his country to come up with a proper response to his advent. The tradition of geniuses entrapped in circumstances, prisoners of their own failings and dupes of their personal eccentricities and foibles, was a well-established one in Brian O'Nolan's Dublin. Instead of attempting to break it or break out of it, he accepted that tradition. Indeed, if anything, he may be said to have perpetuated it; as he accepted and perpetuated too readily also the tradition of the part-time civil-service writer, professional as he was in his journalism and related activities. And besides the aberrant genius who was also a civil-servant, there was the common man, applying only common sense and the defences of a caustic wit to the public and political shortcomings of his country instead of the full range of perception, imaginative and intellectual, which is rightly expected elsewhere of the man of letters.

But although Flann O'Brien and Myles na Gopaleen were writers in conflict with each other; and although the former was more seriously damaged by these entrapments and limitations than the latter (who to some extent rejoiced in them), they both had their triumphs; and among the triumphs of the former is a little, late gem called *The Hard Life*, published four years before his death.

Unlike *The Dalkey Archive*, which was published three years later, but which was probably a re-hash of a work composed some time in the 'forties, it belongs to the last years of his life; and its existence, as in the case of *The Last Tycoon*, increases the sense of tragedy; for he may have been, like Fitzgerald, on the verge of a new lease of creative life for which he simply no longer had the physical stamina.

Not least because to do so would be some sort of an affront to the essentially modest nature of the work itself, one does not wish to make too large a claim for it, so suffice it to say here that all Flann O'Brien's original discoveries about the inconsequential and the banal, all his mastery of Dublin speech and delight in the pointless dialectics of its citizens are again on display. So, too, is his delight in the less sought-after aspects of existence through the exegesis of the particular mode of squalor of which the sub-title gives promise and even on the level of public concern it is amazing how much ground is covered and how topical the book (set as it is at the turn of the century) is proving to be: women's rights, the relaxation and liberalisation of religious dogma, the relationship of nationalism to practical reform and violence as an instrument of change, being among the many topics that are touched on. It is no use growing solemn about it, but those who do not recognise it for the gem it is, are, I suggest, lacking in a particular faculty of recognition.

About *The Dalkey Archive*, though, perhaps the less said the better. If the revelations of personality in *At Swim-Two-Birds* and *The Hard Life* are superbly judged and controlled, in this there appears to be the sort of failure even to notice when they occur which is almost always disastrous in a novel. The elements of *The Third Policeman* which have been taken over are spoiled, such as they are, in the taking; and there is again a lamentable attempt at profundity. Catholicism is treated as a shared joke in the manner of clerics being daring. Only James Joyce and the underwear do something to redeem things.

The impression of course remains that in spite of all the hard work and the effort of one kind or another, the achievement of Brian O'Nolan could have been greater than it is; but although since we live in a particular society and a particular country it is important to discuss, for the future's sake at least, the societal factors in what went wrong, it is at least equally important that criticism should see the total achievement for what it is, leaving out the wastage and the element of flawed promise. How much of the column and the miscellaneous writings will survive the years is doubtful. Probably not much, but they were alive in our time and we in theirs, and a journalist with his eye on eternity is in any case a contradiction in terms. Among the novels (leaving out *An Béal Bocht*) there are two, perhaps three, which have a claim to survival and one which is a complete triumph. *At Swim-Two-Birds* is in all respects an extraordinary achievement: unfailingly ingenious, hilariously funny and a marvellously controlled display of as much as he intended to reveal of its author's personality. The pity is that it was not seen, at the time of its publication, or even within, say, twenty years, as being at least as central to the whole nascent modern tradition as it was in any way related to the work of James Joyce.

BIBLIOGRAPHICAL NOTE

Since the works of most of the authors discussed in this book are either easily available or not available at all, there seemed little purpose in, on the one hand, pointing readers towards what any good general bookshop can supply, such as the Oxford University Press paperback *Castle Rackrent*, edited by George Watson; or, on the other, towards rare, difficult to obtain or out of print editions, such as the three volume Smith Elder *Lord Kilgobbin*.

Among the principal critical, historical or biographical works cited are:

Eamon de Valera *Speeches and Statements by Eamon de Valera* Edited by Maurice Moynihan, Gill and Macmillan

Thomas MacDonagh *Literature in Ireland: Studies Irish and Anglo-Irish* Kennikat Press

P. H. Newby *Maria Edgeworth* Arthur Barker

Terence de Vere White *Thomas Moore: The Irish Poet* Hamish Hamilton

Patrick Buckland *Irish Unionism: The Anglo-Irish and the New Ireland 1885 to 1922* Gill and Macmillan

Conor Cruise O'Brien *Writers and Politics* Penguin

Daniel Corkery *Synge and Anglo-Irish Literature* Cork University Press

Robin Skelton *J. M. Synge and His World* Thames and Hudson

Frank Budgen *James Joyce and the Making of Ulysses* Grayson and Grayson

Stanislaus Joyce *My Brother's Keeper* Faber and Faber

Stanislaus Joyce *The Complete Dublin Diary of Stanislaus Joyce* Edited by George M. Healey, Cornell University Press

W. Y. Tindall *James Joyce: His Way of Interpreting the Contemporary World* Scribner's

J. Mitchell Morse *The Sympathetic Alien: James Joyce and Catholicism* Peter Owen

A. Walton Litz *The Art of James Joyce* Oxford University Press

Augustine Martin *James Stephens: A Critical Study* Gill and Macmillan

Anthony Cronin *Dead as Doornails* Poolbeg